The Revels Plays
COMPANION
LIBRARY

E. A. J. HONIGMANN, J. R. MULRYNE,
R. L. SMALLWOOD and PETER CORBIN general editors

For over thirty years *The Revels Plays* have offered the most authoritative editions of
Elizabethan and Jacobean plays by authors other than Shakespeare. The
Companion Library provides a fuller background to the main series by publishing
worthwhile dramatic and non-dramatic material that will be essential for the serious
student of the period.

The books in the series fall into main groups:
(1) Editions of plays not included in the main series and less exhaustively annotated.
Usually several plays to a volume either by the same author or on a similar theme.
(2) Editions of significant non-dramatic works: masques, pageants, and the like.
(3) Theatre documents and similar source material.
(4) Criticism: collections of essays or monographs.
(5) Stage histories and eye-witness accounts.

Documents of the Rose Playhouse ed. RUTTER
Three Jacobean witchcraft plays ed. CORBIN, SEDGE
John Weever HONIGMANN*
Rare Sir William Davenant EDMOND*

Further titles in active preparation
The Oldcastle controversy eds. CORBIN, SEDGE
* these titles published in the USA by St. Martin's Press

'Art made tongue-tied by authority'

To Douglas, John and Timothy

THE REVELS PLAYS COMPANION LIBRARY

'Art made tongue-tied by authority'

ELIZABETHAN AND JACOBEAN
DRAMATIC CENSORSHIP

JANET CLARE

Tired with all these for restful death I cry,
As to behold desert a beggar born,
And needy nothing trimmed in jollity ...
And right perfection wrongfully disgraced,
And strength by limping sway disabled,
And art made tongue-tied by authority.   (Sonnet 66)

I would to God Shakespeare had lived later . . . that the
muzzle which all men wore on their souls in the Elizabethan
day, might not have intercepted Shakespeare's free articula-
tions, for I hold it a verity, that even Shakespeare was not a
frank man to the uttermost.
                  (Herman Melville, letter to Duyckinck, 1849)

Manchester University Press
Manchester and New York

distributed exclusively in the USA
and Canada by St. Martin's Press, Inc.

published by MANCHESTER UNIVERSITY PRESS
Oxford Road, Manchester M13 9PL, UK
and Room 400, 175 Fifth Avenue,
New York, NY 10010, USA

distributed exclusively in the USA and Canada
by ST MARTIN'S PRESS, Inc.,
175 Fifth Avenue, New York, NY 10010, USA

British Library cataloguing in publication data
Clare, Janet
    'Art made tongue-tied by authority': Elizabethan and Jacobean dramatic censorship.
    – (The Revels plays companion library).
    1. England. Theatre. Censorship, history
    I. Title II. Series
    792

Library of Congress cataloging in publication data
Clare, Janet, 1954–
    Art made tongue-tied by authority: Elizabethan and Jacobean dramatic
censorship / Janet Clare.
        p.   cm.– (The Revels plays companion library)
    Includes bibliographical references.
    ISBN 0–7190–2434–X
    1. English drama–Early modern and Elizabethan, 1500–1600–History and criticism.
    2. Theater–Censorship–Great Britain–History–17th century. 3. Theater–
    Censorship–Great Britain–History–16th century. 4. English drama–17th century–
    History and criticism. 5. English drama–Censorship–History–16th century.
    6. English drama–Censorship–History–17th century.   I. Title.   II. Series.
    PR658.C4C58   1990
    822'.309–dc20   89–77937

ISBN 0 7190 2434 X *hardback*

Photoset by J&L Composition Ltd, Filey, North Yorkshire
Printed in Great Britain by
Bell & Bain Limited, Glasgow

CONTENTS

ILLUSTRATIONS

Reproduced by permission of the British Library.

GENERAL EDITORS' PREFACE

Since the late 1950s the series known as the Revels Plays has provided for students of the English Renaissance drama carefully edited texts of the major Elizabethan and Jacobean plays. The series now includes some of the best known drama of the period and has continued to expand, both within its original field and, to a lesser extent, beyond it, to include some important plays from the earlier Tudor and from the Restoration periods. The Revels Plays Companion Library is intended to further this expansion and to allow for new developments.

The aim of the Companion Library is to provide students of the Elizabethan and Jacobean drama with a fuller sense of its background and context. The series includes volumes of a variety of kinds. Small collections of plays, by a single author or concerned with a single theme and edited in accordance with the principles of textual modernisation of the Revels Plays, offer a wider range of drama than the main series can include. Together with editions of masques, pageants, and the non-dramatic work of Elizabethan and Jacobean playwrights, these volumes make it possible, within the overall Revels enterprise, to examine the achievement of the major dramatists from a broader perspective. Other volumes provide a fuller context for the plays of the period by offering new collections of documentary evidence on Elizabethan theatrical conditions and on the performance of plays during that period and later. A third aim of the series is to offer modern critical interpretation, in the form of collections of essays or of monographs, of the dramatic achievement of the English Renaissance.

So wide a range of material necessarily precludes the standard format and uniform general editorial control which is possible in the original series of Revels Plays. To a considerable extent, therefore, treatment and approach is determined by the needs and intentions of individual volume editors. Within this rather ampler area, however, we hope that the Companion Library maintains the standards of scholarship which have for so long characterised the Revels Plays, and that it offers a useful enlargement of the work of the series in preserving, illuminating, and celebrating the drama of Elizabethan and Jacobean England.

E. A. J. HONIGMANN
J. R. MULRYNE
R. L. SMALLWOOD
PETER CORBIN

PREFACE

It was not until 1968 that the practice of theatre censorship, which became established in the reign of the first Elizabeth, was finally abolished. The system was not of course the same throughout the intervening centuries. The late regime of the Lord Chamberlain, whose duties included regulating entry into the royal enclosure at Ascot and appointing the Keeper of the Royal Swans, was the creation of the Licensing Act of 1737. This book traces the development and the impact of dramatic censorship from its beginnings in the suppression of religious drama to the end of the Jacobean period and it will be concerned with structures quite different from those in more recent use.

It has become axiomatic that the plays of Shakespeare and his contemporaries are components of a particular historical discourse. New historicist critics, in particular, have paid close attention to other modes of writing, examining marginalised works and artefacts to illuminate the issues in dramatic texts. Certain of these scholars have tended to examine Renaissance culture almost exclusively in terms of manifestations of power and have developed perspectives such as that of Stephen Greenblatt on Shakespeare's histories, that the plays represent but ultimately contain subversion. Yet the operation of censorship, which was the instrument of state authority acting upon the playwright and his work, has been largely ignored. This is an unfortunate omission. Before we judge what appears to be a play's structural imbalance, political equivocation or ambivalent ideology we need to take into account the kinds of constraint applied by the state, whether through the theatrical censor or otherwise, which would have been transmitted to the text.

There is a tendency in studies of the politics of Renaissance drama either to dismiss censorship as lenient and posing no serious threat, or to view it as consistently repressive and menacing. Neither view reflects the true nature of a system which under Elizabeth I and James I was dynamic and unstable. We might expect a change in censorship to have occurred after 1603, when the autocratic Queen was succeeded by a monarch who enjoyed a more personal relationship with the dramatists and who, for a time at least, permitted the player relative freedom. But fluctuations in the intensity of censorship and in the issues deemed censorable occurred not only between but during the reigns of the two monarchs. In such a public art as the theatre, dramatic censorship is inevitably linked with local circumstances at the time of performance. This applied equally to revivals of old plays. Even when the text of a play remains constant, its meaning does not. Plays previously judged innocuous may in a different political climate acquire a new and provocative significance. The reverse, of course, is also true and there are instances in all periods of the rehabilitation of formerly subversive texts. My approach then is historically specific. It is based on the assumption that until we locate the text within the historical moment of production and reconstruct the precise pre-occupations of the censor by way of evidence from censored texts we cannot know – other than in the broadest terms – how censorship impinged on the working playwright.

Several isolated cases of censorship are well known. The censorship by the Elizabethan Master of the Revels, Edmund Tilney, of *The Book of Sir Thomas More* is a familiar example, as is the controversy involving Jonson and Nashe after the report in 1597 of a play containing 'seditious and sclanderous matter', later identified as *The Isle of Dogs*. The furore caused by Middleton's *A Game at Chess*, curiously licensed by the Master of the Revels in 1624, is a *cause célèbre* of Jacobean censorship. But these cases are only three of many less documented instances of state interference with drama and, taken independently, they tell us little about the nature of restrictions imposed on the playwrights at each particular time. The censor's strictures on the anonymous *Woodstock*, Fulke Greville's *Mustapha*, Beaumont and Fletcher's *The Maid's Tragedy* and *Philaster*, for example, are less well known but equally important in any assessment of the climate of censorship.

Where do we find the sources for a detailed investigation into early dramatic censorship? The evidence is scattered. Manuscripts bearing traces of the censor's hand provide the only irrefutable evidence of official censorship with a play prior to performance. But there is no Elizabethan or Jacobean collection of manuscript plays submitted to the censor such as the Larpent collection containing the plays sent for licensing from 1737 to 1824. Comparatively few play books have survived. Of those that have come down to us, *Sir Thomas More*, *The Second Maiden's Tragedy*, *Sir John van Olden Barnavelt*, and *The Honest Man's Fortune* give fascinating insights into the censor at work. We find lines deleted which touch on, or could be interpreted as touching on, some matter of social or religious controversy, together with imperatives which convey the Master's powers of enforcement and which sometimes demand such extensive cuts as to necessitate considerable restructuring. Interestingly, certain markings and annotations in scribal hands imply that there was a degree of collaboration between the Revels Office and the theatre in so far as the playhouse scribe anticipated censorship or reformed the play to avoid further objections.

A second area of research involves a comparison of different editions of a play whose textual discrepancies may be traced to the interference of the censor. In prefatory material, or in addresses to the reader, to a patron or dedicatee, dramatists or publishers sometimes drew attention to this background by remarks suggesting, often obliquely, that the integrity of the text has been impaired by official intervention. In general, censored passages appear to have been included in the printed text of a play when the copy text consisted of authorial papers or when its publication occurred at a date considerably later than its first performance. It is probable that when it could be claimed that a play had once been licensed, that play could then be performed and published after a safe interval without observing the strictures of the censor. The different editions of 2 *Henry VI*, *Richard II*, 2 *Henry IV*, *The Malcontent*, *King Lear*, *The Maid's Tragedy* and *Philaster* fall into this category.

Thirdly, amongst Elizabethan and Jacobean state papers, personal correspondence and soliciting letters to patrons, we come upon revealing accounts of the suppression of, or other sanctions against, plays judged scandalous or seditious. The Privy Council minutes contain references to *The Isle of Dogs* which supplement what we know from Thomas Nashe's account in *Pierce Pennilesse His Supplication to the Devill*. Again, in 1606, the diplomat Edward Hoby, writing to Thomas Edmondes, reported the debates in the Commons following the audacious satire in John Day's *The Isle of Gulls*. Later in the reign, Thomas Locke, in his letter to Dudley Carleton, ambassador in The Hague, described how the Bishop of London had prohibited the performance of Massinger and Fletcher's *Sir John van Olden Barnavelt*. Such incidental comments are admittedly sketchy and circumspect in their judgments, but they do help to substantiate conjectures drawn from the condition of the text that a play had been revised in deference to censorship and, more significantly, they provide valuable insights into contemporary discourse on censorship and the interpretation of controversial texts.

Although a number of cases of non-dramatic censorship will be discussed, which serve to illuminate the brief of the Master of the Revels, the focus of this work will be on theatrical censorship. Not only were the procedures and the personnel of the two systems quite different, at least until 1606, but the methods and priorities of theatrical and press censors also differed. Theatre, like sermons, was orientated towards a collective consciousness. As legislation regulating the theatre indicates, successive governments were aware of the potential for mass disturbance in the playhouses intimated in Bacon's perception in *De Augmentis*: 'The minds of men are more open to impressions and affections when many are gathered together than when they are alone'. The Master of the Revels was accordingly likely to react against inflammatory language and subversive iconography. Correspondingly, playwrights could exploit different strategies in the circumvention of censorship from those open to authors of non-dramatic texts. Techniques such as locution of speech, mimicry, parody, and visual imagery are only fully realised in performance and may easily escape the censor engaged in a cursory reading of the text. That actors are accustomed to discovering stage direction in the text, while censors are not, is just one reason why some topical satire went undetected by the censor before performance.

In the wider context of literary censorship, Annabel Patterson has contended that there was an implicit social code governing relationships between authors and authorities, intelligible to all parties at the time as being a conscious and collusive arrangement. But the vicissitudes of stage censorship would have made such an agreement dificult to sustain. Passages in a play may become dangerously topical as the events they describe are overlain by, or re-applied to, fresh political circumstances. Moreover, playwriting is a commercial undertaking and the playwright has to take account of popular demands and tastes (adumbrated in the prologue to *The Isle of Gulls*) as well as the likely response of the censor. Anticipated success no doubt emboldened dramatists to take risks. Indeed, the number of cases of actual interference with texts by the censor and of post-performance intervention militates against a theory of a shared perception as applicable to theatrical censorship.

Censorship does not of course always succeed in stamping out the politically subversive or socially referential. As Annabel Patterson has cogently argued, one of the consequences of censorship is the development of literary codes of reference for contentious issues which the reader learns to decipher. The playwright, however, must depend less on ambiguity and is obliged to have recourse to different strategies of evasion. Although the popular Elizabethan audience contained an intellectually sophisticated element who would have been able to decode oblique political analogies, perhaps the majority, who were not privy to court affairs or to ideological debate, would have appreciated only thinly veiled satire and topical association.

Communicating with an unhomogeneous audience, the playwright has to be more audacious than the writer. The purpose of this study is primarily to re-situate and reappraise those plays which were victims of censorship because of their subject matter or ideology, boldness of language or iconography, or which were censored because of a particular collusion of dramatic material and political event. From such an empirical approach, we can examine how the pressures of censorship shaped the artefacts and rhetorical strategies of plays in the repertoires of the Elizabethan and Jacobean theatres.

This book began its life as a doctoral thesis submitted at the Shakespeare Institute, University of Birmingham, in 1981. I would like to renew my thanks to Dr R. L. Smallwood for his generous and patient assistance during its supervision. Since then I have incurred many debts. I would like to express my gratitude to Japanese friends – in particular, to Seiko Aoyama, Yuji Kaneko, Toshiko Oshio and Soko Tomita – and to colleagues at Ferris University, Yokohama. I am very grateful to Martin Butler, Margot Heinemann, Graham Parry and Lois Potter for reading and commenting on chapters; and to Richard Dutton for generously sharing his research into the mastership of Sir John Astley. I wish to thank especially Douglas Jefferson, Professor Emeritus at the University of Leeds, for his advice, conversation and friendship. The responsibility, however, for any errors which remain is entirely my own.

I should like to acknowledge most gratefully the help I have received from Dr Susan Brock of the Shakespeare Institute, University of Birmingham, from the librarians of Ferris University and from the staff of the reading room, north library and manuscript room of the British Library and of the library of the Victoria and Albert Museum. I am also grateful to the staff of the Photographic Service of the British Library for their efficient assistance.

Portions of this book have appeared in *The Review of English Studies* as an article, '"Greater themes for insurrection's arguing,"': political censorship of the Elizabethan and Jacobean stage, 37, 1987' and in a note 'The censorship of the deposition scene in *Richard II*', 41, 1990. I am grateful to the editor, R. E. Alton, for permission to use part of this material.

Before I had completed Chapter three, my son Timothy was born. Without the continuous involvement of my husband, John Gallagher, with baby and book, and my mother, who has typed more versions of these chapters than she can remember, this work could never have been completed. To them both, heartfelt thanks.

NOTE ON PROCEDURES

I have quoted Shakespeare from the edition of Peter Alexander, (London, 1951), Jonson from the edition of C. H. Herford and Percy and Evelyn Simpson, (11 vols., Oxford, 1925–52), Nashe from the edition of R. B. McKerrow, second edition, revised by F. P. Wilson, (5 vols., Oxford, 1958) and Chapman from the compendium *The Plays of George Chapman: The Tragedies with Sir Gyles Goosecappe*, eds Allan Holaday, *et al.*, (Cambridge, 1987). References to the folio texts of Shakespeare's plays are taken from the Norton Facsimile edited by Charlton Hinman (New York, 1968). Elsewhere, unless otherwise stated, I have quoted from the Revels editions. Where quotations have been transcribed from old spelling the original spelling has been retained, but the long 'ſ', 'i' and 'u' have been normalised and contractions have been expanded. Old-style dates have been altered to conform with the modern calendar year.

Abbreviations used in the notes

APC	*Acts of the Privy Council of England*, ed. J. R. Dasent (32 vols., London, 1890–1907)
Arber, *SR*	*A Transcript of the Registers of the Company of Stationers of London 1554–1640*, ed. Edward Arber (5 vols., London, 1875–94)
Chambers, *ES*	E. K. Chambers, *The Elizabethan Stage* (4 vols., Oxford, 1923)
CSPD	*Calendar of State Papers, Domestic Series*
MSC	*Malone Society Collections*
OED	*Oxford English Dictionary*
PMLA	*Proceedings of the Modern Languages Association*
REED: Chester	*Records of Early English Drama: Chester*, ed. Lawrence M. Clopper (Manchester, 1979)
REED: York	*Records of Early English Drama: York*, eds Alexandra F. Johnston and Margaret Rogerson, (2 vols., Manchester, 1979)
RES	*Review of English Studies*

Introduction

=====

The religious drama

Mid-sixteenth century theatrical censorship in England emerged from the turbulent conditions of the Protestant Reformation and developed alongside other measures which sought to eradicate Catholic iconography[1] and to bring doctrine and ritual into conformity with the new faith. The first substantial evidence of dramatic censorship derives from the sacred drama of the Mystery plays, originally performed on the feast of Corpus Christi, one of the principal holy days of the late medieval Church. These great dramatic narratives were integral to the public display of devotion to the Holy Sacrament; the whole community would take part in the procession through the streets, a prominent part of the Corpus Christi rite, and in the Mass which preceded the production of the cycle. Like the fresco cycles in Romanesque and Gothic churches, the drama rendered the elements of Catholic doctrine in such powerful visual images that it represented a serious impediment to the Reformed faith. Its simple and homely diction which expressed the forms and dogmas of the old faith was altogether more attractive to a popular audience than the sophisticated and unfamiliar arguments of Protestant reformers.

The belief that the regional cycles declined in popularity because they were considered archaic has for some time been discredited.[2] The Mystery plays were deeply rooted in popular culture. They continued to be known familiarly in the singular as the 'Corpus Christi play' even when the festival itself was no longer recognised and when their performance had been transferred to Whitsun. In common with other iconoclastic measures to which hindsight accords a dubious validity, their suppression came to be seen as essential to establishing the true religion in England. But, despite the antagonism of reformers and state intervention, it took several decades to extirpate them altogether.

The Reformation was not at first a popular movement and the changes enforced by the authorities, although drastic, were piecemeal. In the late 1530s, shrines were destroyed and plundered; in the following decade the invocation of saints was forbidden. Purgatory was denied later in the reign of Edward VI (1547–33).[3] The same progressive imposition of the new doctrine is evident in the steady decline of the Corpus Christi plays from the late 1540s to the late 1560s. Under Edward VI royal injunctions set out to eradicate papal influence and traditional practices now denigrated as idolatry and superstition;[4] but as far as drama was concerned the Edwardian government devoted its energies to the promotion of Protestant polemic in the interlude[5] rather than to any sustained effort to suppress the Mystery cycles. At first, the official policy towards the Mystery plays was principally directed at eliminating elements of doctrine associated with the old faith. Although it is difficult to say at what stage in the enforcement of the reformed faith each particular instance of interference occurred, several of the surviving manuscript fragments of the cycles show alterations or erasures which remove specifically Romanist elements. Along with the veneration of saints, the popular cult of the Virgin was much deplored by Protestant reformers as a polytheistic and near idolatrous devotion. Thus, in 1548 in York, we find the suppression of three plays in the cycle which dramatised the death, assumption and coronation of the Virgin.[6]

The Banns of the Chester play, traditionally proclaimed weeks in advance to advertise the play's performance, survive in two distinct transcripts of pre- and post-Reformation texts.[7] By one of the stanzas in the transcript of the early Banns the scribe has written 'erazed in the booke' – a reference to his copy text. The lines in question describe the Corpus Christi procession and the performance by the clergy of a play in honour of the feast:

Also maister Maire of this Citie
with all his bretheryn accordingly
A Solempne procession ordent hath he
    to be done to the best
Appon the day of corpus christi
The blessed sacrament caried shalbe
And A play sett forth by the clergye
    In honor of the fest
Many torches there may you see
Marchaunty and craftys of this Citie
By order passing in theire degree
    A goodly sight that day
They come from saynt maries on the hill

the churche of saynt Iohns untill
And there the sacrament leve they will
    The south as I you say[8]

The Corpus Christi feast was suppressed in 1548 and in subsequent years the plays were transferred to Whitsun. The erased stanza was presumably deleted in the original manuscript as a result of the obsolescence both of the clergy's role in performance and of the procession with the Sacrament. Traditionally, a procession combining religious and civic elements and culminating in the Mass had preceded the cycle. Edwardian (1547) and later Elizabethan (1559) injunctions had, however, forbidden processions 'about the church or churchyard or any other place' before the liturgy.[9] The records show that later processions did take place, but were led by the producers of the play, the craft guilds, disclosing a disjunction of civic and religious ceremonial.

It is evident that some of the differences between the contents of the Banns have been brought about by change in performance due to censorship of plays in the cycle. The early Banns contain a stanza describing a lost play by 'the wurshipffull wyffys of this towne' on the 'Assumption', all mention of which is missing in the later Banns. There are further signs of attempts to preserve the plays by revision and rewriting. The stanza in the late Banns devoted to the bakers' play on the Last Supper refers to the words of the Eucharist as 'a memoriall of that death and passion': words which carry an implicit rejection of the Catholic doctrine of transubstantiation, which affirms that the elements of bread and wine are transformed in substance into the body and blood of Christ. There is a pronounced anti-Catholic gloss to the play on Antichrist, in which the purpose is to expose 'Antechristes the worlde Rounde About': the Protestant identification of Antichrist and papalism was a familiar axiom. In one of the extant transcripts of the late Banns, an additional stanza states that God will not appear in person and that since 'no man can proportion that Godhead' only a voice from 'a Clowdy Coveringe' will be heard. No doubt this repudiation of the anthropomorphic representation of God on the stage of the pageant wagons occurred because of the objections of reformers who regarded any visual image of God as blasphemous.

In the register of the plays, known as the Towneley Cycle, there is further evidence that the texts had been tampered with to remove expressions of doctrine now judged heretical. Against a stanza in play XIX, which depicts the baptism of Christ by John the Baptist, has been written 'corectyd and not playd'.[10] The lines which have been struck through concern the contentious issue of the sacraments. John tells

Jesus that baptism is 'a worthy sacrament' and that there are 'sex othere and no mo'. Far from claiming more, the reformers had argued that there were only three and had embodied this belief in the Ten Articles of 1536. Other alterations in the manuscript reflect a similar concern to remove disputed Catholic material. In pageant XXVI, 'The Resurrection of the Lord', lines in red ink delete Christ's words to Mary Magdelene affirming the doctrine of transubstantiation:

> That ilk veray brede of lyfe
> Becommys my fleshe in wordys fyfe;
> who so it resaves in syn or stryfe
> Bese dede for ever;
> And whoso it takys in rightwys lyfe
> Dy shall he never.   (st. 55)

Transubstantiation was of course a most critical issue. It was rejected under Edward VI and further disputes on the Eucharist were silenced in a proclamation of 1547. The Towneley register is a scribal copy and the annotations are in a later hand. As with instances of suppression in the other cycles, the date of revision is uncertain. Censorship could have been early, soon after the publication of the Ten Articles or perhaps in the wake of events in 1549, when the Edwardian prayer book widened the doctrinal gulf between the old and reformed faiths.

Under Mary Tudor (1553–8) the religious drama was not so much resuscitated, as David Bevington has claimed,[11] as performed with more of the old freedom. Adherence to traditional dogma was prescribed and the plays depicting the death, assumption and crowning of the Virgin were restored to the cycle as part of a return to the old ways of worship. Despite the Queen's zealous Catholicism, there is little evidence in the drama of either rigorous Catholic polemic or a repressive stage censorship. *Respublica*, performed by child actors at Court during the Christmas season in 1553, is the most explicitly anti-Protestant Marian interlude; but the satire is moderate and religious debate is avoided. It is possible that Mary wished to avoid any controversy which might attend the exploitation of drama for overtly polemical purposes. Certainly there is no attempt during her reign to promote a counterblast to the fierce Protestant propaganda found in such plays as John Bale's *King John*. The Queen's proclamation prohibiting the performance of interludes without her 'special license in writing' does not specify the conditions for the grant of consent; but unlike Edward VI's similar injunctions, it appears in the context of a general suppression of religious controversy.[12]

The death of Mary and the accession of Elizabeth I once again brought a reversal of religious dynamics. The fundamentals of early

Elizabethan censorship are contained in a proclamation issued in the first year of the reign, 'Prohibiting Unlicensed Interludes and Plays, Especially on Religion or Policy'.[13] The proclamation went further than previous controls in the way it sought to curb the dramatisation of specific subjects and laid down a new procedure for censorship. In place of the system of licensing by the sovereign or the Privy Council which had prevailed hitherto, surveillance of drama was now entrusted in the cities and towns to the mayor and in the shires to the Justices of the Peace. Local officials were instructed not to permit any play 'wherein either matters of religion or of the governance of the estate of the commonweal shall be handled or treated'. The general principles underlying later Elizabethan and Jacobean censorship which will emerge in the study of textual censorship are here foreshadowed. What is of particular interest, however, is the manner in which Elizabeth I initially departed from the previous practice of centralised censorship in the hands of the sovereign, and in the reign of Edward VI by the Privy Council, in favour of its exercise by local authorities, before later returning to a policy of centralisation with an autonomous censor, the Master of the Revels. As a means of containing the regional religious drama, it was astute policy to vest powers of censorship in local authorities, particularly bearing in mind the problems which a state system would have faced in implementing its decrees in some of the northern catholic strongholds. Once these ends had been achieved and the focus of drama became concentrated in the popular play-houses of the capital, then censorship became the prerogative of a court official.

During the early years of Elizabeth's reign the government, led by Marian exiles, returned to the vigorous pursuit of religious change. The removal of the more overtly Catholic elements in the Mystery plays was not sufficient to satisfy zealous reformers and despite popular opposition there were several attempts during the 1560s and 1570s in the various cities to suppress the sacred drama altogether. That it survived so far into the reign is an indication both of its continuing popular appeal and of the general lack of cooperation the central administration received from municipal authorities. This is well illustrated by reference to the plays in the records of Chester. In 1574, we learn that the 'whitsun playes were plaid at Midsomer', although corrected and amended and with certain plays 'unplaid which were thought might not be justified for the superstition that was in them'.[14] The production was clearly controversial. The mayor, John Savage, and the municipal authorities had given their assent, countermanding the prohibition of Edmund Grindal, Archbishop of

York, a man of puritanical leanings, and the Earl of Huntington, Lord President of the North. Reprisal followed swiftly and was designed to draw maximum attention to Savage's contempt of authority. As he came out of the common hall on the day of his successor's election to the mayoralty, Savage was served with a writ to appear before the Privy Council. His predecessor, John Hanky, and a number of citizens and players were likewise 'troubled for the same matter'.[15] From London, Savage wrote to the city council requesting them to exculpate him from the charge of sole responsibility for allowing the plays. The new mayor, Henry Hardware, replied at great length that neither Savage nor Hanky had done anything 'in their severall tymes of maioralties towchinge the saide plays but by thassent consent and full agreamente of the aldermen sheriffes and comen counsell of the saide Citie'.[16] Savage was pardoned, but his inquisition served as a warning to intransigent communities and demonstrated the increased intolerance of the government towards the old religious drama. After 1575, there is no further recording of the plays in Chester; clearly Hardware, whilst ready to help in exonerating Savage, was not prepared to risk bringing sanctions upon himself by permitting their performance.

That there was much support for the plays within city authorities in the face of government opposition is again evident from the abortive attempt to stage the cycle in Wakefield in 1576. The Burgess Court had already granted the guilds permission to produce the plays, when the Diocesan Court of High Commission intervened and prohibited them on the grounds that they contained many things which 'tende to the Derogation of the Majestie and glorie of god the prophanation of the Sacramentes and the maunteynaunce of superstition and idolatrie'.[17] The same document raised more specific objection to the depiction of the Trinity and the administration of the sacraments of Baptism and Communion.

In York, the records also document official interference with production of the plays, which culminated in their suppression in 1569. The Marian pageants of the cycle had again been suspended in 1561.[18] The following year, the council decided that either the Corpus Christi play or the Creed play should be performed, but only after further consideration and examination. In 1568, it was ordained that instead of the Corpus Christi play the guild would perform the Creed play (which had originally belonged to the Corpus Christi guild before its dissolution in 1547).[19] The text of the Creed play has not survived, but we know that it was intended for instruction and graphically designed to bring a knowledge of the fundamental tenets of the Apostles' creed 'to the ignorant'. Clearly, this was didacticism of the wrong order, for at this stage Matthew Hutton, Dean of York, stepped in and disallowed the play. Dean Hutton's letter to the Mayor of York and the council is one of the most telling testimonies we have concerning the sustained efforts of the government, aided by the ecclesiastical commission, to suppress popular religious drama. He writes of the difficulty of censorship without changing the 'wholle drift of the play' and advises the council not to allow performance.[20] In support of his reaction, Hutton adds that the play, 'thoghe it was plausible 40 yeares agoe', is now outdated and will only be enjoyed by 'the ignorant sort'. Moreover, Hutton's words appear to contain a veiled warning of reprisal should the production proceed, couched in the ostensibly mild observation that he knows not 'how the state will beare with it'. The council accepted Hutton's verdict and subsequently withheld their permission for performance. Evidently, however, there was popular opposition to this prohibition of a traditional dramatic festival, for shortly afterwards we learn that the commons were petitioning the council to allow the customary performance of the Corpus Christi play. Apparently, the members of the council disagreed as to whether or not the pageants should be permitted, before deciding that they should be perused and amended. But the will of the reformers must have prevailed, for there was no religious dramatic festival that year. The Corpus Christi play was performed for the last time in 1569, possibly incorporating the amendments ordered by the council the previous year.

Late in 1569, a final concerted opposition to the English Reformation erupted in the Northern rebellion, led by the Catholic earls, with papal support. The uprising, during which Catholic rituals were temporarily reinstated, posed a serious threat to the new order, illustrating as it did how entrenched were the people of the north-east in the old doctrine and how little support the Queen's religious policies commanded in such areas of traditional loyalty. The uprising was brutally quelled. In such a climate, it is unlikely that the York city authorities would have sanctioned a full scale production of the Corpus Christi play. But there was one last production of religious drama in York in 1572, when the processional Pater Noster play was performed after it had been 'perused amended and corrected' by the council.[21] It was agreed that the production should take place on the Thursday after Trinity Sunday, the feast of Corpus Christi, perhaps in protest against the abandonment of the holy day and its traditional dramatic celebration. But the newly appointed Archbishop Grindal, who was to collaborate in the suppression of the Chester plays, sent for a copy of the play and appears to have appropriated the book: nothing further is heard of it or of any subsequent performance. Yet despite such determined efforts to stamp out the production of sacred drama, it was not easily eradicated from popular memory. The records of the city indicate that the guilds continued to fund the upkeep of the pageant wagons in preparation for or in hope of future performances. In 1579, and once more in 1580, the council agreed that the plays should again be performed and applications were made to the Archbishop for his permission.[22] No positive response was forthcoming. A revival of religious drama must have been contemplated with scant enthusiasm by the apostles of puritanism and their secular counterparts; while affections for the old beliefs could not be smothered overnight, there was every reason to discourage their rekindling in spectacle and performance, the expression of discarded doctrine and the enactment of rejected liturgies.

Censorship of the commercial stage

Whilst ecclesiastical censors were presiding over the suppression of amateur religious drama in the regions, professional secular theatre was establishing itself in London. The first purpose-built playhouse, the Red Lion in Stepney, was erected in 1567, serving as a model for James Burbage's more famous Theatre.[23] The construction of the Theatre in 1567 was closely followed by that of the Curtain (1577) and then by the Rose (1587), built in competition. Situated outside the City walls in Middlesex and Surrey, these first public playhouses escaped the jurisdiction of a hostile council in the Guildhall. The account of the Privy Council's support for the professional stage in the face of opposition from the City fathers is a familiar one: the players, the Council decreed, had to have a permanent house in which to rehearse in readiness for performances at Court. The City authorities grudgingly acknowledged that the Queen 'must bee served at certen times by this sort of people' and, in a letter to the Lord Treasurer, Lord Burghley, conceded that it might be good policy 'to divert idle heads and other ill deposed from other woorse practize by this kynd of exercise'.[24] But from the beginnings of commercial and popular theatre, they deplored the alleged immorality of stage plays and the social disruptions of playgoing. To them it was little more than serving 'Gods enemie in an Inne'.[25]

But these stances – of City opposition and state support – were not consistently polarised. Although keen to protect the players who wore their liveries, the members of the Privy Council expressed motions of unease at the new phenomenon of large crowds converging in public theatres. The fear of public disorder was not confined to the theatre, but arose from the fact that London's population was increasing rapidly, supplemented by large numbers of immigrants, and from an apprehension of the severe problem of crowd control. In April 1580, the Council were investigating breaches of the peace at the Theatre. Playing was frequently prohibited at times when the plague was taking its heaviest toll and it is probable that the Council welcomed this opportunity of regulating the theatres and their audiences. On 17 April 1580, five days after the disorders at the Theatre were reported, the Privy Council ordered the Justices of the Peace of Middlesex to restrain performance until Michaelmas on the basis that playgoing 'might breed or encrease any infection'.[26] In April 1582, they instructed the Lord Mayor to permit only those plays which yielded 'honest recreation and no example of evell'.[27] The crisis came in July 1597 when the Privy Council, hearing reports of riotous behaviour among audiences in the playhouses, took the unprecedented step of instructing a full investigation into performance on the Bankside.[28] Consequently, it was ordered that the playhouses be demolished and playing was prohibited for three months. Curiously, the order appears to have been neither rescinded nor fully implemented, but its impact was selective: only the Swan, where the offending play, *The Isle of Dogs*, had been performed, ultimately fell into disuse, since it remained unlicensed after playing resumed in October. The episode nevertheless indicates that the Queen and her Council were attentive to the rumours and complaints which had been circulating against the theatre.

By the turn of the century the government's attitude towards the popular drama had hardened. Disturbed by the number of playhouses in the vicinity of London and their alleged mismanagement, the Privy Council attempted more comprehensive regulation by means of an order of 22 June 1600, which is recorded in letters sent to the Lord Mayor and Justices of the Peace directing its execution.[29] Only the two new playhouses, the Globe and the Fortune, were to be permitted. The time-honoured custom of performance in the inn-yard was prohibited and playing was restricted to two performances a week. The order was evidently grounded in a degree of misinformation or ignorance. The Fortune was planned as a replacement for the Rose, but here reference is made to the Curtain, which is to be either 'ruyned and plucked downe or to be put to some other good use'. No such demolition took place. The Curtain continued in use for more than twenty years, acquiring a certain notoriety; the Rose, once vacated by the Admiral's Men later in the same year, saw only two further productions by Pembroke's Men until 1602, when Worcester's Men became tenants. There is no evidence that the order produced any reduction in the number of weekly performances. The impresario Philip Henslowe continued to make the same advance payments to the Admiral's Men, presumably for no fewer performances than before. That the Privy Council's injunctions were largely ignored is suggested by the Council's letter to the Justices the following year casting the blame on them for not putting the earlier directives into practice. Though unsuccessful in reducing the opportunities for playgoing, the Council's *communiqués* did nevertheless have the effect of containing any immediate expansion of the theatres.

The government may have been less anxious than might be antici- pated at the relative failure of its attempts to regulate performance because of the earlier introduction of dramatic censorship as a rather more effective means of official surveillance. The most significant measure to affect the professional playwright and players was the enlargement of the Revels Office to become a centralised agency of control. The Master of the Revels thus became the state's dramatic censor, so that local authorities ceased to exercise their former powers of play licensing. When Philostrate, Theseus's Master of the Revels in *A Midsummer Night's Dream*, is given the task of selecting entertain- ment to while away tedious hours before the royal marriage, he is entrusted with only one of the functions of the Office, albeit its original function. The extension of its authority began just after the first playhouses were erected and about the time that the status of actors was being transformed from that of rogues and vagabonds into something akin to a profession. The process culminated in 1581, when full powers of dramatic censorship were formally invested in the Master. The beginnings of this ascendancy are seen in an early patent issued to an acting company, that of Leicester's Men in 1574.[30] The status of the company was undoubtedly enhanced by the gift, whilst the proviso that their 'Commedies, Tragedies, enterludes, and stage playes be by the master of oure Revells for the tyme beynge before sene and allowed' obviously marked a constraint on the production of their plays.

That there had previously been a custom of informal censorship of plays prior to court performance is suggested by an entry in the Revels accounts of 1572, when it was noted that six plays were 'chosen owte of many and ffownde to be best that then were to be had; the same also being often perused and necessarely corrected and amended by all the afforesaide officers'.[31]

As yet, censorship was unsystematic and in the hands of anonymous assistants employed in the Revels Office. A document prepared c. 1573 for Burghley, however, proposed changes in the administration of the Revels. The recommendation begins conservatively enough with the acknowledgement that princes are 'disposed to pastyme' and must therefore 'have thinges accordinge to their pleasure'. However, the author then advises a refashioning of the Office so that power is concentrated in one man of court rank: 'ffirst I woulde wishe for the princes honour, That some one of Countenaunce and of creditt with the prince might beare the name of Master, Suche as the Quenes Majestye thought meetest to receyve her highnes pleasure from tyme to tyme attendaunte in the Courte'.[32] He describes 'the connynge of the office' as resting 'in understandinge of historyes, in judgement of comedies tragedyes and showes, in sight of perspective and architecture'. Here, then, is an intimation of a restructuring of the Office in order to give greater prominence to the Master's assessment of dramatic material and not only the management of court entertainment.

The censors

In 1579 Edmund Tilney was formally appointed Master of the Revels, his relationship to the Howards, who had aided his advancement at Court, presumably also having influenced his appointment.[33] His kinship with Charles Howard, later Lord Chamberlain and then Lord Admiral, would have satisfied the earlier recommendation that the Master should be 'one of Countenaunce and of creditt with the prince'. Tilney's preferment was certainly a departure from former practices. The duties of the Office had previously been performed by Thomas Blagrave, clerk for the Tents and Revels, on the basis of a yearly appointment. In 1581 Elizabeth made an order extending the duties of the Master of the Revels in accordance with some of the recommendations in the report prepared for Burghley. Although Tilney was still theoretically subordinate to the Lord Chamberlain, head of the Queen's household, the powers granted to him in the commission were such as effectively to make him autonomous censor of the drama. The importance of the document is such that it bears extensive quotation:

> And furthermore also we have and doe by these presentes aucthorise and commaunde our said Servant Edmunde Tilney Maister of our said Revells by himselfe or his sufficient deputie or deputies to warne commaunde and appointe in all places within this our Realme of England aswell within ffrancheses and liberties as without all and every plaier or plaiers with their

playmakers either belonginge to any noble man or otherwise bearinge the name or names of usinge the facultie of playmakers or plaiers of Comedies Tragedies Enterludes or what other showes soever from tyme to tyme and at all tymes to appeare before him with all suche plaies Tragedies Comedies or showes as they shall have in readines or meane to sett forth and them to presente and recite before our said Servant or his sufficient deputie whom wee ordeyne appointe and aucthorise by these presentes of all suche showes plaies plaiers and playmakers together with their playinge places to order and reforme auctorise and put downe as shalbe thought meete or unmeete unto himselfe or his said deputie in that behalfe And also likewise we have by these presentes aucthorised and commaunded the said Edmunde Tylney that in case if any of them whatsoever they bee will obstinatelie refuse upon warninge unto them given by the said Edmunde or his sufficient deputie to accomplishe and obey our commaundement in this behalfe then it shalbe lawfull to the saide Edmunde or his sufficient deputie to attache the partie or parties so offendinge and him or them to commytt to warde to remaine without bayle or mayneprise untill such tyme as the same Edmunde Tylney or his sufficient deputie shall thinke the tyme of his or theire imprisonment to be punnishement sufficient for his or their said offences in that behalfe and that done to inlarge him or them so beinge imprisoned at their plaine libertie without any losse penaltie forfeiture or other daunger in this behalfe to be susteyned or borne by the said Edmunde Tylney or his deputie Any Acte Statute ordynance or provision heretofore had or made to the contrarie hereof in any wise notwithstandinge wherefore we will and commaunde you and every of you that unto the said Edmunde Tylney or his sufficient deputie bearer hereof in the due execucion of this our aucthoritie and commaundement ye be aydinge supportinge and assistinge from tyme to tyme as the case shall require as you and every of you tender our pleasure and will answer to the contrarie at your uttermost perills.[34]

It is evident from the Master's commission that the systematic checking of the contents of plays performed at the commercial theatres was seen as a necessary means of state control. Quite new to the Office are the powers vested in Tilney to licence and suppress plays at his discretion and the right to imprison players or playwrights who disregarded his authority. The stipulated procedure that players should 'presente and recite' their plays before the Master of the Revels was, however, later modified so that the censor made his reformations in the play book. The fact that there is no immediate evidence of Tilney's censorship following his appointment may well be because the process was oral and therefore went unrecorded.

The financial transactions recorded in Henslowe's *Diary* include payments to Tilney for the licensing both of performances at the Rose and of plays. It seems initially Henslowe paid Tilney a sum of five shillings each week, but that after 1597 he made payments on a monthly basis.[35] That Tilney enjoyed a monopoly on licences may well help to explain why the Council's restrictions on the number of performances appear to have been waived. In general, it was the companies who paid the Master the sum of seven shillings for the licensing of each play (later increased to one pound and then two pounds). Henslowe records both direct payments to Tilney and advances to personnel of the Admiral's Men, such as the leading actor William Downton, for the discharge of licensing fees.[36] In a few cases, as we shall see, there must have been lengthy negotiations between the theatre and the Revels Office, as following the Master's demands for change the company were obliged to return the manuscript to its author or to bring in a different playwright to revise the play.

The unprecedented authority now conferred upon Tilney as Master of the Revels is quite definitively recorded by documentary testimony. Details in the patents granted to the adult companies under Elizabeth I, and later James I, reiterate the powers given to him in his commission. There is, for example, a note appended to the indenture of licence granted to the Earl of Worcester's Men in 1583 which advises municipal authorities on the procedure of censorship for travelling companies: 'No play is to bee played, but suche as is allowed by the sayd Edmund, and his hand at the latter end of the said book they doe play'.[37] Tilney's prerogatives continue to be recorded in later patents, such as the 1606 indenture to the company of players patronised by Prince Henry (formerly the Admiral's Men); but, as we shall see, there was some deviation from the practice in the early Jacobean period. Moreover, in the same patent granted to the Prince's Men, Sir George Buc, who had been promised the Revels in Elizabeth's reign and had been granted the legal reversion in June 1603, was named alongside Tilney as entitled to the benefits of the Office. This suggests that the volume of work was becoming too much for one censor. For no apparent cause, the patent granted to the King's Men in 1603 omits any reference to the 'auctoritie, power, priviledges and profittes' of the Master of the Revels. Since however there is evidence, albeit after 1606, that Buc was licensing plays for the King's Men, it would be wrong to infer from the omission that they were exempt from official censorship. The most feasible conjecture for the absence of the proviso, which will be considered later, is that the accession of the Scottish James VI initially disrupted the Elizabethan system of censorship.

Buc was not Tilney's cousin, as is sometimes stated, but he was related to the influential Howards and probably owed the Mastership to the Lord Admiral.[38] His early career reveals a man of various abilities and ambitions. He entered the Middle Temple in 1585, with the son of the Bishop of London as surety. Three years later he was serving against the Armada. A historiographer of some merit, his works included the pro-Plantagenet *History of the Life and Reigne of Richard III*, significantly only published in 1646, and a study of his own genealogy, *The Ancientry of Buck*. He was elected a Member of Parliament in 1595. Before his first nomination for the Revels in 1597, he was put forward by the Lord Admiral for the position of French Secretary. Howard's letter to Cecil in 1595 recommending Buc for the post (which went to Thomas Edmondes) also refers to the Queen's wish to promote him. Advancement, however, came more rapidly with the accession of James I, who made him a Gentleman of the Privy Chamber; knighted in the royal garden at Whitehall on 23 July 1603, he was amongst the inordinate number of courtiers to benefit from James's largesse. Having already proved himself a loyal servant of the Crown, Buc would have been a more attractive candidate for the Revels than the other contenders, the barrister Edward Glascock, whose patent of reversion dated May 1603 was stayed, and an earlier rival the playwright John Lyly, who had begun to contend for the reversion of the office as early as 1588.[39] From the state's standpoint, theatre personnel and writers make ineffectual censors, a maxim borne out by the experience of the years 1604–6, when Samuel Daniel was temporarily acting as censor for the Children of the Queen's Revels. To satisfy the diverse interests of audience, patrons and the Crown whilst being conscious that extensive textual censorship jeopardises the play in performance, is the dilemma of a dramatic censor intimately connected with the theatre. Buc, on the other hand, was primarily concerned to show his gratitude and loyalty by protecting the King's interests and by shoring up royal authority against outbursts of dramatic satire. He appears to have pursued the duties of the Office conscientiously and, relative to his successor, with moderation until his alleged madness brought about his removal in 1622.

The succession was again already spoken for; Sir John Astley, who had held the reversion to the Revels Office since 1612, now realised his interest. Astley remained titular Master until his death in 1640, but he discharged the duties of the office for a mere sixteen months.[40] On 20 July 1623 he leased the Mastership to Henry Herbert, brother of the poet George Herbert, for the sum of £150 per annum. The episode is a singular illustration of the fact that the Revels Office, once acquired, was a proprietary right capable of being assigned to a purchaser. There is no evidence that the transfer of privileges required, or received, the Crown's specific approval. Nevertheless, the Earl of Pembroke, a relation of Herbert's, was as Lord Chamberlain in a position to encourage the enterprise and to recommend the new incumbent to the King. James was evidently content to ratify the transaction and Herbert received his knighthood almost immediately. Nevertheless, his tenure of the post depended, at least initially, on Astley's remaining alive. It was only in 1629 that Herbert was granted (jointly with Simon Thelwall) a legal reversion to the office which he already *de facto* held, enabling him ultimately to inherit the mastership in his own right on Astley's death.

Izaak Walton, in his *Life of Mr. George Herbert*, briefly refers to Henry Herbert's career: '[he] became a menial servant to the Crown in the daies of King *James*, and hath continued to be so for fifty years: during all which time he hath been Master of the Revels; a place that requires diligent wisdom, with which God hath blest him'.[41] Unlike his brother George, who according to Walton had 'ambitiously thirsted' for a public role before taking orders and withdrawing from 'empty, imaginary, painted pleasures', Henry Herbert was keen to enhance his position within the royal household. The records, which continue after the Restoration when Herbert was fighting to retain his former privileges, show that he relinquished none of his ambition.

It was not until Herbert's assumption of the Revels in 1622 that, owing to his practice of recording personal memoranda in an office book, we have detailed chronological information about the censor's response to individual plays.[42] Herbert undoubtedly wielded the authority of his office with rigour and diligence and protected his official prerogatives. In a note of 1633 after his suppression of Massinger and Fletcher's *The Tamer Tamed*, he distinguished between former and present practices: 'It concerns the Master of the Revells to be carefull of their ould revived playes, as of their new, since they may conteyne offensive matter, which ought not to be allowed in any time.'[43] Old plays had to be re-submitted to him on the grounds that they might be full of 'offensive things against church and state', since in former times 'the poets took greater liberty' than was currently allowed. Diplomatically couched in Herbert's indictment of the audacity of earlier dramatists is a complaint against the comparative leniency of his predecessors. The note contains additional information about measures introduced by Herbert with a view to tightening up the processes of control. Copies of all new plays are to be deposited with the Master so that he can check what has been allowed or disallowed and the players should not begin to learn their parts until he has licensed the play. The terms of the instruction suggest that the theatre companies, in the absence of any means of checking that lines formerly suppressed did not subsequently find their way back into texts, had exploited this flaw in the system.[44]

The work of Tilney, Buc and Herbert would seem to have been assisted by a degree of unofficial censorship in the playhouse, probably by the playhouse bookkeeper mediating between the playwright and his text and the censor. Herbert referred to this practice in 1633 when he returned the book of *The Tamer Tamed* to Edward Knight, the bookkeeper of the King's Men, with the following order: 'In many things you have saved mee labour: yet wher your judgment or penn fayld you, I have made boulde to use mine. Purge ther parts, as I have the booke.'[45] It is impossible to know how far this was a matter of routine. There is evidence in several dramatic manuscripts that the plays have not only been censored by the Master of the Revels, but revised in deference to censorship by a different hand: *Woodstock* and *The Second Maiden's Tragedy* and Massinger and Fletcher's *Sir John van Olden Barnavelt* evince signs of editing with the possible objections of the censor in mind. Such caution suggests some awareness of the permissible extent of a play's political critique. That any such confederacy was limited is, however, quite obvious from the number of cases of official censorship discussed in the following chapters in which playwrights intentionally or otherwise went beyond the bounds.

A note on press censorship

Elizabethan drama was subject to two largely unrelated types of censorship: censorship by the Master of the Revels before the performance of a play and censorship by an ecclesiastical licenser prior to publication. Our focus is on theatrical censorship which was governed by rather different considerations from those of literary censorship. But as much of the evidence for dramatic censorship is textual, some clarification of the different systems is necessary. Moreover, from cases of state interference with the publication of certain works, we can more fully apprehend the general climate of censorship as well as the specific concerns of the Master of the Revels.

Whereas the bureaucratic regulation of the stage was a feature of the later years of Elizabeth I, coexisting with the expansion of the professional theatre, the origins of the state system designed to control the output of the presses can be found in the early Tudor period. The interference of the Church with theatre production diminished with the suppression of sacred drama; but its influence over printed matter increased during the Elizabethan period and was consolidated in the

Star Chamber decree of 1586.[46] The preamble of the decree rational-
ised the introduction of more stringent state control of the press on the
grounds that there had been abuses and disorders in the printing and
selling of books. Henceforth, all printers had to notify the Master and
wardens of the Stationers' Company of their possession of printing
presses; printing was to be restricted to London and the universities
and if secret presses were found they would be defaced. With the
injunction that all books must be 'first seen and perused by the
Archbishop of CANTERBURY and Bishop of LONDON', a system of
official press censorship was instituted. The impractical nature of a
procedure whereby two prominent ecclesiastics were expected to
operate as licensers for all printed books was rectified two years later
when similar authority was delegated to ecclesiastical subordinates.
Entries in the Stationers' Register, which records books approved for
publication, show that from 1588 a number of subordinate clerics
were also inspecting and authorising works for print.[47]

In 1606 there is evidence that the Revels was beginning to extend its
power still further. From entries in the Stationers' Register, it appears
that Buc's authorisation was now accepted as licence for the publication of plays, an area which officially had been quite distinct from
theatrical censorship. A number of plays printed in the 1590s,
including *Richard II*, refer in their Register entry only to the licence of
the warden of the Stationers' Company, who had presumably been
influenced by the imprimatur of the theatrical censor. It may then be
conjectured that, even before Buc's name began to appear in the
Register, stationers had been tacitly accepting Tilney's stage licence in
lieu of ecclesiastical sanction, but it was with Buc that the practice
became established. Whatever the circumstances which were to lead
ultimately to the coalescence of dramatic censorship, in performance
and in print, under the sole direction of the Master of the Revels, the
extension of the censor's authority is an event of critical importance: it
confirms the secularisation of dramatic censorship under absolute
state control.

Censorship by decree

As with theatrical censorship, the Privy Council or the sovereign could
override the official system of press control. On 1 February 1587, the
Privy Council instructed the Archbishop of Canterbury to halt the
circulation of the second edition of Holinshed's *Chronicles* and to
ensure that certain parts of the work were revised.[48] The Council's
orders were provoked by their belief that the chronicles contained

'sondry thinges which we wish had bene better considered' and, more revealingly, 'reporte of matters of later yeeres that concern the State, and are not therefore meete to be published in such sorte as they are delyvered'. Then, in 1599, in the wake of one of the Council's most repressive acts of literary censorship when satires and epigrams were burnt in the Stationers' Hall, it was further enjoined that 'no Englishe historyes be printed excepte they bee allowed by some of her majesties privie Councell'.[49] Books which had been printed without licence were ordered to be burnt. Acts of royal intervention outside the regular system of press control continued to occur under James I. One such instance presents the ironical spectacle of the King suppressing, at parliamentary insistence, a tract which upheld the pre-eminence of the royal prerogative. In March 1610 Parliament directly confronted the King's absolutist assumptions by compelling him to issue a proclamation against John Cowell's *The Interpreter*, published in 1607. Although Cowell, a civil lawyer, had defined the power of the Crown in similar terms to those postulated by James himself in his treatise *True Law of Free Monarchies*, he was condemned by the King for wading too deeply into 'the deepest mysteries that belong to the persons or State of Kings or Princes'.[50] The book was publically burnt and Cowell was declared a traitor.

The playwright's response

There was little scope for writers of the sixteenth century to have formulated anything so privileged as principles of artistic freedom; but oblique references to the fetters of censorship and to the system of spies and informers it engendered give some insight into the frustrations of working under such conditions. Shakespeare, apart from his reference to 'art made tongue-tied by authority' in his world-weary sonnet 66, is remarkably silent on the matter. Other writers were not so reticent. Of necessity, comments on the government and its censorship remain guarded; but spies encouraged in their activities by the authorities are vehemently denounced. One such figure was the notorious inquisitor Richard Topcliffe, who informed the Privy Council of alleged sedition in *The Isle of Dogs*. Not surprisingly, Nashe and Jonson frequently attacked informers who sought to blacklist writers by, as they alleged, wilfully misconstruing their work. In the Preface to *Pierce Pennilesse*, one of his earliest works, Nashe glosses what he sees as one of the paradoxes of 'this moralizing age, wherein every one seeks to shew himselfe a Polititian by misinterpreting'.[51] A similar complaint is lodged in the epistle 'to the

Gentlemen readers' of *Strange Newes of the Intercepting Certaine Letters*, when Nashe rails against 'upstart interpreters', the description suggesting a parvenu on a new path of social advancement, who have extorted 'unreverent' meanings out of his lines. In *Summer's Last Will and Testament*, Nashe's entertainment played before a private audience, the fool, Will Summers, speaking as Prologue, addresses the 'moralizers' who 'wrest a never meant meaning out of every thing, applying all things to the present time', and advises them to direct their attention to the 'common Stage' of the public playhouses. Through the character of Winter, Nashe acts as devil's advocate:

> Then censure (good my Lord) what bookemen are,
> If they be pestilent members in a state:
> He is unfit to sit at sterne of state,
> That favours such as will o'rethrow his state:
> Blest is that government where no arte thrives,   (III. p. 278)

From a modern perspective, Winter appears as the embodiment of repressive impulses in an autocratic regime; but in the late sixteenth century, when government policy was just beginning to counter the subversive potential of a more accessible literature, there is a striking novelty in such a representation.

Jonson likewise denounced informers and agents who allegedly sought to distort his literary purpose. In his epigram 'On Chevril', he inveighs against the critic who with his 'petulant pleadings threatens the starre-chamber, and the barre' by personalising the poet's satire.[52] The dedication of Volpone to 'the two famous universities' contains a warning that 'Application, is now, growne a trade with many' and 'wise and noble persons' should not be too credulous of or familiar with 'invading interpreters' who 'cunningly, and often, utter their owne virulent malice, under other mens simplest meanings'. Again, in the Induction of *Bartholomew Fair*, Jonson makes a similar assault on informers who wrongfully seek to identify the play's characters. The audience are enjoined not to harbour any 'State-decipherer' or 'politique Picklocke of the Sceane' who may attempt to see libels in the characters of the fair. There is, of course, more than an element of disingenuousness in such protestations, since the avowals of innocence and assaults upon 'picklocks' of the scene are part of a dual strategy, designed to repel the attentions of the censor while simultaneously exciting the interest of the initiated spectator in decoding those apparently forbidden meanings.

Critiques of the inefficacy or perniciousness of censorship which are now commonplace are to be found lucidly articulated in several plays of the period. In Marston's *The Dutch Courtesan*, Crispinella astutely comments that, as with literary censorship, any official prohibition is counter-productive: 'those books that are call'd in, are most in sale and request'.[53] Safely within the classical worlds of *Poetaster* and *Sejanus*, Jonson expressed his ideal of a state where artistic freedom is guaranteed by the clemency and wise judgement of the ruler. In *Poetaster*, Virgil's reputation is undermined by the lies of envious detractors, but Augustus Caesar intervenes in support of the poet. Virgil's panegyric to Caesar and his scorn of 'the malicious, ignorant, and base Interpreter' who seeks to misrepresent the author's purpose reflects Jonson's own view of the vulnerability of his profession. Virgil's comment that it is not the controlled anger of the satirist but an active intelligencing system which is the true sign of malaise in the state is developed in *Discoveries*, where Jonson argues that a healthy society both needs and permits sharp satirical correctives.[54] Again, in *Sejanus*, tyrannous censorship is seen as one manifestation of the corruption of Rome under Tiberius. The historian Cordus is accused on a fabricated charge of being 'a sower of sedition in the state' and his works are ordered to be suppressed and burnt. The case against censorship is vigorously argued. Arruntius contends that if 'th' age were good' criticism could be voiced without repercussions. With Sabinus he attacks the 'brainlesse diligence' of the senators, who earn only shame for themselves and for the writer an 'eternall name'. Yet such an enlightened analysis was far from becoming a matter of public debate.

There are similarities in the responses of artists working under the two separate systems of literary and theatrical censorship. Historiographers generally exercised caution in their editing of material. Most playwrights were circumspect in their choice and deployment of historical sources. There were however more dangerous ways of evading the restrictions imposed on literary and dramatic works. Printers of recusant books set up secret presses or, more often, worked abroad, frequently using false imprints further to mislead the authorities.[55] Subversive discourses, such as the Jesuit Robert Parsons's *A Conference about the Next Succession to the Crown of England* (1594), in which he not only discussed the prohibited subject but upheld the deposition of wicked princes as righteous and lawful, was published pseudonymously in 'N', probably Antwerp. Actors attempted to circumvent the system by not submitting their play to the Master of the Revels or by producing a play substantially different from that which he had licensed. Such transgressions when detected attracted harsh penalties. Presses were destroyed and books burnt; theatres were closed, plays suppressed and actors arrested.

What the state cannot legislate for, however, is the act of interpretation applied to literature and drama: a privilege perceived as a
dangerous liberty by Lord Chief Justice Coke at the trial of the Jesuit
poet Robert Southwell in 1595, in his warning against the misappro-
priation of texts: 'And them likewise we met withall, and made it a
felony to publish them, and a felony to keep them. A good point, my
masters, to be observed. Beware how you read them!'.[56]

As recent studies have shown, reading techniques had indeed
developed in response to writing strategies so constructed as to evade
censorship. Readers were familiar with codes of reference which
enabled the writer to comment on prohibited matters. The relationship of the audience with the play text is somewhat different. As
Marston says in his address to the reader in *The Fawn*, the life of the
play 'rests much in the actors' voice' and 'consists in action'. The play
is decoded in performance and, as we shall see, it was sometimes only
after a play's meaning was thus publically exposed that objection was
taken and reprisals occurred.

Notes

1 See Margaret Aston, *England's Iconoclasts* (Oxford, 1988), I, *Laws
  Against Images*, pp. 1–18, 294–343.
2 The conclusions of H. C. Gardiner's investigation of the last days of the
  religious drama, *Mysteries' End: An Investigation of the Last Days of
  the Medieval Religious Stage* (New Haven, London, 1946) although
  polemical, have not been disputed by later theatre historians and have
  gained general acceptance.
3 See J. J. Scarisbrick, *The Reformation and the English People* (Oxford,
  1984), pp. 61–2.
4 'Injunctions for Religious Reform; Ordering Homilies to Be Read from the
  Pulpit', *Tudor Royal Proclamations*, eds. Paul L. Hughes and James F.
  Larkin (3 vols., New Haven, London, 1964–9), I, pp. 393–403.
5 Anti-papal interludes comprised part of the coronation entertainment.
  The Revels' account lists the cost for cardinals' hats, cord and fur for
  friars, caps of crimson and black for priests and a crown and cross for a
  pope. See A. Feuillerat, *Documents Relating to the Revels in the Time of
  King Edward VI and Queen Mary* (Louvain, 1914), pp. 5–6.
6 See *The York Plays*, ed. Richard Beadle (London, 1982), p. 27.
7 See F. M. Salter, 'The Banns of the Chester Plays', *RES*, 15 (1939), 432–
  57 and *RES*, 16 (1940), 1–17, 137–48. Salter dates the composition of the
  early Banns between 1521–34 and the late Banns as at 1575 for the last
  performance of the plays in Chester.
8 Salter, *RES*, 16 (1940), 141.
9 *Tudor Royal Proclamations*, I, p. 399 and II, p. 122.
10 *The Towneley Plays*, ed. George England, side-notes and Introduction by
   Arthur W. Pollard (London, 1897), p. 201.

11 David M. Bevington, 'Drama and polemics under Queen Mary', *Renaissance Drama*, 9 (1966), 105–24, at 105.
12 'Offering Freedom of Conscience; Prohibiting Religious Controversy, Unlicensed Plays, and Printing' (*Tudor Royal Proclamations*, II, pp. 5–8). In the Edwardian proclamation of 1551 'Enforcing Statutes against Vagabonds, Rumor Mongers, Players, Unlicensed Printers' it was stipulated that no interludes or plays should be performed 'unless the same be first allowed by his majesty or his Privy Council in writing signed with his majesty's most gracious hand or the hands of six of his said Privy Council' (*Tudor Royal Proclamations*, I, p. 517).
13 *Tudor Royal Proclamations*, II, pp. 115–6.
14 *REED: Chester*, p. 110.
15 *REED: Chester*, p. 109–10.
16 *REED: Chester*, p. 114.
17 See A. C. Cawley, 'Organization of the Corpus Christi plays', *The Revels History of Drama in English* (London, 1983), I p. 37.
18 *REED: York*, I, pp. 331–2.
19 See Alexandra F. Johnston, 'The plays of the religious guilds of York: the Creed play and the Pater Noster play', *Speculum*, 50 (1975), 55–90.
20 *REED: York*, I, p. 353.
21 *REED: York*, I, p. 365.
22 *REED: York*, I, p. 390.
23 Recent legal research has brought the Red Lion into prominence, replacing the traditional view that the Theatre was the first public playhouse. See Janet S. Loengard, 'An Elizabethan lawsuit: John Brayne, his carpenter, and the building of the Red Lion theatre', *Shakespeare Quarterly*, 34 (1983), 298–310.
24 'Remembrancia of the City of London', *MSC*, I (Oxford, 1907), pp. 68–9, 74–6.
25 The Lord Mayor to the Privy Council, 13 April 1582, *MSC*, I (1907), p. 54.
26 *APC 1578–80*, XI, p. 449.
27 *MSC*, I (1907), p. 53, E. K. Chambers takes the order as evidence that the Lord Mayor still had power to 'allow' plays in spite of the new authority vested in the Revels Office. See E. K. Chambers, *Notes on the History of the Revels Office Under the Tudors* (London, 1906), p. 76.
28 See below, pp. 51–4.
29 *APC 1599–1600*, XXX, pp. 395–8.
30 See Chambers, *ES*, II, pp. 87–8.
31 Chambers, *Notes*, p. 23.
32 Chambers, *Notes*, p. 33.
33 See W. R. Streitberger's detailed study 'On Edmond Tyllney's biography', *RES*, 39 (1978), 11–35.
34 See A. Feuillerat, *Documents Relating to the Office of the Revels in the Time of Queen Elizabeth*, (Louvain, 1908), pp. 51–2.
35 See Henslowe's *Diary*, eds R. A. Foakes and R. T. Rickert, (Cambridge, 1961), pp. xxviii–xxix.
36 See *Documents of the Rose Playhouse*, ed. Carol Chillington Rutter (Manchester, 1984), p. 130.
37 Chambers, *ES*, II, p. 222.

38 For the details of Buc's varied career and Court connections see Mark Eccles, 'Sir George Buc, Master of the Revels', *Thomas Lodge and Other Elizabethans*, ed. C. J. Sisson (Cambridge, 1933), pp. 409–506.

39 *Ibid.*, pp. 431–4 and Chambers, *Notes*, pp. 57–60.

40 For the details of Astley's tenure see Richard Dutton's forthcoming article 'Patronage, politics and the Master of the Revels: the case of Sir John Astley, Master of the Revels 1622–40', *English Literary Renaissance* and his forthcoming book on the Revels Office. I am grateful to Dr Dutton for allowing me to read his article in advance of publication.

41 *The Lives of John Donne, Sir Henry Wotton, Richard Hooker, George Herbert, Robert Sanderson* (Oxford, 1927), p. 262.

42 See *Dramatic Records of Sir Henry Herbert*, ed. J. Q. Adams, (New Haven, 1917). Herbert's office book is not extant; Adams's edition is based on transcript by Edmond Malone.

43 *Dramatic Records*, pp. 20–1.

44 In 1633, when Herbert licensed Mountfort's *The Seaman's Honest Wife* (or *The Launching of the Mary*) he appended a note to the licence instructing the bookkeeper to present him with the fair copy, presumably to check that his reformations had been incorporated into the prompt book.

45 *Dramatic Records*, p. 21.

46 'The newe Decrees of the Starre Chamber for orders in printinge', Arber, *SR*, II, 807–12.

47 In 1588 Whitgift appointed twelve persons to license books for printing, see Arber, *SR*, III, 690.

48 *APC 1586–7*, XIV, pp. 311–2.

49 Arber, *SR*, III, 677.

50 *Stuart Royal Proclamations*, eds. James F. Larkin and Paul L. Hughes (Oxford, 1973), I, pp. 243–5.

51 *The Works of Thomas Nashe*, I, p. 154.

52 *Ben Jonson*, VIII, p. 44.

53 *The Dutch Courtesan*, ed. Martin Wine (London, 1965), III. i. 39–40.

54 *Ben Jonson*, VIII, p. 634.

55 See A. C. Southern, *Elizabethan Recusant Prose 1559–1582* (London, 1978), pp. 338–59.

56 See Christopher Devlin, *The Life of Robert Southwell* (London, 1967), p. 309.

CHAPTER I

Fractured images:
the censor and the history plays
of the 1590s

Nay, what if I proove Playes to be no extreme; but a rare exercise of vertue. First, for the subject of them (for the most part) it is borrowed out of our English Chronicles ... what can be a sharper reproofe to these degenerate effeminate dayes of ours? (*Pierce Pennilesse His Supplication to the Devill*)

I have shown art and learning in these verses, I assure ye; and yet if they were well searched they're little better than libels. But the carriage of a thing is all, sir: I have covered them rarely. (The schoolmaster, *Woodstock*)

No evidence has survived to indicate that Tilney's commission of 1581, which virtually transformed his office from purveyor of royal entertainment to government censor, had any immediate effect. The apparent political conservatism of the repertoires of the Queen's Men, and less markedly of Strange's Men, during the 1580s presumably warranted little official interference.[1] Indeed, by the end of the same decade, the state was endorsing the support of the theatre in combatting anti-establishment propaganda. The cause of conflict was the vehement doctrinal controversy known as the Martin Marprelate affair, which arose from a number of scurrilous prose pamphlets mocking the bishops and the *via media* of the Church of England. The source of government alarm lay as much in the popular appeal of pamphlets written in a virulent, colloquial style as in their advocacy of a single Puritan form of church organisation. For a year, the authors and printers eluded detection by frequent removals of the printing press. In response, contravening their own prohibition of the representation of matters of religion or policy, the government supported anti-Martinist propaganda in the form of dramatic satire composed by Lyly, Nashe and Greene and performed by the Queen's Men and Paul's Boys. Richard Bancroft, canon of Westminster and a vigorous opponent of Puritanism, seems to have played a large part in promoting the plays, a fact which Whitgift, Archbishop of Canterbury, recalled in 1597 when recommending him for the bishopric of

London: 'by his advice that course was taken, which did principally stop Martin's and his fellows' mouths'.[2] From the beginning of the campaign, however, there was some uneasiness at allowing players and playwrights the freedom to deal with church matters in a satiric vein. Francis Bacon, writing at the time of the controversy, condemned the use of the stage and the policy of treating the Martinists with 'their own weapons', commending an anonymous bishop for his comment on the first Marprelate pamphlet that 'a fool was to be answered, but not by becoming like unto him'.[3] Despite such reservations, the plays were performed in the private and public theatres and playgoers were able to see the grotesque spectacle of Martin, with 'a cocks combe, an apes face, a wolfs bellie', having his blood spilt upon the stage in a mock letting of humours.[4] Such plays seem to have succeeded in undermining the popular appeal of Puritan propaganda. In one of the anti-Martinist pamphlets (August 1589), Martin ruefully acknowledges to his sons that the commons are 'now wearie of our state mirth, that for a penie, may have farre better by oddes at the Theater and Curtaine and any blind playing house everie day'.[5]

The plays ran for about five months before the government began to have doubts about the wisdom of its policy. Lyly, in *Pappe with an Hatchet* (October 1589), referred to comedies recently composed which were not allowed to be played even though the portrait of Martin was more restrained than in former plays. In November 1589 constraints were applied on the satire which had so recently been stimulated. The reaction is found in Privy Council letters to Whitgift, the Mayor of London and Tilney, setting out matters judged unfit for stage representation. The instructions to Tilney stipulate that, in company with two nominees of the Lord Mayor and the Archbishop of Canterbury, he is 'to stryke oute or reforme suche partes and matters as they shall fynd unfytt and undecent to be handled in playes, both for Divinitie and State'.[6] Companies who present unlicensed plays are threatened with extinction. After 1589, no more is heard of Paul's Boys for a decade: a fact which has prompted the reasonable conjecture that they were suppressed in direct consequence of their performance of the anti-Martinist plays.[7] In the light of the tacit support given to the bishops in their original sponsorship of the anti-Puritan drama, such reprisals cannot be seen as anything but an arbitrary penalty, perhaps born of panic. The episode does, however, reveal the government's recognition that satire, despite its effectiveness to undermine opposition, is potentially anarchic and once loosed cannot be consistently harnessed to orthodoxy and state interests. Conversely, this is perhaps the earliest illustration of the unpredictable nature of a new censorship borne upon the tides of policy and breaking upon the works of dramatists who had assumed themselves immune.

The role of the censor 1581–1603: an overview

Apart from the general duty to supervise the presentation of political or religious issues, we have no precise knowledge of Tilney's working brief. His preoccupations as dramatic censor can only be deduced from the major concerns of state policy and from actual cases of censorship. We know, for example, that in 1581 'AN ACTE against sedicious Wordes and Rumors uttered againste the Queenes moste excellent Majestie' made it punishable by death to circulate 'any manner of Booke Ryme Ballade Letter or Writing, conteyning any false sedicious and slaunderous Matter' which might lead to 'the encoraging stirring or moving of any Insurreccon or Rebellion, within this Realme'.[8] Laws concerning treason and seditious libel made incitement to rebellion or speculation on the succession capital offences. A proclamation of 1587 prohibited the spread of seditious rumours.[9] This policy of keen surveillance of any potentially subversive activity extended to restrictions on the publication of history of topical interest. The censorship of Holinshed's *Chronicles* has already been mentioned: the cancelled pages in the second edition of the *Chronicles* included references to the house of Cobham, John Stow's account of the Babington plot of 1586 and his discussion of recent events in Scotland and Ireland. Again, Hayward's *The First Part of the Life and Raigne of King Henrie IIII* was initially licensed by the bishop's chaplain in 1599, but was soon after suppressed. Attorney General Coke, who conducted the prosecution of Hayward, entertained no doubts about the historian's intentions, as is evident from his note that 'the Doctor selected a story 200 years old, and published it last year, intending the application of it to this time'.[10] Equally suspect was history which rejected the traditional providential interpretation in favour of a secular analysis of political actions. Several of Machiavelli's works, for example, which most clearly projected such ideas were refused licence: *I Discorsi* and *Il Principe* were printed only in Italian, without licence and with the false imprint of 'Palermo' at the press of John Wolfe in 1584.[11]

Tilney would assuredly have been as conscious of the potential of the history play to project meanings into the present as were the judiciary and the Privy Council. Bibliographical evidence from a number of plays which belong to the last decade of the sixteenth century does, indeed, suggest that they were censored because they staged issues which were topical or referential; since it was perceived that these plays had the potential to kindle or inflame public disorder, and since the momentum of playgoing itself could not be halted, censorship became the principal agent of containment. To this period, notably, belong two history plays – *Sir Thomas More* and *Woodstock* – which have survived in manuscript and which exhibit different forms of censorship. New light can be shed on the texts of *Doctor Faustus* by placing them in the context of contemporary censorship. The structural imbalance and textual anomalies in the printed edition of *Jack Straw* are likewise suggestive of censorship. In the light of what is known about Tilney's functions, discrepancies between different editions of 2 and 3 *Henry VI* and *Richard II* can also be attributed to his incursions. In this context, the state reaction to the lost but much cited production of *The Isle of Dogs* assumes a greater significance and lends credence to more tentative evidence in other suspected cases of textual censorship.

Any attempt to construct a precise and detailed chronology of Tilney's dealings with plays in the repertoires of the companies from the late 1580s, when he began to exercise his authority, through the next decade is bound to be frustrated. Such an account is precluded by the patchiness of the information available to us. Dates of performance of plays from this period are notoriously difficult to determine and whilst some texts present certain or cumulative evidence of censorship, others have to remain the subject of conjecture. Instances of interference from the Revels Office will therefore be discussed chronologically when a date can be determined or reliably estimated. Where evidence for censorship or for a play's date is scant, it will be located within the context of plays apparently censored from similar premises. This approach will facilitate examination of the predominant concerns of censorship in the 1590s and some of the strategies which playwrights adopted in response.

Doctor Faustus

One of the earlier Elizabethan plays which it is contended met with censorship is *Doctor Faustus*.[12] There is no direct evidence of this; but the status of the so-called 'A' version as a performance-based text, combined with the political referentiality of one of the passages absent in 'A' and present in the 'B' version, suggests interference by Tilney.[13] The provenance of 'A' – published, though probably not for the first time, in 1604 – as an Elizabethan stage version is indisputable. Its title page refers to performance: 'as it hath been Acted by the Right Honorable Earle of Nottingham his servants'; and it has been recognised that, in contrast to the 'B' text, 'A' accommodates the probable limitations of staging in the first London theatres.[14] Unfortunately, nothing is known about the stage history of the play before it was performed at the Rose and entered into Henslowe's accounts in 1594; but Greg's reasonable conjecture that it was briefly the property of Pembroke's Men before it came to the Admiral's Men has not been substantially contradicted.

One of the passages present in the 'B' version of 1616, but not in 'A', is the early part of the scene in Rome depicting the humiliation of Saxon Bruno. It has been assumed that this passage, as with the rest of the additional material, represents later work independent of Marlowe, for which Henslowe paid Rowley and Bird.[15] It has been dismissed as 'hack work' and the language described as 'grisly bombastical rhymed verse couplets'.[16] But the scene does contain resonances of Marlowe in the graphically drawn confrontation between the rival popes and the comic ritual of the papal court, as well as specific verbal echoes. Allowing for the likely depredations of Tilney, there is a case for arguing that the entire scene originated with Marlowe, part of it being suppressed before early performance but later recovered with some adulterations by Rowley.

The scene in Rome has a different tone in each of the two texts. The 'A' text's version is merely an opportunity for Faustus to play practical jokes on the Pope: a crudely realised piece of slapstick which submits to official anti-Catholic propaganda as well as to the prejudices of a predominantly Protestant audience. In the 'B' text, the cause of the celebration of St Peter's feast is not the 'belly-cheare' of the 'A' text, but the political triumph of the Pope's victory over Bruno, a rival pope whose claim had been put forward by the German Emperor. The Pope's hubris is conveyed by his treading on the back of Bruno, who reacts to this humiliation with dignity. In his words 'thus I fall to *Peter*, not to thee', he acknowledges the holiness of the Office, but not of its present incumbent.

There is much in this scene as it appears in the 'B' text which would have had disquieting implications for the Elizabethan government. In the later text, the Pope excommunicates the Emperor, curses the people who submit to him and, designating him as 'that haughty Schismatique', threatens to depose him from his 'Regall Government'. An Elizabethan audience would almost certainly have seen reflected in the Emperor's excommunication that of the Queen by Pius V in 1570, which paved the way for rebellion by freeing English Catholics from loyalty to the Crown.[17] In view of the Elizabethan prohibition of dramatic material relating to church and state, this episode with its references to excommunication and the absolute authority of the Papacy would surely have provoked the opposition of the censor. The suppression of the Pope's lines would not account for the omission of the entire Saxon Bruno episode; it would, however, have been difficult to stage the scene effectively in their absence.

The idea that the 'rival pope' episode had been written in or before 1593, but was censored for the stage version which lies behind the 'A' text, is substantiated by details gathered from other sources. The fact that at 1,517 lines the play is exceptionally short, in itself suggests that lines must have been lost. On external grounds, it is feasible that Marlowe took the name Bruno – not in the source – from the Dominican philosopher and iconoclast Giordano Bruno, who had visited England in 1583 and debated with the doctors of Oxford.[18] There was much in the hermiticism of Giordano Bruno, his unorthodox Catholicism leading to a life of exile and the stake, and his interest in magic which would have engaged Marlow and is pertinent to *Doctor Faustus*. On 26 May 1592, Bruno was incarcerated in the prisons of the Holy Office.[19] If we accept the view of most editors that *Doctor Faustus* was Marlowe's last play before his death in 1593, it may be inferred from the dramatisation of Saxon Bruno's confrontation with the Pope, his imprisonment and his contrived escape, that Marlowe intended an allusion which would have appealed to the more initiated in his audience.

Stylistically, a claim may also be made for Marlowe's hand.[20] Although not uncommon, the reference to the Papacy as St Peter's Chair, by Raymond King of Hungary in the 'B' version of the scene, is one also made by Machiavel in the Prologue to *The Jew of Malta*. Marlowe in *Tamberlaine* was fond of the motif of trampling on one's enemies. The image of the Pope stepping on Bruno recalls Tamberlaine's ascent of the throne on the back of Bajazeth.

There is then, from the criteria of both style and content, a case for Marlowe's composition of the Bruno episode. It seems reasonable to suppose that it does not appear in the 'A' text because Tilney suppressed its protrayal of a triumphant Pope threatening to depose his allegedly heretical enemies in terms which could readily be applied to the Queen and ordered its revision, thus promoting the anti-papal satire which remains. Marlowe's original scene was presumably recovered to increase the attraction of an old Elizabethan play. Its restoration took place at a time when the threat of excommunication carried less immediate impact and when the English Catholic body was no longer regarded by Catholic governments of Europe as a major oppositional force.

The book of Sir Thomas More

The *cause célèbre* of Elizabethan censorship is the case of the play book of *Sir Thomas More*, whose authorship is usually attributed to Anthony Munday. The book, which came before the Master of the Revels in the early 1590s,[21] is the earliest extant manuscript to demonstrate state interference with secular drama. It is well known that Tilney's hand is to be seen at intervals throughout the play book, excising whole scenes and substantial sections of dialogue, making marginal comments and interlineations.

The material which Tilney suppressed falls into two categories: the displays of xenophobic disorder in the anti-alien riots and More's role in opposing Henry VIII's break with Rome. Even so, the latter issue is rather summarily represented by Munday in the first place and the play is silent about More's opposition to the Acts of Supremacy and Succession. Despite the potential for controversy in the character and career of More, his dramatic representation should therefore have caused the censor little concern. The More of the play is no tragic hero or Catholic martyr, but a figure of folk memory. Considering Munday's anti-Catholic activities, including the writing of pamphlets and his part in the capture of the Jesuit priest and poet Robert Campion, this is not surprising. It may well have been that his former services to the government permitted him to bring More to the stage, eliminating any possible suspicion of his motives and loyalties. There is, however, evidence of censorship in the Council meeting of scene x, the one scene in which Reformation loyalties inescapably intruded. The session is interrupted by the arrival of Sir Thomas Palmer from the King with instructions that More should subscribe to certain unspecified articles, presumably a vague reference to the Ten Articles or to the Injunctions of 1536 which alluded to 'the Bishop of Rome's usurped power'.[22] Tilney has drawn a diagonal line through the portion of the scene which depicts More and the Bishop of Rochester, alone amongst the councillors, refusing to sign. He has further signified his disapproval by a long, thin cross in the left hand margin and the note 'ALL ALTR' in the right-hand margin. No attempt has been made to revise the scene, probably because it was recognised that it would have been impossible to present More's political and religious intransigence in a manner acceptable to Tilney without distorting the portrayal. Significantly, the events which led to More's downfall are

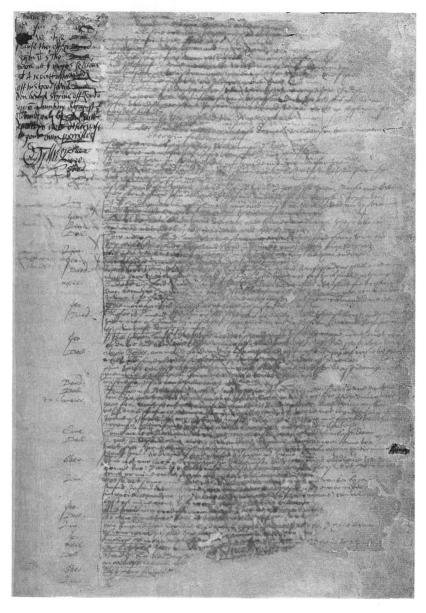

1 *Sir Thomas More*: the insurrection scene. Tilney's orders for the revision of the play.

greatly compressed and any suggestion of his participation in religious conflict is avoided.

Tilney's initial and principal objection, however, was to the representation of the May Day riots against foreigners who had taken refuge in London and were blamed for causing economic disadvantage to the indigenous population. These are dramatised in scenes i and iv and in a truncated scene v (f. 3r–3v, 5v). The entire first scene in which a rowdy group of citizens protests against the rights and privileges taken by strangers in the city, has been marked for omission by means of marginal rules and crosses. (Plate 1). No doubt Tilney disliked the dynamic of the opening assembly and the articulacy of its spokesman, John Lincoln, who composes an address to be read during the annual Spittle sermons which makes compelling reference to the citizens' plight now that 'aliens' dominate the economic life of the city. The peroration urges the commons to unite and seek the redress of their wrongs:

> wherfore, the premisses considered, the redresse must be of the comons, knit and united to one parte. And as the hurt and damage greeveth all men, so must all men see to their willing power for remedie, and not suffer the sayde Aliens in their wealth, and the naturall borne men of this region to come to confusion.   (fol. 3v)

Tilney's curt directives indicate how he wished to shift the emphasis from the cause and course of the rebellion to the righteous quelling of it:

> Leave out the insurrection wholy and the Cause ther off and begin with Sir Thomas Moore att the mayors session with a reportt afterwards off his good service don being Shrive off London uppon a mutiny Agaynst the Lumbards only by A short reportt and nott otherwise att your own perilles E. Tyllney   (fol. 3r)

Clearly, Tilney was not remotely interested in the effects of his censorship on the play: entire scenes are to be omitted, whatever their dramatic significance or theatrical impact, and replaced simply by reports of the events they describe. In the scene following the beginning of the riot Tilney's censorship is more piecemeal. In a discussion between the Earls of Shrewsbury and Surrey and Sir Robert Cholmeley in which they comment on the restiveness of the commons (fol. 5r), Tilney continues to indicate his disapproval of the presentation of popular unrest: a large, elongated cross has been placed against Shrewsbury's speech in which he refers to 'dangerous times', 'frowning Vulgare brow', 'distracted countenaunce of greefe', and 'the displeased commons of the Cittie', accompanied by the marginal imperative 'Mend this'. The expression of sympathy for the commons' cause by others has provoked Tilney's further displeasure. He has drawn marginal rules against a speech by Surrey, who prophesies that the 'saucie Aliens' will pay for their pride, and also against Cholmeley's measured criticism of the King's advisers, who have failed to inform him of the 'base abuse and dayly wrongs' experienced by his subjects. A large cross reinforces his objection to the passage. Manifestly, Tilney wanted to redirect the citizens' hatred to less controversial scapegoats: almost all references to 'aliens' and 'french-men' have been excised and an alternative victim, the Lombard, substituted.[23] The riot is resumed in scene four, where Lincoln incites the mob to fire the houses of the strangers, and in the incomplete scene five, where the apprentices join the insurgents to go 'a Maying'. Both scenes have been marked for omission in their entirety, although this may have been done in the playhouse in deference to Tilney's injunctions, since the style of the marginal rules and of the form of the square cross are different from Tilney's markings elsewhere.

The explicit preoccupations of Tilney's censorship help to date the play as c. 1592–3. The ever-present antagonism against immigrants reached its peak in the last decade of the century.[24] In April 1593, the City council were authorised to discover the provenance of virulent tracts indicating that 'artyficers and others who holde themselves prejudiced in theire trade' were planning to attack the foreigners.[25] The following month, the Privy Council were taking more extreme measures to counter further threats in 'seditious libels' posted on the wall of the Dutch churchyard in Austin Friars, the centre of Dutch preaching, which warned that unless the strangers had departed by July, 'Apprentices will rise to the number of 2,336. And [they] ... will down with the Flemings and strangers'.[26] In reaction the Council ordered the houses of suspected persons to be searched for in-criminating evidence. Suspects were to be cross-examined and if they 'refuse to confesse the truth' they were to be tortured in Bridewell, 'as often as you shal thinck fit'.[27] Tilney's censorship, then, can be seen as part of wider measures to prevent the fuelling of hostility against the foreign communities from which the state derived so much economic benefit.[28]

It has been argued that *Sir Thomas More* was composed as late as 1603 and that the reason for censorship lay in the resurrection of fears associated with the rebellion of the Earl of Essex.[29] The case rests ultimately on a 1603 entry in Henslowe's *Diary* recording a payment to two of the five revisers identified in the manuscript, Chettle and Heywood, for an unnamed play. Whether this entry is a reference to

Sir Thomas More must remain open to question. Certain sections of the play may have been revised in 1603; but to claim the date of the original composition as 1603 involves minimising the likelihood of a more contemporary relevance in the anti-alien riots and gives insufficient weight to Tilney's initial sweeping injunction against the insurrection and 'the mutiny agaynst the Lumbards'.

One of the intractable problems surrounding the manuscript is the status of the so-called additions which are to be found on separate leaves and bound up with the original folios. Most of these were clearly made for theatrical use, and are not therefore of concern here. Only one of the six additions has any direct bearing on Tilney's censorship, namely, that numbered II on folios seven to nine. The addition is a composite work in three different hands, designated as B, C and D by Greg, the last being often attributed to Shakespeare.[30] The section in hand 'B' is in part a transcript of the cancelled riot scene in scene iv with the addition of a new character, the clown, who exhibits a rumbustious xenophobia. Hand 'C's contribution is a scene in the Guildhall in which a messenger announces the progress of the rebels and More prepares to meet and appease 'with a calm breath this flux of discontent'. The Guildhall scene may have been part of the original play which would have been comprised in the lost folios following the cancelled apprentice riot of scene v: it is there in Holinshed's *Chronicles*, which Munday follows quite closely in his depiction of the early stages of the May Day riots. Interestingly lines at the beginning of the scene in which Sir John Munday arrives hurt, a witness to the strength of the apprentices and their cudgels, have been deleted. The inclusion of the lines suggests that hand 'C' was unaware of the fact that the apprentices play no part in the revised insurrection scene. Addition II ends with the contribution of hand 'D', in which More enters and entreats the rioters to be calm and compassionate. His advocacy is emotive as he describes the foreigners' plight should they be forced to leave England. He proceeds to argue passionately that if order is imperilled 'men lyke ravenous fishes woold feed on one another'. The warning which finally persuades Lincoln and his supporters to be 'rul'd' by More, however, lies in his heightened speech on kingship and divine right, with its assertion that by rising against the King, who has been lent 'his throne', 'his sword' and 'his owne name' by God, they are in fact rising against God himself. The argument is clinched with the insinuation that their desperate offensive against legitimate temporal authority is jeopardising their very souls. Casting aside the grievances of the commons, emphasis is now placed on proper respect for sovereignty and on the political commonplace that rebellion is a heinous act which is opposed to the order of a divinely sanctioned universe.

There has been much debate about whether the additions were made prior to the play's submission to Tilney or following his censorship and consequent upon it. Different hypotheses have been advanced to accommodate an apparent disregard (in the hand 'B' version of scene iv) of Tilney's injunction against the representation of the insurrection. Several commentators have followed the lead of Greg that revision could not have taken place after Tilney had perused the play book, on the grounds that there is nothing in addition II which would have satisfied his political objections. It has been suggested that the additions, motivated by literary or theatrical considerations, were undertaken simultaneously with Tilney's perusal of the book.[31] Another theory allows for double submission of the manuscript to the Revels Office, Tilney's comprehensive condemnation being registered on its second examination.[32] Giorgio Melchiori notes changes in the tone of the insurrection in addition II and suggests self-censorship in the playhouse at an early stage before submission to Tilney.[33] On the other hand Scott McMillin, in a thoroughgoing analysis of the text from the premiss of production, has contended that the revisions were made at different stages and that their main purposes were theatrical, specifically to allow for a reduced cast.[34] Hand 'D', he maintains, was working well in advance of the other revisers and in ignorance both of Tilney's censorship and of the later recasting of scenes for a production by the Admiral's Men. The supposedly revised insurrection scene is, therefore, according to McMillin, no revision at all, but early supplemental writing uncopied by Munday.

Gary Taylor has argued on internal and linguistic evidence that the revisions date from the following decade.[35] This thesis provides a further objection to an hypothesis, such as Greg's, which accommodates the additions within the original text. The principal weakness of any such hypothesis lies in the fact that there are no traces of Tilney's interference on the additional leaves. In every scene which deals with politically sensitive material, Tilney has left clear signs of his displeasure. It would be curious if, had he perused addition II or even part of it, he had left not a single mark.

It seems evident, then, that the revisions post-date Tilney's censorship although precisely when they appeared cannot be ascertained. Since the censor had not taken exception to the extent of prohibiting it altogether, it seems reasonable to assume that the company would have attempted to reform the play soon after, if not immediately upon Tilney's injunctions, when its very topicality would have guaranteed its theatrical success.

Scholars have been driven to argue for either pre-censorship or Jacobean revision because of a general conviction that the additions, specifically II, are not responsive to Tilney's censorship. In determining the relationship of the additional passages to the original text, however, too much stress has been placed on the apparent failure to obey Tilney literally in the revised riot scenes. That the insurrection is dramatised and not reported has been taken as evidence that the supplementary writing is in no way responsive to Tilney's stipulations. Had the revisers followed Tilney to the letter, however, they would have lost nearly a quarter of the play. Examined from a different perspective, the recast form of the insurrection serves to illuminate the kind of strategies which playwrights employed to circumvent censorship in an attempt to maintain a measure of dramatic integrity. The tenor of the riots in the revised scenes, from what we can tell, has subtly changed. The danger of actual violence is tempered by the clown's absurd exhortations and the humour serves to defuse the effect of the rioters' aspirations. The causes of unrest are trivialised when Lincoln, adopting the clown's insult, plays on the foreigners' liking for parsnips, overlooking their economic advantages. At this stage the rebellion has become almost a travesty of its former self. Indeed, the Lincoln of the censored first scene of the play who displayed some skill in oratory has been replaced by the demagogic figure confronting More. The leader who in scene one inspired the commons, admits in the hand 'D' revision, that he is unable to exert any control over them, provoking More's rejoinder: 'Then what a rough and ryotous charge have you to Leade those that the devle Cannot rule'. Significantly, the participation of the apprentices in the rebellion – the most sensitive because the most topical reference – has not been recast to compensate for the cancelled scene v.

There are further signs of deference to the specifications of Tilney's censorship in the Guildhall scene, where the foreigners are referred to as 'Lumbards'. It is true that the word 'strangers' remains in the hand 'D' passages in which More persuades the insurgents to capitulate; but, as part of More's rhetorical strategy to elicit sympathy for the aliens, the context is quite different. The pejorative aspect of the word 'strangers' was not universal; the term could indeed be reclaimed by those more favourably disposed. Sir John Woolley, for example, deployed affecting advocacy in his defence of the immigrants in Parliament in 1593: 'In the days of Queen Mary when our cause was as theirs is now, those countries did allow us that liberty which now we seek to deny them. They are strangers now, we may be strangers hereafter. So let us do as we would be done to'.[36] Again, hand 'D' depicts More unhistorically subduing the riot. In doing so, he reasserts the ideological basis of order and degree; it is recognition of this doctrine, rather than penitence at their 'mountanish inhumanyte', which effects the insurgents' submission. While More's realisation of the fate of foreigners plodding towards the ports brings local colour into an episode resounding with orthodox ideas, the purport of the addition would seem to be essentially a palliative to recover Tilney's favour. Gestures have been made towards diminishing the censor's underlying apprehensions; the rebels have been discredited whilst the rebellion itself, vital to the play's theatrical life, has been preserved.

Whether or not Tilney was satisfied with such dramatic compromises is another matter. The fact that, apart from a solitary reference to the actor Thomas Goodale as messenger, we have no solid evidence for the production or the publication of *Sir Thomas More* may suggest the censor's continuing disapproval and a certain reluctance to be associated with a play that had incurred such strong antagonism from the censor.

The life and death of Jack Straw

The first and only edition of the anonymous *Jack Straw* was printed in 1593. The play book must therefore almost certainly have been perused by Tilney before that of *The Book of Sir Thomas More*; but in the light of his censorship of the insurrection in the *Sir Thomas More* manuscript, there is a strong case for arguing that a censored prompt book underlies the printed text of *Jack Straw*.[37] The play deals with the eponymous leader of the Kentish faction in the Peasants' Revolt of 1381. Straw is heralded as 'a notable Rebell in England' on the title page; yet as it stands, the rebellion is accorded only perfunctory attention. Exposition of the rebels' cause at the beginning of the play – founded on the burden of extortionate taxation – is minimal and the dramatisation of the rebellion itself so cursory that it is reasonable to assume that material was deleted from the original play book. There is no significant mention of tax abuse, as there is in Holinshed or Stow. The peasant farmer, Jack Straw, refuses to pay the poll tax for his daughter demanded by the King's collector of taxes, on the basis that she is under age and 'therefore goes cleare'. A brawl ensues in which the collector is killed and rebellion is proclaimed. The playwright, however, does not appear fully engaged with the popular cause. Issues and motives are summarily sketched and do not adequately account for Nobs's vehement proclamation of rebellion:

> By gogs bloud my maisters, we will not put up this so quietly,
> We owe God a death, and we can but die ...
> Wele so deale of ourselves as wele revenge this villainy.   (ll. 53–9)

Yet there is also a notable inconsistency in Nobs's involvement in the rebellion, since he proceeds to speak critically of the rebels' ambitions and prophesies their probable fate on the gallows.

The second act, depicting the course of the rebellion, is characterised by a series of extremely brief episodic scenes: Nobs stealing Tom Miller's goose; the rebels proclaiming their intention to march to London; the King's arrival to conciliate them, followed by his abrupt departure. The total effect is one of fragmentation. This is particularly so in the final scene of the second act which simply comprises 'Nobs with a Fleming':

> Sirra here it is set downe by our Captaines that as many of you as cannot say bread and cheese, in good and perfect English, ye die for it, and that was the cause so many strangers did die in Smithfield.
> Let me heare you say bread and cheese.
> Brocke and Keyse   (ll. 616–21)

The fact that there is no elaboration elsewhere of any theme of hostility towards strangers leaves this scene oddly hanging. In the context of Tilney's censorship of those scenes in *Sir Thomas More* dealing with the insurgents' reactions against foreigners, it may be conjectured that before the play was inspected by the Master of the Revels, its original version would have included the acts of violence and victimisation described by Holinshed:

> On the same day also they beheaded manie others, as well Englishmen as Flemings, for no cause in the world, but onelie to satisfie crueltie of the commons, that they were in their kingdome ... breaking into the church of the Augustine friers, they drew forth thirteene Flemings, and beheaded them in the open streets; and out of the parish churches in the citie, they tooke foorth seventeene ... But they continuing in their mischeefous purpose, shewed their malice speciallie against strangers, so that entring into everie street, lane, and place, where they might find them, they brake up their houses, murthered them which they found within, and spoiled their goods in most outragious manner.[38]

If the author of *Jack Straw* had sought to reproduce the brutal details set out in his sources, the scenes could not have escaped the censor's intervention. At a time of anti-alien riots in the city the stark analogies to be drawn would have invited the play's censorship.

Although it must remain a matter of speculation whether the rebellion in *Jack Straw* had been as extensively treated as in its source, before the play was submitted to the Revels Office, the proposition plausibly accounts for the compression of the play and the glossing over of the rebels' cause. Structurally, the scant detail of the rebellion itself is disproportionate to the attention given to the orthodox sentiments voiced by the Queen Mother and the protracted treatment of Richard's clemency towards the rebels. In theatrical terms the rebellion, such as it is, plainly has more vitality than the lengthy expositions of hierarchical doctrine by the King and his councillors which comprise much of the rest of the drama.

2 Henry VI

In the case of *Jack Straw*, there is only one version of the play and speculations about textual censorship can only remain as such. Most of Shakespeare's history plays, on the other hand, exist in more than one edition and there is, therefore, a stronger case for arguing that particular passages in one, or other, show signs of interference from the censor. *Parts 2* and *3 of Henry VI* exist in two substantially different editions, although, interestingly, comparisons between the respective texts of each Part do not betray the same patterns of censorship.[39]

The discrepancies between *The First Part of the Contention of the Two Famous Houses of York and Lancaster*, published in 1594, and *2 Henry VI* in the folio text are such that it used to be thought that *The Contention* was the source play for *2 Henry VI*. This view has been almost universally rejected, to be replaced by the theory that the 1594 quarto is defective because of its origin as a text reported from performance and suffering accordingly, among other features of a bad quarto, from differences in idiom.[40] Recent reappraisals of the quarto text arising from increased attention to theatre production have brought fresh insights. It has been closely argued that *The Contention* reflects *2 Henry VI* prepared for performance by Pembroke's Men in 1592–3, probably when they were forced to tour the provinces.[41] The provenance of the folio text appears to be autograph which, judging by the inclusion of the names of the actors, Bevis and Holland, at the beginning of Act IV Scene ii, has been prepared for performance.

We might expect then that any censorship by the Master of the Revels would have been transmitted either to both texts, making it difficult to determine what alterations, if any, were made to meet his demands, or to the quarto. In fact, the evidence does not seem to point that way. There are omissions and variant passages in the folio which can only reasonably be accounted for by censorship of the copy text. The lines in question contain references to the deposition of Henry VI

or to the Irish rebellion which York is sent to quell and from which
mission he acquires an army. Moreover, passages in the later text,
including sections depicting Cade's rebellion (notably IV. ii), have
been set from a reprint of the quarto, from which we can infer that
there was some textual irregularity in the printers' basic copy. Such
recourse to the earlier edition could well have happened because the
compositors were working from a manuscript which amongst other
textual problems included excisions and alterations by the Master of
the Revels.

It is notable that in several instances, when the Yorkists expose their
scorn for the King and his supporters, the tone is rather more muted in
the folio text. *2 Henry VI* does not contain Warwick's exhortation in
Act II scene ii that York should usurp the crown by inciting popular
support:

> Then Yorke advise thy selfe and take thy time,
> Claime thou the crowne, and set thy standard up,
> And in the same advance the milke-white Rose,
> And then to gard it, will I rouse the Beare,
> Inviron'd with ten thousand Ragged-staves.
> To aide and helpe thee for to win thy right,
> Maugre the proudest Lord of Henries blood,
> That dares deny the right and claime of Yorke   (C4v)

In its place the folio text has Warwick's flat promise: 'My heart
assures me, that the Earle of Warwick/Shall one day make the Duke of
Yorke a king.' (p. 482). Further, the encounter between Clifford and
York before their single combat has changed its tenor in the folio text.
In *The Contention* they exchange vehement insults, concluding with
York's taunt at the King, 'Come fearfull Henry grovelling on thy face,
Yeeld up thy Crowne unto the Prince of Yorke' (H3r). The exchange
has been altered in the folio to the expression of mutual admiration.
The contemptuous jibe at Henry is absent. As Andrew S. Cairncross,
the Arden editor, argues, the variant passages suggest revision undertaken to mute language 'considered derogatory to the Queen, the
Court, or certain members of the nobility'.[42] Moreover, quite apart
from the personal abuse of a king with whom Elizabeth shared a
common if remote ancestry, the exchanges of *The Contention* herald a
violation of the concept of sovereignty which would have carried
unwelcome resonances.

There are further traces of censorship in the representation of the
Irish rebellion. In Act III scene i, news of the revolt is brought while the
Queen, Suffolk and York are plotting the death of Duke Humphrey. In
The Contention, the messenger speaks of 'the wilde Onele' being up in

arms and the Irish are variously stigmatised as stubborn, uncontrolled, proud and ambitious. The folio text has only one such specific reference: the Cardinal's reminder to the squabbling Suffolk and York that 'the uncivil kerns of Ireland are in arms'. There is no mention of O'Neill as commander of the rebels. Bearing in mind the excision of comments on recent events in Ireland from the second edition of Holinshed's *Chronicles*, in 1587, it seems almost certain that references to the Irish were deliberately cut to the minimum necessary to accommodate the demands of the plot. The omission of the allusion to O'Neill is further explained by its specific contemporary resonance. In the 1590s Hugh O'Neill, Earl of Tyrone and head of one of the great Anglo-Irish clans, was engaged with Spanish support in mobilising forces against the English with the ultimate aim of making Ulster an independent kingdom. In 1595, he assumed the title of 'the O'Neill' and in Ulster was accorded almost monarchical status. He was declared a traitor; fears intensified as successive attempts to subdue the rebels miscarried.[43] By the end of the decade it was forbidden 'on pain of death, to write or speak of Irish affairs'.[44] Accordingly, it is most likely that the short but crucial account of the Irish rebellion was censored in the latter part of the decade as the current Irish troubles came to present ever more serious threats to Crown ascendancy.

The scenes one might expect to have suffered censorship are those depicting the popular rebellion led by Jack Cade; but there are only limited traces of interference. The quarto text does give immediate prominence to the rebellion on the title page as 'the notable Rebellion of Jacke Cade', in contrast to the first page of the folio text which refers only to 'the death of Good Duke Humfrey'; but in both transmissions of the text, Cade's uprising is seen as little more than a travesty of popular rebellion, with Cade's ambitions presented as a parody of York's. A counter-revolutionary view is implicit in the portrayal of Cade the demagogue and his fickle supporters, where there is little to bear out York's account of Cade's fierce valour (III. i. 356–81), a tribute also found in Holinshed. Whether the feebleness of the rebellion is due to the anticipation of the Master's disapprobation or is a consequence of the rejection by the Revels Office of an original, more robust portrayal, it seems evident that censorship, or the consciousness of it, was involved. A few lines omitted in the folio would seem, moreover, to be lost to actual censorship of a Master of the Revels anxious to rid the text of any seditious sentiments. Cade's brag, 'bid the king come to me ... or otherwaies ile have his Crowne tell him, ere it be long' is absent and the rally to his followers, 'now weele march to London, for to morrow I meane to sit in the kings seate at Westminster' has become in the folio the more modest vaunt that in London the rebels will have the mayor's sword borne before them. The idiom of the quarto is not mere hyperbolic rant but expresses in some measure the angry defiance of rebels with a personal stake in their cause; as such it echoes the language of the London apprentices who in 1595 joined with 'certain soldiers or masterless men' and threatened that the Lord Mayor should not 'have his head upon his shoulders within one hour'.[45] If, as seems probable, the lines were censored in the text underlying the folio, it may be inferred that Tilney was again anxious to modify the popular and subversive idioms of the times.

The Contention, representing the play in one of its acting forms, is usually regarded as a text inferior to the folio, whose provenance was autograph. But the fact that the folio text has suffered some interference from the censor should make us doubt its ultimate integrity (and for an editor its total dependability as copy text).

3 Henry VI

The relationship between the texts of *The True Tragedy of Richard Duke of York*, published in 1595, and *3 Henry VI* is analogous to that of *The Contention* and *2 Henry VI*, in that the quarto records early performance of the play by Pembroke's Men. With the last play of the trilogy, however, it is the earlier text which transmits Tilney's censorship. *The True Tragedy* is considerably shorter, omitting as it does many rhetorical passages and long tracts of introspection such as the greater part of Gloucester's soliloquy (III. ii. 124–95) in which he declares his ambitions. Such omissions can readily be attributed to cuts made prior to performance; but the content of certain other passages suggests that they have been suppressed by Tilney. Into this category falls the exchange in Act IV scene vi, in which Henry, on being released from the Tower, relinquishes power to Warwick and Clarence as protectors of the realm. Compared with the scene in *3 Henry VI*, the version in *The True Tragedy* contains minimal negotiation:

> *King.* Thus from the prison to this princelie seat,
>   By Gods great mercies am I bought
>   Againe, *Clarence* and *Warwicke* doe you
>   Keepe the crowne, and governe and protect
>   My realm in peace, and I will spend the
>   Remnant of my daies, to sinnes rebuke
>   And my Creators praise

War. What answers *Clarence* to his soveraignes will?
Cla. Clarence agrees to what king Henry likes.   (D8r)

The episode in the folio is much fuller: Henry interprets his release by
Warwick as providential and a sign that he should surrender his power
to the earls; Warwick and Clarence then discuss the terms of the
abdication and raise the issue of the succession. The contention that
this scene was censored is further substantiated by the non-appearance
of the deposition scene in *Richard II* in all Elizabethan editions of that
play. It is sometimes assumed that the absence of the scene relates to
Queen Elizabeth's known identification with Richard II. But no such
precise analogy needs to be drawn. The question of the succession had
become, by the mid-1590s, an extremely delicate issue and the Queen
had expressly forbidden its discussion. It seems highly improbable that
in the political climate of the 1590s, the Master of the Revels would
have allowed full theatrical realisation of a monarch surrendering
power and bringing about a new line of succession.

   A bibliographical study of the different texts of *2 Henry VI* and *3
Henry VI* fails to offer any coherent view of the operation of
censorship in the early 1590s. Our limited knowledge of the history of
Pembroke's Men during the years 1591–94 provides no further
assistance. All we can say with any certainty is that the different
editions encapsulate the plays at arbitrary moments of early production and that they incorporate the demands of the censor as the
date and the occasion of performance dictated.

Thomas of Woodstock

The date of the anonymous manuscript play commonly entitled
Thomas of Woodstock can be placed between *2 Henry VI* and
Richard II, that is c. 1593–94, on the basis of source and derivation
respectively.[46] The manuscript has been carefully annotated in preparation for production, although there is no record of performance
or of the company to whom it belonged. The play is of particular
interest in that, besides evidence of playhouse revision in response to
Elizabethan censorship, there are signs, to be considered later, of
Jacobean censorship in the hand of George Buc. Quite clearly, the
manuscript does not have the same interest as *The Book of Sir Thomas
More*. While its final leaf, which would ordinarily contain the licence
of the Master of the Revels, is missing, there is no indication that
Tilney ever perused the manuscript: there are no marginal comments
in his hand and the style in which lines are excised does not resemble

the censor's markings in *More*. What we appear to have is a fair copy transcribed from the author's original and annotated by various hands including the playhouse bookkeeper.

From the colour of the ink, it is evident that the various cuts were made by more than one hand. There is, however, a consistency in the content of certain of the excised lines which suggests that the cuts have been made in compliance with Tilney's instructions. The language of the play is subversive in its expression of open hostility to the King. Woodstock accuses Richard of wilfully neglecting his sovereign duty: 'See here King Richard: whilst thou liv'st at ease/Lulling thyself in nice security,/Thy wronged kingdom's in a mutiny.' (II. ii. 40–2). Two short horizontal rules signify the deletion of the lines. Richard's abuses of power provoke a rare unity of purpose between the nobles and the commons. Significantly, assages in which rebellion is presaged are marked for omission. The first of these occurs in Lapoole's soliloquy after the murder of Woodstock at Calais. Lapoole, the governor of the port, who has stage-managed the murder, reports that, 'The gentlemen and Commons of the realm/ Missing the good old duke, their plain protector,/ Break their allegiance to their sovereign lord/ And all revolt upon the barons' side' (V. i. 285–8). Another passage in which rebellion is proclaimed, this time by the magnates, is marked for removal in a different hand:

> *Bagot.* Stay, my dear lord; and once more hear me, princes.
>   The king was minded – ere this brawl began –
>   To come to terms of composition –
> *Lanc.* Let him revoke the proclamations,
>   Clear us of all supposed crimes of treason,
>   Reveal where our good brother Gloster keeps,
>   And grant that these pernicious flatterers
>   May by the law be tried, to quit themselves
>   Of all such heinous crimes alleged against them,
>   And we'll lay down our weapons at thy feet.
> *King's Men.* Presumptuous traitors!
> *Lord's Men.* Traitors!
> *King.* Again we double it: rebellious traitors!   (V. iii. 110–22)

The deletion of these episodes suggests an attempt to diminish the elements and language of insurrection as part of the fabric of the play.

A further excised passage (II. iii. 27–70) embodies the Queen's lament for the state of the realm. In conversation with the Duchesses of Gloucester and Ireland she grieves at the burdens suffered by the commons because of the King's misgovernment. In response, the Duchess of Gloucester reassures her that 'England's not mutinous' and that 'none dares rob him of his Kingly rule', despite the fact that 'much misled by flatterers', Richard 'neglects, and throws his sceptre care-lessly'. To compensate for the oppressive levies exacted by her 'wanton Lord' from the commons, the Queen promises to redress their grievances by distributing her own revenue, a gesture which invites Cheyney's contrast, 'a virtuous queen, although a wanton King'. The decision to omit this passage must have taken place during an early stage of transcription, since the characters' lines have not been differentiated by speech prefixes. Once again, the material suggests that it was considered advisable to take out such a direct critique of sovereignty. In particular, allusions to the commons' grievances against the King brought about by exorbitant taxation and the political influence of flatterers may well have been perceived as carrying dangerously contemporary associations.

In the scene of Woodstock's murder, two significant cuts – apparently in different hands – have been made to lines spoken by Lapoole. The Governor, who has hitherto shown no trace of remorse for his complicity in the murder of the good Duke, suddenly recognises a conflict between the imperatives of conscience and his duty to the King: 'Horror of conscience, with the King's command/ Fights a fell combat in my fearful breast' (V. i. 35–6). The second excision – which is made by the same hand as is responsible for deleting part of his soliloquy – removes lines which show Lapoole recoiling in horror from his deed: 'A seven times crying sin. Accursed man!/ The further that I wade in this foul act/ My troubled senses are the more distract,/ Confounded and tormented past my reason' (V. i. 41–4). In view of their powerful expression of inner conflict, to cut these two passages for the purpose of theatrical abridgment would seem misconceived and any other artistic reasons are hard to deduce. But in the early 1590s the lines would have carried an oblique but nonetheless disturbing referentiality. Elizabeth had signed the death warrant of Mary Stuart in 1589. The Queen's attempt to extricate herself from any involvement in regicide by claiming that her Secretary of State, William Davison, had sent off the warrant without her authority was common knowledge and fundamentally distrusted by Catholic ob-servers.[47] It is a reasonable conjecture that the deletion was made to forestall the drawing of coded analogies between the two events.

In the manuscript of *Woodstock*, we appear to have a version of the text prepared for performance, and then reconsidered in the light of objections raised by the Master of the Revels on his perusal of the foul papers. We know from Tilney's presence in *The Book of Sir Thomas More* that he did not methodically suppress or amend provocative material, but that he dealt in broad directives: 'leave out the insurrection', 'mend this', 'all alter'. Certain passages in *Woodstock* seem therefore to have been omitted in accordance with the censor's instructions to remove explicit reference to rebellion and the more overt denunciations of King Richard; such material may well have been perceived as bearing a generalised likeness to current affairs of state, or at least as offering a dangerous precedent to disaffected subjects.

Edmund Ironside

From the only other surviving play manuscript ascribed to the early 1590s, *Edmund Ironside*, little evidence of censorship can be deduced. As with *Woodstock*, the play book represents a scribal copy of authorial papers and as such would already incorporate Tilney's strictures and licence, but it would seem improbable that the censor interfered extensively with the text of the play. In the conflict between Saxon and Dane, the drama veers away from controversial issues. The dramatic focus is the depiction of the crude stage Machiavel, Edricus, and his self-seeking strategems, yet he is hardly an agent of subversion. Despite claims by the editor Eric Sams concerning the relative political audacity of the play, there is little in its account of rivalries and treachery which would have alarmed Tilney.[48] The extant manuscript does, nevertheless, bear many marks of revision and the play has been abridged by almost 200 lines by an annotator who appears to have been preparing it for performance. The cuts appear quite arbitrary and only two of the deleted passages might be singled out as embodying politically sensitive or offensive sentiments: first, Edmund's pronouncement that the destruction of the Kingdom may ensue not from foreign aggression but from internal strife: 'England, if ever war thy face doth spoil/ thank not thy outward foe but inward friend/ for thou shalt never perish till that day/ when thy right hand shall make thy heart away' (ll. 377–80). And, secondly, the Bishop of York's strong denunciation of the Archbishop of Canterbury for his support of Canute: 'a rebel, a profane priest, a Pharisee/a parasite, an enemy to peace.' (ll. 834–5). The latter instance of excision suggests a literal-minded reaction against an explicitly derogatory reference to the episcopate, without regard to the context and the Archbishop's role. Since the removal of these lines has been made by the same hand as is responsible for the cuts elsewhere, it may be concluded that, if censorship was involved at all, this could only have been in anticipation of some further official objection and that lines were taken out as part of the general pruning process whilst the play was being prepared for production.

The contentions of Eric Sams, who favours Shakespearean author-ship of *Edmund Ironside* c. 1589, have been treated with a certain amount of scepticism, as must his views of the censorship prevailing when the play was composed. Sams contends that objection would have been taken to its 'bawdry, oaths, Satanism, blasphemy and a caricatured Primate of All England' (p. 24); but we have no evidence from other cases of dramatic censorship that such issues were of particular concern to Tilney. Blasphemy and oaths were censored in play texts, but not before 1606, when profanation on the stage was prohibited by statute. The prohibition of matters of faith and divinity in the drama relates to doctrinal controversy, rather than to the dramatic appearance of historical or pseudo-historical ecclesiastics, or their intrigues. It is, moreover, inaccurate to imply that Whitgift as Archbishop of Canterbury would have had anything to do with the original licensing of *Edmund Ironside*. Certainly, for the brief period when the anti-Marprelate plays were being produced, the Archbishop had authority to check the contents of plays, but the implication within the Privy Council's injunctions is that this power of censorship related specifically to the anti-Marprelate satire and was exercised for a brief period only. Conversely, the manuscript of *Edmund Ironside*, unlike those of *Sir Thomas More* and *Woodstock*, gives little insight into the workings of censorship and, again unlike his fellow play-wrights, the author of *Edmond Ironside* cautiously avoids parallels between the dramatic context and contemporary politics.

Richard II

This was not, however, judged to be the case when Shakespeare's *Richard II* came before the censor in 1595. Shakespeare goes further than the author of *Woodstock* in that he not only dramatises the grievances of the rebel Bolingbroke and the populace who endorse his violation of royal sacrosanctity, but lingers over the King's forced abdication. Such a scene, with its subordination of traditional ideo-logy and its inversion of monarchical ritual, invited strong reaction from the Master of the Revels. Although the evidence remains internal and bibliographical, censorship undoubtedly took place. It is well known that the deposition scene failed to appear in print in the Elizabethan editions of the play, or in subsequent reprints, and was not published until well into the reign of James I, in the 1608 quarto. The title page of this quarto advertises the additional material in the play and draws attention to its recent staging: 'With new additions of the Parliament Sceane, and the deposing of King Richard. As it hath been lately acted by the Kinges Majesties Servantes, at the Globe'.

If audiences had been familiar with the spectacle of the deposition on stage during the previous decade, it seems unlikely that the publisher, Mathew Lawe, would have coupled new publication with its being 'lately acted'.

The copy text for the quarto of 1597 is claimed to be autograph, and not a copy which has been annotated for theatre use. This may have been the manuscript sent to Tilney before the preparation of the prompt book. The manuscript appears to have been quite carefully edited, so that the omission of the deposition scene causes few anomalies in the dramatic narrative. The scene is cut from the moment when the Earl of Northumberland accuses the Bishop of Carlisle of treason for his support of Richard (IV. i. 150–3) and resumes with Bolingbroke's announcement of his intended coronation (IV. i. 319–20).[49] Richard's abdication becomes a *fait accompli*; his entry and his attempt to upstage Bolingbroke, before his histrionic surrender of power, are lost. There is, however, nothing incongruous about the early, compressed version of the scene; even the Abbot's words, 'A woeful Pageant have we here beheld', which in the full textual version refer to Richard's abdication, arrest and conveyance to the Tower, can now be taken to refer to the arrest of Carlisle on Northumberland's charge of treason. Nevertheless, 'pageant' most obviously refers to Richard's ritualistic abdication, and the fact that the line was left to stand suggests that responsibility for the excisions lay with the censor, who would not have concerned himself with the dramatic consistency of whatever survived his attentions.

The text of the deposition scene as it appears in the fourth quarto of 1608 is, with its mislineations and verbal errors, a poor one. Had the scene been performed on the stage at intervals since the play's composition as editors have implied, it would surely have been possible for Matthew Lawe, who secured copyright from Andrew Wise in 1603, to have obtained a fair copy prepared for stage use. The condition of the text, accordingly, tends to show that the printers did not have recourse to a playhouse text long in the possession of the King's Men and suggests that their copy must have been taken from an unauthorised source. The provenance of the scene in the 1608 quarto would, therefore, seem to be a hasty transcript compiled from dictation or memory and released to the printers, following the recovery of the scene for a Jacobean revival. The folio text, on the other hand, corrects the inaccuracies of the quarto and with its more precise stage directions seems to represent a more authoritative version of the scene.

Critics and editors have been hesitant about discussing the full implications of the scene's omission and what we may deduce about the state's fear of the theatre as an arena for inflammatory spectacle. The Arden editor, Peter Ure, comments that the scene is likely to have been performed on the stage, but was cut out of the printer's manuscript, 'probably because political conditions towards the end of the century made dethronement of an English monarch a dangerous subject for public discussion'.[50] It is difficult to see why what was 'a dangerous subject for public discussion' was not equally hazardous when presented in the theatre, where its reverberations might be felt across a wider range of public opinion. The Cambridge editor, Andrew Gurr, tends towards Ure's view: 'Perhaps the stage version of the play never lost the deposition scene, so that the playhouse always had a full version of the text'; and remarks that Tilney's record as a censor is undistinguished in comparison with press licensers.[51] But, as we have seen, evidence pieced together from the *Sir Thomas More* manuscript and anomalies in other texts suggests that Tilney was anxious to have the portrayal of seditious events abridged, or reported rather than enacted. Gurr's point that Lawe's use of a theatrical transcript signifies that the scene was appearing on stage in 1608, and by implication earlier, seems to ignore the more immediate evidence of the title page. We know from the reference to 'new additions' that the scene was being played and, as we have seen, the phrasing of the advertisement makes a strong case for its recent restoration to the play. Whereas it would have been judged dangerous in the last decade of Elizabeth's reign, when the question of the succession loomed large yet was a prohibited area of discussion, such fears would have been less predominant following the uncontested succession of James I. Nor is there evidence that ecclesiastical censorship was, on the whole, more stringent than censorship of drama by the Master of the Revels. Hayward's history of Henry IV, which was as much concerned with the deposition of Richard II as Shakespeare's play, was licensed without any objection by the Bishop of London's chaplain. Moreover, the Stationers' Register entry for *Richard II* in 1597, granting Andrew Wise copyright, shows that the play was amongst those works printed on the strength of the wardens' authorisation and without specific ecclesiastical sanction.[52]

The scene's undoubted literary and dramatic qualities have been invoked to support the case for its inclusion during the play's early stage history. Ernest Talbert, notably, discusses the artistry and compelling lyricism of the scene and comments that this 'may well have restrained any tendency toward delation on the part of those who watched its performance even in a year of official scrutiny and theatrical turmoil' and that 'Shakespeare could have expected his artistry to be supported by that of the Lord Chamberlain's actors'.[53] But it is doubtful whether the actors' recognition of the scene's lyrical qualities would in itself have persuaded them to take such risks. One may also assume that the Master of the Revels would hear from his sources if the players were to disregard his strictures so flagrantly as to perform the momentous episode.

From his treatment of the events leading to the deposition, it is evident that Shakespeare was conscious of dealing with intractable political issues which demanded cautious representation. There is much that is said elsewhere in *Richard II* to counter the subversive ideology of royal deposition. In the first act, Gaunt refuses to respond to the plea of the Duchess of Gloucester to revenge her husband's murder, stating the familiar belief in the king's sacrosanctity. Reminiscent of More's quasi-homily, in the section of *Sir Thomas More* attributed to Shakespeare, is Carlisle's outburst of orthodox sentiment immediately before Bolingbroke assumes power, in which he argues the heinousness of Bolingbroke's crime and predicts a pattern of nemesis:

> And shall the figure of God's majesty,
> His captain, steward, deputy elect,
> Anointed, crowned, planted many years,
> Be judg'd by subject and inferior breath,
> And he himself not present? O, forfend it, God,
> That in a Christian climate souls refin'd
> Should show so heinous, black, obscene a deed!   (IV. i. 125–31)

The lines reflect the Yorkist sympathies and interpretations expressed in some of Shakespeare's chronicle sources; but more pertinent is their articulation of the Tudor doctrine of non-resistance embodied in the Elizabethan Church homily 'Against Disobedience and Wilful Rebellion'. Shakespeare could have found part of the content of the speech, without the augury, in Samuel Daniel's epic poem *The First Foure Bookes of the Civile Warres*; but, by deviating from the source and placing the speech just before the moment of deposition, he appears to anticipate any counter-charge that the play upholds Bolingbroke's usurpation.

In the deposition scene itself there are signs of circumspection in the handling of source material. Each of the chroniclers, Edward Hall and Raphael Holinshed, records thirty-three articles presented by Parliament which propound Richard's misgovernment. Holinshed attributes the King's fate to the grievances advanced in this form: 'The articles objected to King Richard, whereby he was counted worthie, to be deposed from his principalitie'. In the play, Northumberland alone makes an oblique reference to the articles, which goes unheeded. The corollary of justification in Richard's deposition is thus avoided by both Richard and Bolingbroke. Only in the staging of the actual dethronement, an elaboration from a bare reference in Holinshed, does Shakespeare abandon his cautious handling of the sources, thereby eliciting the interference of the Master of the Revels and suppression of the most theatrical moment in the play.

The Isle of Dogs

In contrast with the textual inferences of censorship in *Richard II*, evidence of the government's reaction to Jonson and Nashe's lost play, *The Isle of Dogs*, can only be pieced together from Privy Council records and literary sources. Fragmentary details of the controversy appear in Henslowe's *Diary* and in Nashe's *Lenten Stuffe*; it was also recalled by Jonson over twenty years later in his conversations with the Scottish poet William Drummond. The affair is illuminating for the information it provides about an attempt to circumvent censorship and the response of authority to an overstepping by playwrights and actors of the bounds of the permissible.

The unease which the government was beginning to feel about the nature of plays being presented in the public theatres and their influence on a large and volatile audience is illustrated in measures taken by the Privy Council on 28 July 1597.[54] In response to information of 'verie great disorders committed in the common playhouses both by lewd matters that are handled on the stages and by resorte and confluence of bad people', directives were addressed to the Justices of Middlesex: they were to prohibit playing within three miles of the city until All Hallowtide (1 November) and further to send for the owners of the Curtain, Theatre and other common playhouses and instruct them 'to plucke downe quite the stages, gallories and roomes that are made for people to stand in, and so to deface the same as they maie not be imploied agayne to suche use'. The order was dispatched on the same day as the aldermen sent one of their standard letters of complaint about the immorality of plays and the breaches of public order occurring in and around the theatres; but, as Carol Chillington Rutter has pointed out, it is clear that the Privy Council were not responding to any specific complaints from the City.[55] It is unlikely that there would have been time for the Privy Council to have received and responded to the *communiqué* from the Guildhall and there is,

besides, nothing in this letter to suggest urgency. More probably, the
Council were acting on information conveyed through their own
intelligencing network.

Investigations continued, apparently conducted by the hated
Richard Topcliffe. From a letter dated 15 August 1597, sent by the
Privy Council to Topcliffe and the Middlesex Justices, it appears that a
particular play had been brought to the Council's attention. It is
recorded that several of the players and one of the offending playwrights had been imprisoned and that the rest of the actors were to
suffer reprisal as fitting 'theire leude and mutynous behavior'.[56] The
Council's determination to prevent circulation of the play is conveyed
in the order to Topcliffe to discover how many copies had been
distributed and to whom. Nashe's involvement in the offence is
indicated by the Council's final instruction to examine papers found in
his lodgings. Although the controversial play, its venue and the
company who performed it, are all unnamed in the instructions to
Topcliffe and the Justices, Henslowe helps to complete the picture. As
early as August 1597 he began to sign up players from Pembroke's
Men, who had been responsible for staging *The Isle of Dogs* at the
Swan. On 10 August 1597, Henslowe records in his *Diary* that he had
taken on the actor William Borne for a period of three years
'beginynge Imediatly after this Restraynt is Recaled by the lordes of
the counsell which Restraynt is by the menes of playinge the Ieylle of
dooges'.[57] Henslowe's note is somewhat misleading, since the Privy
Council seems to have ordered the closure of the theatres on the basis
of reports alone before more specific information about *The Isle of
Dogs* had reached them; but it indicates that the cause of the scandal
was well known on the Bankside. The unnamed actor and 'maker' of
part of the play referred to in Topcliffe's brief was Ben Jonson. We
know that he was released from the Marshalsea prison on 8 October
1597, along with two actors from Pembroke's company, Gabriel
Spencer and Robert Shaw, and that he spoke to Drummond of his
internment under Elizabeth. His account suggests that his fellow
prisoners had been engaged to inform upon him: 'In the tyme of his
close Imprissonment under Queen Elizabeth his judges could gett
nothing of him to all their demands bot I and No, they placed two
damn'd Villans to catch advantage of him, with him, but he was
advertised by his keeper.'[58]

Nashe escaped punishment by fleeing to Great Yarmouth, where he
compiled his defence – or special pleading – which appears in *Lenten
Stuffe*. In his preamble to the whimsically entitled 'Praise of the red
herring' he reminisces on the 'troublesome stir' and 'generall rumour'

spreading throughout England in the wake of what he depicts as the prodigious birth of *The Isle of Dogs*: 'I was so terrifyed with my owne encrese (like a woman long travailing to bee delivered of a monster) that it was no sooner borne but I was glad to run from it.'[59] In an appended side-note, he casts the blame upon the actors who created the last four acts, 'which bred both their trouble and mine to'. Nashe protests that he was unjustly incriminated, although his self exculpatory reference to the actors having commandeered the text must obviously be treated with some caution. His testimony does, however, correspond with the Council's instructions to Topcliffe to question the imprisoned actors about the part their fellow actors had had in the devising of the 'sedytious matter'. If the actors had completed various portions of the work themselves, then Jonson as a 'maker' of the play, as well as an actor in it, must have provided the main impetus. Certainly he suffered the heaviest reprisals of all those persecuted in the matter. Nashe's account of the play's composition further suggests a degree of improvisation in the playhouse, so that there may well have been no official play book to submit to Tilney before performance. This would help to explain the ostensibly harsh reaction of the authorities: not only had the players transgressed the bounds of toleration in performance, but they had compounded their offence by ignoring the requirement of the Master's licence.

Despite the sweeping nature of its dictates, the Privy Council's order had effect only to the extent that playing ceased at all of the London venues, and then only for some three months. Even Francis Langley's Swan, where the *Isle of Dogs* had been staged, did not suffer the ultimate penalty of demolition, though it subsequently declined into disuse.[60] Many of the members of Pembroke's Men, who had been resident at the Swan, joined Henslowe's company, the Lord Admiral's Men, at the Rose, since Langley was denied a licence to resume playing when other theatres did so in November 1597. Until his death in 1601, Langley made valiant efforts to revive his company, but it appears that he was unable to purge his original offence of having mounted the *Isle of Dogs*. Although the Swan remained in occasional use for a variety of dramatic and other entertainments until 1614 or thereabouts, it was no longer home to an established company.

Why the demolition order of 1597 was neither fully implemented nor rescinded remains open to question. Glynne Wickham has argued that the Privy Council did not actually intend that the theatres be destroyed and that the order was given in the knowledge that under the law of real property no one was in a position to enforce it.[61] Even if the legal owners of each playhouse could be identified (and the ownership of the Theatre and that of the Curtain were in dispute), they could not be compelled to 'pluck down' their investments without payment of compensation. The motive behind such an ineffectual injunction may have been, as Wickham has argued, to appease the City. This conjecture is based on the familiar presupposition that the Council, unlike the hostile City aldermen, were inveterately well disposed towards the theatre. As letters from the Guildhall testify, the City fathers were indeed consistently inimical to playgoing and the disruptions it caused. But at a time of phenomenal growth in London's population, the Privy Council were also profoundly apprehensive about the potential for protest and riot amongst the crowds who amassed at the public theatres. The Council were no doubt seriously alarmed to hear of the particular outbreaks of unrest which occurred in the wake of the *Isle of Dogs*. By suspending performances, punishing individual actors in Pembroke's company and withholding its licence from the Swan, they succeeded in containing the immediate threat. They must have known that the total demolition of the theatres was a draconian penalty which could not be readily implemented; but the order could be seen as a deterrent in the form of a suspended sentence on theatre personnel which might be activated if they should in future produce further provocative material on their stages.

The closure of the theatres in 1597 is an appropriate point at which to take stock of the first decade of censorship. Most of the evidence which has come to light relates to Tilney's censorship of the history play; this in turn discloses a readiness to see in historical events an image of the present. That the past could be exploited in this way was, of course, a convention familiar to playwrights and audiences and one which, as the Protestant interludes demonstrate, could be useful for state purposes. Playwrights could safely encourage such an awareness in their audience when directed at approved targets, as Greene does in the Induction to *James IV* (c. 1590). Here, the misanthropic Scot, Bohan, draws a comparison between the corruption of a former generation in the Court of Scotland and that of the present day: 'In the year 1520 was in Scotland a king, overruled with parasites, misled by lust, and many circumstances too long to trattle on now, much like our court of Scotland this day.'[62] Where referentiality had political immediacy, however, the censor was ready to suppress it. Government fears of insurrection – epitomised in Robert Cecil's words: 'When has England felt any harm by soldiers or gentlemen, or men of worth? . . . Some Jack Cade or Jack Straw and such rascals are those that have endangered the kingdom'[63] – extended to its representation on the stage. This was particularly true of the troublesome years of the

1590s, characterised by simmering resentments among the populace which regularly erupted in outbreaks of turbulence.[64] That plays could not endorse rebellion whatever its cause is clear from the censorship of *Sir Thomas More*, *Woodstock*, *Jack Straw*, *2 Henry VI* and, as we shall see, *2 Henry IV*. As he perused history plays which dealt with notable uprisings, Tilney, mindful of his commission, would have judged their effect on the volatile audience of the Elizabethan popular playhouse,[65] which included numbers of unruly apprentices, the dispossessed and the disaffected.

More so than any other genre, the Elizabethan history play, with its concessions to the censor, is a captive text. State surveillance of drama accounts for the failure of dramatists to respond fully to their historical material: the perfunctory treatment of More's refusal to jeopardise his loyalty to Rome, for example, or the underwritten role of Richmond in *Richard III*. Again, the absence of the signing of Magna Carta and the careful treatment of the King's excommunication, in both *King John* and *The Troublesome Reigne*, were probable due to an awareness that the interdict imposed on the realm in 1208 by Pope Innocent III would have been referential to the excommunication of Elizabeth I.

To secure the authorisation of plays concerned with intractable political themes, playwrights, as we have seen, developed certain strategies of evasion. The schoolmaster in *Woodstock* parodies such dramatic equivocation in his verses when he lambasts the issue of blank charters and the King's favourites, but ends incongruously with the line 'God bless my lord Tresilian'. With somewhat greater subtlety, dramatists covered their tracks by importing sentiments which echoed the dominant Tudor ideology, such as the homiletic corrective in the revision of *Sir Thomas More*, Carlisle's lines at Richard II's deposition and the speeches on obedience following the defeat of the rebels in *Jack Straw*. The same imperatives may account for the diffusion of history in plays like *Edmund Ironside* and Peele's *Edward I* by the elements of romance and folklore. Accordingly, the traditional view that almost all Elizabethan history plays acquiesce in the ideology exemplified in the prescribed church homily 'Against Disobedience and Wilful Rebellion' has increasingly come under siege. More radical readings of the texts are substantiated by evidence of a censorship which sought to suppress material judged seditious or inflammatory and to secure artistic orthodoxy.

Notes

1 See Alfred Harbage and Samuel Schoenbaum, *Annals of English Drama, 975–1700* (revised edition, London, 1964). Many of the plays are lost; but romantic comedies and popularist histories predominate.
2 Quoted by R. B. McKerrow, *The Works of Thomas Nashe*, V, p. 44.
3 'Advertisement touching the controversies of the Church of England', *The Works of Francis Bacon*, ed. James Spedding (14 vols., London, 1857–74), VIII, p. 77. The pamphlet was not published until 1640.
4 See Lyly, 'Pappe with an Hatchet', *The Complete Works of John Lyly*, ed. R. W. Bond (3 vols., Oxford, 1902), III, p. 408 and Nashe, 'A counter-cuffe given to Martin Junior', *The Works of Thomas Nashe*, ed. McKerrow, I, p. 59.
5 'Martins Months Minde', *The Complete Works of Thomas Nashe*, ed. A. B. Grosart (6 vols., 1883–84), I, p. 179. Nashe's authorship is rejected by McKerrow.
6 See *APC 1589–90*, XVIII, pp. 214–6.
7 See Chambers, *ES*, II, pp. 18–19 and W. R. Gair, 'La compagnie des enfants de St. Paul, Londres (1599–1606)', *Dramaturgie et société: Rapports entre l'oeuvre théâtrale son interprétation et son public aux XVIᵉ et XVIIᵉ siècles*, ed. Jean Jacquot (2 vols., Paris, 1968), II, 655–74, at 655.
8 23 Eliz. c. 2, *Statutes of the Realm* (London, 1819), IV, p. 659.
9 *Tudor Royal Proclamations*, II, pp. 534–5.
10 *CSPD 1598–1601*, CCLXXV, p. 449.
11 The works circulated in manuscript. See Felix Raab, *The English Face of Machiavelli* (London, 1964), pp. 52–3.
12 In an essay published posthumously, *Faustus and the Censor*, ed. John Henry Jones (Oxford, 1987), Sir William Empson vigorously argues that Marlowe's known heretical views are incompatible with the orthodox theology of the play. He contends that there was an earlier version of *Faustus* suppressed by Tilney and that the surviving texts embody numerous changes made at the behest of the censor. Whilst Empson's view is expressed with characteristic verve it rests on the dubious premiss that Tilney sacrificed *Faustus* to gratify the Archbishop in 1589, when the privileges of the Revels Office were under threat (pp. 50–1). Besides, if the play was suppressed in 1589, it is odd that there is nothing on record about it.
13 I use W. W. Greg's familiar distinction. All quotations are from his *Parallel Texts* (Oxford, 1950).
14 See Glynne Wickham, 'Exeunt to the cave: notes on the staging of Marlowe's plays', *Tulane Drama Review*, 8 (1964), 184–94, at 187.
15 Leslie M. Oliver, 'Rowley, Foxe, and the *Faustus* additions', *Modern Language Notes*, 60 (1945), 391–4, first pointed out that a 'source' for the scene was Foxe's *Acts and Monuments*, which Rowley had used in *When You See me You Know Me*. But surely Marlowe would also have known Foxe's immensely popular work. Fredson Bowers, 'Marlowe's *Doctor Faustus*: the 1602 additions', *Studies in Bibliography*, 26 (1973), 1–18 and Constance Brown Kuriyama, 'Dr Greg and *Doctor Faustus*: the supposed originality of the 1616 text', *English Literary Renaissance*, 5

(1975), 171–97, have convincingly argued that the 'B' text does indeed contain the additions. This does not preclude the possibility that censored material was later recovered.

16 Empson, p. 174 and Kuriyama, p. 190.

17 This was tentatively suggested by F. S. Boas in the first scholarly edition of the play (London, 1932) and accepted by Oliver. Neither considered the possibility of early censorship.

18 See Frances A. Yates, *Giordano Bruno and the Hermetic Tradition* (London, 1964), pp. 167–8 and Hugh Trevor-Roper, *Catholics, Anglicans and Puritans: Seventeenth Century Essays* (London, 1987), pp. 28–9.

19 Yates, p. 348.

20 See Wilbur Sanders, *The Dramatist and the Received Idea: Studies in the Plays of Marlowe and Shakespeare* (Cambridge, 1968), p. 353.

21 This date can only be conjectured (although substantiated by details of censorship). See Greg's Introduction to the *Malone Society Reprint* (Oxford, 1911); I. A. Shapiro, 'The significance of a date', *Shakespeare Survey*, 8 (1955), 100–6 and Peter W. M. Blayney, '*The Booke of Sir Thomas Moore* re-examined', *Studies in Philology*, 69 (1972), 167–91. All quotations are from the *Malone Society Reprint*. The manuscript, Harley 7368, is in the British Library.

22 See *Documents of the Christian Church*, ed. Henry Bettenson, (Oxford, 1943), pp. 323–5.

23 'Strangers' and 'aliens' were the usual generic term for the immigrants. The French and Dutch communities predominated. See Andrew Pettegree, *Foreign Protestant Communities in Sixteenth Century London* (Oxford, 1986).

24 Pettegree, pp. 291–3.

25 *APC 1592–3*, XXIV, pp. 200–1.

26 Quoted by Pettegree, p. 292.

27 *APC 1592–3*, XXIV, p. 222.

28 Both the City authorities and the Privy Council were appreciative of the benefits brought by the foreigners. In the 1590s, the strangers' contributions to help their co-religionists abroad were channelled through the Privy Council. Pettegree comments: 'The strangers and the government were, ultimately, tied together by strong ties of mutual interest, and this was to prove the most effective protection of the strangers' privileges' (p. 295).

29 Carol A. Chillington, 'Playwrights at work: Henslowe's, not Shakespeare's, *Book of Sir Thomas More*', *English Literary Renaissance*, 10 (1980), 439–79.

30 The papers of the celebrated symposium on the internal evidence for Shakespeare's part in the play were edited by A. W. Pollard, *Shakespeare's Hand in the Play of Sir Thomas More* (Cambridge, 1923). For recent discussion of the question see *Shakespeare and Sir Thomas More: Essays on the Play and its Shakespearian Interest*, ed. T. H. Howard-Hill (Cambridge, 1989).

31 G. Harold Metz, 'The Master of the Revels and *The Booke of Sir Thomas Moore*', *Shakespeare Quarterly*, 33 (1982), 493–5.

32 See B. W. Black, '*The Book of Sir Thomas Moore*: a critical edition', (unpublished doctoral dissertation, University of Michigan, 1953), p. 95;

R. C. Bald, 'The Booke of Sir Thomas More and its problems', Shakespeare Survey, 2 (1949), 44–65 at 51; and Blayney, 'The Booke of Sir Thomas Moore re-examined', p. 190.

33 Giorgio Melchiori, 'The Booke of Sir Thomas Moore: a chronology of revision', Shakespeare Quarterly, 37 (1986), 291–308 at 299.

34 Scott McMillin, The Elizabethan Theatre and The Book of Sir Thomas More' (New York, 1987), pp. 74–95.

35 'The date and auspices of the additions to Sir Thomas More', Shakespeare and Sir Thomas More, pp. 101–31. One difficulty with a theory of Jacobean revision for the King's Men is that it cannot adequately account for the marginal note in addition V, 'Messenger T. Goodal'. It is known that Thomas Goodale was with Strange's Men in the early 1590s; he disappears from records after 1599. He may, as Taylor suggests, have later become a hired man with the King's Men, but there is no evidence that he had any connection with the company.

36 Quoted by Pettegree, p. 291.

37 The play is only 1,210 lines in length. The printer, Danter, seems to have been aware of its brevity in his preparation of the text. See the Introduction to the Malone Society Reprint, prepared by Kenneth Muir and F. P. Wilson (Oxford, 1957). All quotations are from this edition.

38 Raphael Holinshed, The Third Volume of Chronicles, (London, 1587), p. 431.

39 For the quarto I use the Malone Society Reprint of The First Part of The Contention (Oxford, 1985), and for The True Tragedy (in fact an octavo), the Shakespeare Quarto Facsimile (Oxford, 1958).

40 The theory was first put forward by Madeleine Doran, Henry VI, Parts II and III (Iowa, 1928) and accepted by most subsequent editors.

41 See Scott McMillin, 'Casting for Pembroke's Men: the Henry VI Quartos and The Taming of A Shrew', Shakespeare Quarterly, 23 (1972), 141–59 and William Montgomery, 'The contention of York and Lancaster: a critical edition', (2 vols., unpublished doctoral thesis, Oxford University, 1985), 2, pp. xxxi–xxxii.

42 2 Henry VI, ed. Andrew Cairncross (London, 1957), p. xxvii.

43 A New History of Ireland, eds T. W. Moody, F. X. Martin, and F. J. Byrne (Oxford, 1976), III, pp. 115–29.

44 CSPD 1598–1601, CCLXXI, p. 225.

45 Calendar of the Manuscripts of the Marquis of Salisbury, (24 pts, London, 1883–1976), V, pp. 249–50.

46 See Woodstock: A Moral History, ed. A. P. Rossiter (London, 1946), pp. 66–72. All quotations are from this edition. The manuscript, Egerton 1994, is in the British Library. David Lake, 'Three seventeenth-century revisions: Thomas of Woodstock, The Jew of Malta and Faustus B', Notes and Queries, 228 (1983) 133–43, argues from the premiss of linguistic style that Woodstock is a Jacobean play. If this were the case the extant manuscript must represent the actual prompt book perused and reformed by Buc rather than, as is argued here, an Elizabethan transcript re-examined by the censor prior to a Jacobean revival. But the manuscript, unlike others examined by Buc for the first time, bears few signs of his presence.

47 Davison was imprisoned and brought to trial. Catholics, according to

information conveyed to Walsingham, were of 'the opinion that the course taken by the Queen against Mr. Davison is to convey herself in a cloud' (*CSPD 1581–90*, CC, p. 406).

48 *Shakespeare's Edmund Ironside*, ed. Eric Sams (Aldershot, 1985), pp. 21–5. Quotations are from this edition.

49 The text of the quarto deposition scene is printed in *Richard II, 1597, Shakespeare Quarto Facsimile* (Oxford, 1966).

50 *Richard II*, ed. Peter Ure (London, 1956), p. xiv.

51 *King Richard II*, ed. Andrew Gurr (Cambridge, 1984), p. 9.

52 Arber, *SR*, III, 89. Leo Kirschbaum, *Shakespeare and the Stationers*, (Columbia, Ohio, 1955), points out that even after the Star Chamber decree the wardens continued to exercise the licensing powers which they had assumed before that time (p. 40). It was quite common for plays to be entered under the hands of the wardens: six plays were thus entered on 15 May 1594.

53 Ernest William Talbert, *The Problem of Order: Elizabethan Political Commonplaces and an Example of Shakespeare's Art* (Chapel Hill, 1962), pp. 194–5. David Bergeron, 'The deposition scene in *Richard II*', *Renaissance Papers* (1974), 31–7 argues that lines 154–317 of Act IV are a later addition. His argument ultimately comes to rest on the conviction, similar to Talbert's, that 'no actor, director, spectator, or reader would truly want to be deprived of this new appearance of Richard at his formal abdication'. But when have a censor's sensibilities been so attuned?

54 *APC 1597*, XXVII, pp. 313–4.

55 *Documents of the Rose Playhouse*, pp. 114–6.

56 *APC 1597*, XXVII, p. 338.

57 See *Documents of the Rose Playhouse*, pp. 118–20.

58 *Ben Jonson*, I, p. 139. Herford and Simpson suggest that Jonson is here alluding to his imprisonment, while awaiting trial for the murder of Gabriel Spencer in 1598, and that the spies were agents assigned to entrap him because of his recent conversion to Catholicism (I, pp. 18–9).

59 *The Works of Thomas Nashe*, III, pp. 153–4.

60 See Chambers, *ES*, II, pp. 412–3.

61 Glynne Wickham, 'The Privy Council order of 1597 for the destruction of all London's theatres', *The Elizabethan Theatre*, ed. David Galloway (London, 1969), pp. 21–44, at p. 23.

62 Robert Greene, *The Scottish History of James the Fourth*, ed. Norman Sanders (London, 1970).

63 *CSPD 1598–1601*, CCLXXIII, p. 352.

64 See Peter Clark 'A crisis contained?: the condition of English towns in the 1590s', *The European Crisis of the 1590s*, ed. Clark (London, 1985), pp. 50–4. Some protests were aimed at particular targets, such as the foreign and refugee communities; other disturbances were engendered by general discontent at worsening economic circumstances in the capital and other towns. Genuine fears existed of a fundamental breakdown in public order.

65 See Andrew Gurr, *Playgoing in Shakespeare's London* (Cambridge, 1987), pp. 54–6, 132–7.

CHAPTER II

'Little better than libels': the censorship of history and satire, 1597–1603

Mitis. Asper, (I urge it as your friend) take heed, The dayes are dangerous,
full of exception, And men are growne impatient of reproofe.
(*Every Man Out of His Humour*, 1599)

it may seeme not impertinent to write of the stile of a history ... what
thinges are to be suppressed at large: how credit may be won and suspition
avoyded: what is to bee observed in the order of times ... what liberty a
writer may use in framing speeches, and in declaring the causes, counsailes
and eventes of thinges done: how farre hee must bend himselfe to profit ...
but this were too large a field to enter into.
(John Hayward, Address to the Reader,
The First Part of the Life and Raigne of King Henrie IIII, 1599)

The theatre continued to flourish during the last years of Elizabeth's
reign as part of both popular and aristocratic culture. The public
playhouses reopened within four months of their enforced closure in
July 1597 in the wake of *The Isle of Dogs*. Paul's Boys also resumed
playing in 1599–1600, the company apparently having been prohibited since 1590 for their complicity in the Marprelate controversy,
and in late 1600 the Chapel Children were resuscitated at Blackfriars.[1]
More plays were performed at Court during the winter of 1600–1
than at any time during the reign[2] and on 31 March 1602, following
the promotion of their patron to the Privy Council, a third company,
Worcester's Men, was granted official licence to perform in London.[3]
A new generation of playwrights – including Jonson, Marston and
Chapman – began their turbulent careers as dramatists writing for the
children's companies as well as for the adult players. The reopening of
the theatres and the increasing social prestige of the actors did not,
however, signify any relaxation of censorship. On the contrary, the
evidence suggests that the proscriptive measures of the early 1590s
were intensified as a result of the *fin-de-siècle* political tensions
generated by anticipation of the Queen's death and the factionalism
which accompanied the uncertain succession.

The Queen's physical decline was causing more pronounced fissures in the body politic than had yet appeared. The Earl of Essex was in secret correspondence with James VI of Scotland and was engaged in creating a faction in support of James's claim to the throne.[4] In opposition to the young Earl were the sons of the elder statesmen, Lords Burghley and Cobham, Robert Cecil and Henry Brooke. Francis Cordale, writing of affairs in England in the summer of 1599, commented that in their desperation the Commons saw in Essex a liberator from their oppressions: 'they would follow any who would be likely to procure them some immunities for never were they more oppressed, and subject to all servile conditions'.[5] Among symptoms of troubles, wrote Bacon in his essay 'Of Seditions and Troubles' are 'libels and licentious discourses against the state'. Libels and rumours did indeed proliferate at this time.

The term 'libel' in its modern usage connotes a false written statement which is defamatory of personal reputation, giving rise to the civil remedy of damages; but for Bacon and his contemporaries, the concept of public libel carried the thrust of sedition and de-stabilisation as well as slander. The ambit of the offence is conveyed by a royal proclamation of April 1601 offering a reward of £100 for information about libels 'tending to the slander of our royal person and state, and stirring up of rebellion and sedition within this our realm'.[6] This dual aspect of libel – the private wrong of defamation and the crime of seditious communication – became the focus of censorship, dramatic and non-dramatic. By the end of the century, satire and political history were equally fertile sources of potentially libellous material and both were the subject of keen surveillance.

The blueprint for theatrical censorship can be detected in two acts of non-dramatic censorship at the turn of the century, namely, the bishops' ban on formal verse satire and the suppression of John Hayward's history of the ascendancy of Henry IV. In June 1599, one of the few documented instances of Elizabethan artistic repression took place when the Archbishop of Canterbury and the Bishop of London issued a decree to the Master and wardens of the Stationers' Company prohibiting the printing of satires and epigrams. The prelates also forbade the printing of English history without the prior consent of the Privy Council and reiterated that no plays should be printed without authority.[7] To demonstrate their condemnation of the fashionable genre (a number of satires having gone into successive editions), Marston's *Pygmalion* and *The Scourge of Villanie* and Davies's *Epigrams* were burnt in the Stationers' Hall. What prompted the bishops to take issue with verse satire at this time? As Richard

McCabe has argued, they were evidently acting as ministers of state rather than moral guardians: the primary target of their injunctions was social satire, not obscenity or lewdness.[8] Of the suppressed books, Thomas Cutwood's *Caltha Poetarum* was the only work which overtly relished its lascivious moments. Others launched assaults on contemporary abuses such as religious hypocrisy and opportunism, courtly sycophancy and the devious operation of the law, as personified in Marston's *The Scourge of Villanie*. Hall's *Byting Satyres* contain virulent complaints against the enclosures which had been the cause of riots in London in 1592 and which were a continual source of agrarian discontent. At a time of economic hardship and of increasingly strong, factional rivalry, such exposure of the self-interest and pretensions of particular groups and individuals in the form of verse satire was, no doubt, perceived as fuelling social discontent.

A further measure of increased cultural surveillance is the bishop's stipulation that before publication all histories must be approved by a member of the Privy Council. Significantly, this restriction was imposed almost immediately after the controversy aroused by the publication of John Hayward's *The First Part of the Life and Raigne of King Henrie IIII*, which resulted in the suppression of the book, followed by the trial of the author and his imprisonment for three years. The history was licensed in the ordinary way by the Bishop of London's chaplain, Samuel Harsnett, in February 1599. The initial objection was to the dedication to Essex, who was described as 'magnus ... et presenti judicio, et futuri temporis expectatione'. Writing to his friend, Dudley Carleton, in Ostend the following month, John Chamberlain reported:

> The treatise of Henry IV. is well written; the author is a young man of Cambridge, a lawyer. There is much talk about it, why such a story should come out now, and exception is taken to the Latin epistle, dedicated to the Earl of Essex. I can find no harm in it, but it was commanded to be cut out of the book.[9]

Harsnett later claimed in his defence that the offending lines had been added after he had licensed the book.[10] In any event, however, Hayward's decision to dedicate his work to Essex and his attempt to evade literary censorship by incorporating the dedication at a later stage with the discourse in the epistle to the reader on the value and purpose of historiography, betrays a lack of that judgement which he commends in the characters of his history. At such a time, it was hardly judicious to give the appearance of promoting the Earl's cause.

Essex, opposed by the powerful Cecil faction, was in the Queen's disfavour even before he left for his ill-fated campaign against the Earl of Tyrone in Munster in July 1599. According to one interested observer, it was 'muttered at Court that he and the Queen have each threatened the other's head; undoubtedly all kindness is forgotten between them'.[11] The case against Hayward, however, was not confined to the untimely dedication. At his trial in February 1600, the historian was interrogated by Lord Chief Justice Popham in a way which reveals the Crown's apprehension of how the writing of history may be manipulated to disclose the present:

> Who made the preface to the reader?
> Wherein he conceives that book might be not only precepts but patterns for private direction and for matters of state, and instruct young men more shortly, and old men more fully?
> Where he had any warrant to set down that King Henry IV. never taxed the subject, nor left 900,000 in his coffers?
> In what point were the oaths unlawful taken by King Henry IV. of his subjects?
> When were any forces sent in his time into Ireland?
> What moved him to set down that any were in disgrace for their service there, or that the nobility were then had in contempt, or that they were but base that were called about that King, or that the subjects were bound for their obedience to the State, and not to the person of the King?
> What moved him to maintain, with arguments never mentioned in the history, that it might be lawful for the subject to depose the King, and to add many persuadings in allowance thereof?
> What moved him to allow that it is well for common weal that the King was dead?[12]

Popham's examination significantly concentrates on those features of Hayward's account – such as the Irish expedition and the precarious nature of the King's personal authority – which appear to have been disproportionately emphasised or even imported from their contemporary parallels. It is clear that Hayward is being accused not of poor or incompetent historiography – for which even the most negligent historian could hardly expect to be judged a criminal – but of the wilful abuse of his craft for an ulterior motive. The Lord Chief Justice implies that contemporary correspondences were intended for detection rather than made explicit. In Hayward's history, the veiled criticism works by projecting a contrasting mode of government: that Henry IV did not tax his subjects invited an allusion to Elizabeth's heavy taxation prior to the Irish campaign. The decoding of the parallel illustrates a certain ingenuity on the part of both appreciative readers and hostile critics. Popham evidently considered, however, that the history might have an impact beyond an educated few: 'Might he think that this history would not be very dangerous to come amongst the common people?'. This question carries one of the clearest intimations of how closely the authorities were disposed to view the publication of political histories and, by extension, the history plays of the period.

Although Hayward claimed in his defence that the facts could be found in his sources, Sir Edward Coke, the Attorney General, contended according to his notes of the trial that Hayward had intended the application of his history to the current time.[13] Hayward's innovative methodology of inserting anachronistic detail, which he argued was 'lawful for any historiographer', fuelled the substance of Coke's accusations. As the Attorney General's *précis* of the book and his selection of certain passages illustrate, it was the perceived topicality of its subject matter and its ideological subversiveness which caused the suppression of the history and Hayward's imprisonment: but the authorities may well have been alarmed by the appearance of this new analytical history – dramatic in style, sceptical of human motive and imaginative in circumstantial detail.[14] It was too close to the Continental tradition heralded by the prohibited Machiavelli, which rejected the providential design of the chronicle tradition.

By the time of Essex's trial in February 1601, following his abortive rebellion, it was generally accepted that Hayward had written a history which mirrored the Earl's career. Essex's opponents were able to exploit the prefiguration to their own purpose in drawing up his full indictment. In a speech to the Star Chamber, Robert Cecil gave his version of Essex's putative strategy, involving a pact with Tyrone who would land on English shores with 8,000 men, in order that 'the Queen be put aside, and all made a prey to Irish kerns'. Yet Cecil's vividly exaggerated representation of what was essentially an unco-ordinated rebellion gained credence from the correlation with Henry Bolingbroke, drawn from Hayward's history:

> These things appeared by the book written on Henry IV., making this time seem like that of Richard II., to be reframed by him as by Henry IV. He kept this book 14 days to peruse, and when he knew many copies where dispersed, sent to the Metropolitan to have it called in as a dangerous book. He would have removed Her Majesty's servants, stepped into her chair, and perhaps had her treated like Richard II.[15]

Although Essex denied any such seditious intent or designs on the Crown and repudiated Cecil's allegations, it was to no avail. The state was thus, ironically, able to exploit the contemporary nuances of Hayward's history for its own purpose as evidence against Essex and the objectives of his rebellion. It had ultimately proved useful ammunition for those who had sought to suppress it.

Essex and his faction had, of course, encouraged such analogies suggested throughout the trial by watching on the eve of their rebellion a command performance of *Richard II* by the Chamberlain's Men. That they chose to preface their uprising by crossing the river to the Globe to attend a play depicting a successful usurpation was entirely consonant with an uprising which according to one historian was 'more suited to the stage of the Globe than the streets of the capital'[16]; but their attendance also actualised the fears inherent in the play censorship of the previous decade that the stage was capable of fuelling insurrection. Although posterity may perceive the hopeless theatricality of Essex's attempt to seize power, at the time, its defeat could not but be regarded as a deliverance from the brink of a national calamity. The Privy Council ordered sermons against the rising to be given recalling the fate of Richard II:

> If he had not been prevented, there had never been a rebellion in England since Richard II. more desperate or dangerous. The rebellion in the North was far off, and thereby not so perilous. The great Armada of Spain was but a thunderclap, the noise being greater than the danger, and Her Majesty's subjects faithfully united to encounter it. But in this attempt, so many noblemen and gentlemen of good sort are combined, as the event must needs have been most fearful to the State.[17]

It was, of course, expedient for the Cecil faction to intensify the danger as a means of demonstrating both its loyalty to the Queen and, by implication, its approval of primogeniture and the proposed succession of James VI of Scotland.

Curiously, the complicity of the Chamberlain's Men in the series of events leading to Essex's desperate bid for the Crown did not produce any reprisals against the professional theatre. Although Augustine Phillips, one of the actors, had to testify to Coke that the impetus for the performance came from the Essex faction, the company were not arraigned. According to Phillips, the Chamberlain's Men were loath to stage the play on the grounds that it was 'so old and so long out of use that they should have small company at it', but the proffered forty shillings, 'more than their ordinary', prevailed and the play was performed.[18] Annabel Patterson has cited the government's leniency towards the players as an example of *non-censorship*, exemplifying the notion of an implicit contract between authors and authorities.[19] But the case does not fit into the usual categories of Elizabethan theatre censorship, namely, pre-performance censorship of the play book or suppression of the play following unlicensed performance. Private performances of plays were permitted and the play had already been censored and approved by Tilney. Coke did make the performance an issue in his case against the insurgents; but Phillips's testimony that the company were induced to perform for financial remuneration may have persuaded him that they were not accomplices in their audience's motives. Since the commons had withheld their support from what was an exclusively aristocratic uprising, the government may have seen no reason to penalise the popular theatre by placing further restrictions on its operations. However, after three editions in 1598 and 1599, no further edition of *Richard II* appeared until 1608, following a Jacobean revival. During this interval the play had presumably assumed the stigma of a seditious text.

In other respects, though, Essex's nemesis did have ramifications for dramatic censorship: for several years it provoked an increased vigilance towards plays which might revive memories of his popular appeal and it induced playwrights to be circumspect. Even after the Queen's death, Samuel Daniel was questioned about his motives for writing *Philotas*, which was seen as reflecting Essex's rise and fall from royal favour.[20] Representation of the careers of royal favourites was clearly an area to be treated with caution. An apparently innocent passage in an earlier play might yet on revival unwittingly evoke dangerous associations. In Dekker's *Old Fortunatus*, Fortunatus, returning from his travels with the magic purse, reports to his sons what he has witnessed in some courts:

> In some Courts shall you see ambition
> Sit piecing *Dedalus* old waxen wings,
> But being clapt on, and they about to flie,
> Even when their hopes are busied in the clouds,
> They melt against the Sunne of majestie,
> And downe they tumble to destruction:
> For since the heavens strong armes teach kings to stand,
> Angels are plac'd about their glorious throne,
> To gard it from the strokes of Traitrous hands ...   (II. ii. 200–8)

The lines were printed in 1600 and may have been spoken at the Court performance at Christmas 1599 recorded on the title page. But in a number of extant copies of the 1600 edition, the leaf containing the passage has been excised.[21] After 1601, when the fall of Essex exemplified Bacon's view of the 'slipperiness' of great place,[22] the lines would have acquired a new and unsettling significance. 'I cannot but tremble when I hear of the very least offence which may breed dislike in Her Majesty's thoughts, either towards them whom I attend or towards myself,' wrote Dr Edward Stanhope, Chancellor to the Archbishop of Canterbury and Bishop of London, in December 1599 to his brother, Sir John Stanhope, later of the Privy Council. Stanhope's concern was caused by the Queen's offence at ministers who had not observed 'Essex's restraint as they ought to have done' and had mentioned him in their sermons and 'prayed for him by name'.[23] Theatre and public sermons had the same popular audiences and were subjected equally to official surveillance. Stage allusions to Essex, genuine or imagined, would certainly have been censored if they had been appreciated by the Master of the Revels, as was the case with *Henry V*. Once it was perceived that the passage in *Old Fortunatus* contained echoes of Essex, it would have seemed expedient to remove it.

Fulke Greville's comments on Essex's disgrace and its repercussions for the writer are instructive. In his *Life of Sir Philip Sidney*, published posthumously, he remarks that, confronted with the downfall of one so exalted, it behoves the writer to be cautious: 'This sudden descent of such greatnesse, together with the quality of the Actors in every Scene, stir'd up the Authors second thoughts, to be carefull (in his own case) of leaving faire weather behind him'.[24] Greville took no risks. He consigned his tragedy of Anthony and Cleopatra to the flames, for fear that it would be 'construed, or strained to a personating of vices in the present governors and government'. There was just cause for such precautions. According to Greville, the Earl's opponents 'took audacity to cast Libels abroa in his name against the State, made by themselves; set papers upon posts, to bring his innocent friends in question'. Certainly Greville's long association and friendship with Essex drew the suspicions of Robert Cecil, who successfully checked his advancement in the reign of James I. His drastic burning of a play which he feared would be subjected to a hostile contemporary interpretation is again indicative of a political climate where it was prudent for playwrights to practise a degree of self-censorship.

To examine how play production was affected by such constraints during the closing years of the reign, we now turn to those plays which bear traces of textual censorship. Of the texts which show some evidence of interference by the Master of the Revels, all are histories or satires: *2 Henry IV*, *Henry V*, *The Merry Wives of Windsor*, *Every Man Out of His Humour*, *Cynthia's Revels* and *Poetaster*. There are no details of the censorship of Chapman's lost satire, *The Old Joiner of Aldgate*; but the proceedings in the Star Chamber which it provoked and the arguments used in defence by Chapman and the theatre managers provide rare insights into a case of libel centred on a stage play.

2 Henry IV

2 Henry IV incurred censorship on two accounts: its copious and not unsympathetic exposition of the rebel cause; and the original choice of the name Oldcastle for the fat rogue Falstaff. Since these two instances of censorship were unrelated and ensued from different sources of state intervention, they will be discussed independently. The Falstaff/ Oldcastle controversy, which impinges on five plays and involves two theatre companies, will be included in the later discussion of dramatic satire.

Stephen Greenblatt has produced a brilliant analysis of the production and containment of subversion and disorder in Shakespeare's history plays, concluding:

> It is precisely because of the English form of absolutist theatricality that Shakespeare's drama, written for a theater subject to state censorship, can be so relentlessly subversive: the form itself, as a primary expression of Renaissance power, helps to contain the radical doubts it continually provokes.[25]

Applied to the exercise of power, the plays are indeed subversive in their rejection of traditional moral views of princely virtue in favour of a ruthless pragmatism. But in its treatment of rebellion *2 Henry IV* does not enclose its subversion as assiduously as Greenblatt suggests and for this reason it elicited the interference of the Master of the Revels. The play would have come before Tilney in 1597 or 1598. Some two years later, Hayward was being accused at his trial of 'omit[ting] every principal point that made against the traitor or rebels' in his history of Henry IV.[26] It may therefore be expected that a play depicting the turmoils of rebellion – albeit at a time before Essex's disaffection – would have been regarded with a degree of suspicion by Tilney. That the rebellion gains respectability from the leadership of a righteous Archbishop would have been an immediate reason for the censor's intervention.

There is indeed evidence of censorship: a number of passages dealing with the aims of the rebels appear only in the folio text. The fact that such passages are almost entirely concerned with the insurgents' cause, their grievances and strategies, points clearly to their suppression at some time before the publication of the quarto in 1600. In Act I scenes i and iii, several cuts are made to the rebels' lines, with the combined effect of diminishing the extent of their grievances and, in particular, underplaying the Archbishop of York's involvement with their cause. It is significant, for example, that the quarto omits most of Morton's final speech in the first scene of the play (I. i.

189–209) reporting the Archbishop's endorsement of the rebellion, which has brought new life to the cause. Under his influence, the insurgents' fears of divine retribution are dissipated:

> For that same word 'rebellion' did divide
> The action of their bodies from their souls;
> And they did fight with queasiness, constrain'd ...
> This word 'rebellion' – it had froze them up,
> As fish are in a pond. But now the Bishop
> Turns insurrection to religion.

Morton's words were almost certainly removed because they dared to articulate the subversive idea of a rebellion gaining momentum from the belief that it is divinely sanctioned. The Archbishop first appears in Act I scene iii and notably his lines have been drastically cut. His final speech in the scene, in which he rallies the rebels and points to the prevailing disenchantment with Bolingbroke, is omitted:

> Let us on,
> And publish the occasion of our arms.
> The commonwealth is sick of their own choice; ...
> What trust is in these times?
> They that, when Richard liv'd, would have him die
> Are now become enamour'd on his grave.
> Thou that threw'st dust upon his goodly head,
> When through proud London he came sighing on
> After th' admired heels of Bolingbroke,
> Criest now 'O earth, yield us that King again,
> And take thou this!' O thoughts of men accurs'd!
> Past and to come seems best; things present, worst.   (ll. 85–108)

Similarly, the Archbishop's measured reply to Prince John's admonition at Gaultree Forest (IV. i. 55–79) – in which he presents what he considers to be the grievances of the commonwealth and the rebels, once supporters of Henry IV – has presumably been censored, since it is also absent in the quarto. It is not difficult to conceive the reasons for the interest taken by the censor in these passages. The Church of the Elizabethan Settlement was expected to collaborate with the government and to denounce the evil of rebellion; Tilney would not wish to see a member of the episcopate portrayed in active support of such a cause. Further lines missing from the quarto are likewise concerned with the uprising, notably Lord Bardolph's comment on the contingencies of rebellion (I. iii. 21–4) and his expository speech on the rebels' strategies (I. iii. 36–55), whereby in words which seem set to shock the censor, he elevates the present insurrection to 'this great work-/ Which is almost to pluck a Kingdom down'. The other two excised passages (I. i. 166–79 and II. iii. 23–45) refer back to the beginnings of the rebellion in *1 Henry IV*. The first has Morton admonish Northumberland for the weakening of his resolve where once, in full knowledge of the risks of rebellion, he had urged Hotspur forward in 'stiff-borne action'; in the second, Lady Percy upbraids Northumberland for deserting her husband, 'the mark and glass, copy and book,/That fashion'd others'. It seems unlikely that censorship was directly responsible for the omission, since Hotspur's part is uncensored in both texts of *1 Henry IV*. Nevertheless, the dramatic purpose of the speech is to revive memories of the rebels and of Hotspur's intrepid exploits in their 'bold enterprise'. It may well have been considered prudent to cut lines which placed an heroic gloss upon an assault against the Crown.

It has been argued that the 1600 quarto of *2 Henry IV* was censored, but as a result of press rather than theatrical censorship.[27] Alfred Hart contends that the play suffered at the hands of ecclesiastical censors immediately before publication in 1600 and that lines thought to be referential to Elizabeth and Essex were then excised. But the Stationers' Register entry makes no reference to ecclesiastical licensers. George Walton Williams has suggested that the omission of lines from the text was conditioned by the references they contain to Richard II: the only allusion to Richard II retained in the quarto is that made by King Henry (III. i. 64), a scene supplied by a cancel sheet in the second issue of the play only. The omission of the scene of Richard's deposition in *Richard II* adds weight to the argument. But this cannot be regarded as a complete explanation for the play's censorship: the most celebrated identification of the Queen with Richard II was voiced by Elizabeth herself in 1601 during a conversation with the antiquary William Lambarde, some time after the probable censorship of *2 Henry IV* and publication of the edited quarto.[28] The subversive content of the passages, with their cogent defence of rebellion, would seem a more probable reason for their disappearance. Whether all the cuts came about through official censorship cannot be determined. The authorial papers which lie behind the quarto text would not presumably have been submitted to Tilney, although it is possible that, in the wake of *The Isle of Dogs* controversy and in a climate of more intense surveillance, his reformations were circumspectly incorporated into the foul papers. This was not a time for playwrights to show their mettle.

No further edition of the play appeared until the folio text of 1623, which contains the excised passages. We have no way of knowing when in the play's theatrical life the lines were restored, but once the succession had been settled and any fears of rebellion had receded, they would no longer have carried quite the same threat.

Henry V

The last of Shakespeare's chronicle history plays, *Henry V*, was written and performed in 1599. The eulogy to Essex in the Chorus before Act V, which anticipates his triumphant return from Ireland, indicates that composition was early in the year, almost certainly before the restriction on the publication of history imposed by the bishops in June. Although the injunction that English history must first be allowed by a member of the Privy Council refers to the publication of non-dramatic history, it connotes a keener surveillance of all writing and presentation of historical materials. It is perhaps significant that no authorised version of *Henry V* appeared in print until that of the folio text.

Philip Edwards has described the play as taking 'its life from the exhilaration of battle in prospect'.[29] Jonathan Dollimore and Alan Sinfield have likewise argued that the French campaign and the union at the close is 'a re-presentation of the attempt to conquer Ireland and the hoped-for unity of Britain'.[30] If this is so, and the fact that Ireland dominated the Privy Council agenda in 1599 supports this view, then the play is the most suggestively topical of Shakespeare's histories. While the success of Essex's expedition was confidently anticipated, the analogy would have been quite acceptable to the censor; but once the hopes invested in Essex and his campaign had failed to materialise, so that the dynamic of the play and its celebration of the military hero no longer reflected the turn of contemporary events, then we might expect qualifications in the censor's response. The brevity of the 1600 quarto does indeed suggest Tilney's interference. Passages which are omitted include all the lines of the Chorus, Act I scene i, which expound the devious reasons for the Church's support of the war, several of the French scenes, Henry's rousing speech before Harfleur and the introduction of the Irish captain Macmorris in Act III scene ii. These passages would not all necessarily have been victims of censorship. But the substance of certain of them, and the nature of the text itself, being based on performance, point to censorship as a likely cause.[31] Commentators have noted as one of the marks of Henry's campaign, the unity of the English, Welsh, Scottish and Irish contingents against the common enemy. Philip Edwards observes that 'quite unhistorically, Shakespeare introduced his quartet of the Welsh Fluellan, the Irish Captain Macmorris, the Scottish captain Jamy, and the English Gower as a tribute to the Tudor idea of Britain as a union of peoples setting out to conquer foreigners' or, quoting Richard Simpson, 'as if to symbolise the union of the four nations under one crown, and their co-operation in enterprises of honour, no longer hindered by the touchiness of separatist nationalism'.[32] Jamy the Scottish captain, and the Irish captain Macmorris may not, however, have appeared on the Elizabethan stage, since the passage in which they are introduced in Act III scene ii does not exist in the quarto. In this text, there is only a brief dialogue between Gower and Fluellen about the use of gunpowder; no reference is made to an Irishman, introduced by Gower in the folio as 'a very valiant gentleman' and the discourse which follows between Jamy, Fluellen and Macmorris is missing. In this exchange, Macmorris is ridiculed by Fluellen for the deficiency of his military tactics in directing the mining operations. When Fluellen is on the point of criticising his nation, Macmorris is indignantly defensive: 'Of my nation? What ish my nation? Ish a villain, and a bastard, and a knave, and a rascal. What ish my nation? Who talks of my nation?' (III. ii. 115–8). Fluellen deflects Macmorris's indignation, but the tension remains unresolved. The passage was almost certainly excised by the Master of the Revels. It seems probably that it was the appearance of the Irish captain and not, as Gary Taylor suggests, the Scottish Jamy, who enters with Macmorris but has comparatively little to say, which elicited the interference of the censor.[33] Tilney may have struck out the lines simply because of their Irish referentiality at a time when discussion of Irish affairs carried the death penalty,[34] or he may have considered that the invention of an Irish element helped to evoke particular associations which, in view of Essex's failure, were quite inappropriate.

If one of the quarto omissions can be accounted for by censorship, then it seems probable that other omissions had a similar cause. The Chorus is omitted throughout, which at first seems puzzling. It does not present undue difficulty with casting and to have cut this populist and exuberant celebration of nationhood in the interests of theatrical abridgment would have been inapt. The fifth Chorus makes an explicit analogy between Henry and Essex:

> Were now the General of our gracious Empress –
> As in good time he may – from Ireland coming,
> Bringing rebellion broached on his sword,
> How many would the peaceful city quit
> To welcome him! Much more, and much more cause,
> Did they this Harry.

To have included these lines in any production in late 1599 would have been to invite government reprisal and accusations of propaganda in support of the Essex faction. But it is not just these lines which induce comparisons between Essex's Irish campaign and Henry's

French war. Throughout, the Chorus orchestrates the audience's response to the expedition and heightens the sense of momentous occasion. The optimism it expresses would have reflected the expectations held by many of Essex's waging a successful campaign in Ireland. Lines, such as 'Then should the warlike Harry, like himself,/Assume the port of Mars' (Chorus I) and 'Now all the youth of England are on fire ... For now sits Expectation in the air' (II), together with the accounts of Henry's departure to Harfleur (III) and of the English camp (IV), could be applied to any popular military hero and any campaign. Throughout 1599, these passages would have evoked thoughts of Essex's venture; but when reports of wastage of men and resources, irresolution and an apparently dishonourable truce with Tyrone became widespread, the analogy would have become subversive of actual events. By endorsing the national expectation of a favourable outcome to the campaign, Shakespeare had allowed himself to anticipate too confidently the pattern of Essex's fortunes. The censor may well have licensed this most topical of plays on the condition that lines which directly or indirectly promoted such allusions were removed in performance. The Chorus, with its peculiar mood and substance, was the obvious excision.

One further scene may have suffered at the hands of the censor. The quarto omits the first scene of the play depicting the conspiracy between the Archbishop of Canterbury and Bishop of Ely, in which they propose to support Henry in the French war in the hope of deflecting him from his purpose of stripping the Church of various lands bequeathed to it. The scene exposes starkly the vested interest of the Church in its support of aggressive initiatives against the French. Alan Sinfield and Jonathan Dollimore have drawn attention to an interesting correspondence: in 1588 Archbishop Whitgift had encouraged the clergy to be generous in their contributions to the Armada campaign, on the grounds that it would avert criticism of amassed Church wealth.[35] But to open the play with the Primate of all England and an influential member of the Privy Council laying schemes of dubious integrity may well have stimulated Tilney's interference or, at least, expedient cutting in the playhouse.

Leonard Tennenhouse, noting the demise at the turn of the century of chronicle history plays, together with romantic comedy and Petrarchan poetry, attributes their decline to the obsolescence of the rhetorical strategies they employed.[36] Political imperatives, he argues, shape aesthetic imperatives and, with the accession of James I through primogeniture, there was no longer quite the same necessity to idealise state authority. Tennenhouse compares the chronicle histories, which present authority exercised by a victorious contender who appropriates the symbols of power held by rivals, with Shakespeare's Jacobean history, *Henry VIII*, in which genealogy authorises art.

The obvious differences between Shakespeare's handling of history in the two tetralogies and in *Henry VIII* have been argued in different terms elsewhere and need not be further treated here.[37] But, as has been mentioned, one reason for Shakespeare's withdrawal from the English chronicles as source, ignored by Tennenhouse, lies in the restrictions, of June 1599, placed on the publication of English history. Even if the injunction did not directly impinge on dramatic history, it suggests a more restrictive attitude towards the genre. Recent experience of censorship over *Richard II*, *2 Henry IV* and *Henry V*, no doubt attracted Shakespeare to the greater freedom offered by North's Plutarch, to which he would shortly turn for *Julius Caesar*. Moreover, there is more continuity between Shakespeare's Elizabethan and Jacobean histories than Tennenhouse perhaps allows. In *Coriolanus*, Shakespeare was again preoccupied by the dramatically effective realisation of rebellion against the state engendered by popular grievance. Here he presents a less restricted view of civil unrest and dramatises a rebellion which has at its roots a justified cause. This relative lack of inhibition may well have been due to the relaxation of censorship during the early Jacobean period and a shift in the concerns of the Master of the Revels.

The satirist and the censor

We have noted how the concept of libel was broad enough to encompass the public element of seditious language, critiques of entire social groups or professions, and the private aspect of defaming an individual. It is, of course, difficult to prove the intentionality of the latter two manifestations and playwrights were aware of this; in prologues and addresses to the reader they persistently proclaimed their innocence. Jonson continually refined the argument that he was attacking the sin, not the sinner. In a scene which appears only in the folio text of *Poetaster*, there is a dialogue between the poet Horace and the eminent lawyer Trebatius, which is drawn from the second book of Horace's *Satires*. Horace, whose stance on the role of the poet would seem to reflect Jonson's own, discusses with Trebatius the moral validity of satire and the dangers inherent in its composition. Horace affirms that he 'will write *satyres* still, in spite of feare'. Trebatius counsels caution:

take heed, as being advis'd by mee,
Lest thou incurre some danger: Better pause,
Then rue thy ignorance of the sacred lawes;
There's justice, and great action may be su'd
'Gainst such, as wrong mens fames with verses lewd.   (III. v. 125–9)

The satirist's rejoinder, which draws a distinction between a malevolent libel and the righteous expression of moral censure, is a true Jonsonian one:

Hora. I, with lewd verses; such as libels bee,
    And aym'd at persons of good qualitie.
    I reverence and adore that just decree:
    But if they shall be sharp, yet modest rimes
    That spare mens persons, and but taxe their crimes,
    Such, shall in open court, find currant passe;
    Were CAESAR judge, and with the makers grace.   (III. v. 130–6)

The view, however, that the state would so differentiate appears a counsel of optimism. Certainly, during the final years of the Queen's reign, the censor was responsive to alleged cases of satirical libel. While the implications for public order of such satire are not immediately apparent, it would seem that the state perceived the libellous tendency as an evil to be extirpated and to this end bracketed all forms of libel together.

The revival of interest in verse satire towards the turn of the century promoted its popularity as a dramatic genre, particularly in the repertoires of the children's companies. An early contention by O. C. Campbell that, as a result of the 1599 ban on verse satire, 'authors associated with the prescribed movement devised a form of comedy which effectively preserved its salutary purposes and methods'[38] is not closely knit. It is questionable whether there existed, as Campbell discerns, such a clearly defined 'movement' and, if so, of whom it comprised. Only Marston amongst the authors of the prohibited satires later turned to the theatre. The popularity of dramatic satire would seem to have more to do with the factional politics of the period, a time when libels, obliquely cast, were endemic, and with the re-emergence of the boys' companies who, as Rosencrantz's words attest, were luring audiences away from the public theatres with their sharply satirical and witty productions. But the adult companies were also involved in cases of alleged defamation which elicited some textual censorship of their plays.

The Falstaff/Oldcastle controversy

A familiar case of assumed topical satire featured in the repertoire of the Chamberlain's Men, initiated by Shakespeare's original appellation of Falstaff as Sir John Oldcastle in the two parts of *Henry IV*. Interest in the affair goes beyond mere textual censorship, in this case after Tilney's original licence, in that it suggests the exploitation of satirical references by the Essex faction against their court rivals led by Lords Cobham and Burghley. The case also reveals the kind of pressure which could be exerted covertly in the censorship of drama. Although the facts are fragmentary, there is sufficient evidence to allow a reconstruction of the probable background, if not the motivation, which lay behind Shakespeare's original use of the name Oldcastle for Falstaff.

That Falstaff was at first so named, there is no doubt. In *1 Henry IV* Hal puns on the name by addressing Oldcastle, alias Falstaff, as 'my old lad of the castle' (I. ii. 41). In the quarto of *2 Henry IV* there is the speech prefix 'Old' before one of Falstaff's rejoinders to the Lord Chief Justice (I. ii. 113–6). Since the copy text of the latter quarto comprised Shakespeare's foul papers, it appears either that Shakespeare was still thinking of Falstaff as Oldcastle during the early stages of composition and here reverted unthinkingly to the original name, or that throughout the second part Falstaff was still Oldcastle, but that this one prefix escaped alteration when the controversy broke out. When the change took place is not so important a question as why. There is no contemporary record of the renaming of the knight as being mandatory. In the early 1620s, however, Richard James, in a dedicatory epistle addressed 'To my Noble friend Sir Henry Bourchier' and attached to his edition of *The Legend and Defense of the Noble Knight and Martyre Sir Jhon Oldcastel*, attests to the fact that a complaint was voiced by the family which had inherited Oldcastle's title of Lord Cobham:

> ... in Shakespeare's first shewe of Harrie the fift, the person with which he undertooke to playe a buffone was not Falstaffe, but Sir Jhon Oldcastle, and that offence beinge worthily taken by personages descended from his [title], as peradventure by manie others allso whoe ought to have him in honourable memorie.[39]

It has been reasonably assumed by editors, and by David McKeen in his comprehensive study of the House of Cobham, that William Brooke, Lord Cobham – who became Lord Chamberlain on 8 August 1596 following the death of Lord Hunsdon, the patron of Shakespeare's company – objected to this apparent defamation of the Lollard martyr Oldcastle, and the travesty of his title.[40]

If, as seems probable, it was William Brooke and not his less influential son Henry who accused the company of vilifying the House of Cobham on the stage, the complaint and the consequent change from Oldcastle to Falstaff must have been made before 5 March 1597, the date of William Brooke's death. Both Gary Taylor and Robert J. Fehrenbach have argued that the change was made before the Christmas Court performances of 1596, when they suggest *1 Henry IV* was performed.[41] Taylor confines the Brookes' objections to the first part of *Henry IV*, contending that by the time Shakespeare came to write *2 Henry IV*, after *The Merry Wives of Windsor* in early 1597, Falstaff was Falstaff from the start. However, A. R. Humphreys, who believes that *2 Henry IV* was composed immediately after *1 Henry IV* and before *The Merry Wives of Windsor*, argues that Shakespeare was forced to make the change from Oldcastle to Falstaff in both parts and that he revised the epilogue to include the disclaimer 'Oldcastle died a martyr and this is not the man'. The epilogue is indeed over-long and cumbersome and, as Humphreys has said, it is unlikely that all its disjointed sections would have been delivered at every performance.[42] This is no proof, of course, that Oldcastle ever appeared in performances of the play, but does indicate that in certain circles the identification of Falstaff with Oldcastle was still being made or exploited, to the extent that Shakespeare was compelled to make a public denial of any such intention.[43]

In the absence of certain evidence about Shakespeare's association with any Court faction, we can only surmise whether he set out deliberately to travesty the House of Cobham. It has been argued by Alice Lyle Scoufos that throughout the trilogy Shakespeare, by exploiting typological exegesis, has constructed a sophisticated satire of the Cobhams, rivals of the Essex-Southampton group.[44] McKeen is much more cautious and conjectures that Shakespeare found the Knight in *The Famous Victories of Henry V* and enriched the character without considering the fact that it might cause offence amongst those who revered the memory of Oldcastle. It has been assumed that Lord Cobham was hostile to the theatre[45] and that it was therefore Shakespeare's intention to poke fun at one of its critics. There is, however, no concrete evidence that Cobham was personally antagonistic towards the theatre; it is notable that he did not sign the 1596 petition addressed to the Privy Council protesting against Burbage's plans to set up a theatre in the Blackfriars precinct. Nevertheless, William and Henry Brooke were bitterly hostile to Essex, for whom on the evidence of *Henry V*, Shakespeare, like his sometime patron Southampton, had some admiration. The possibility can therefore be advanced that Shakespeare was entering, albeit marginally, the arena of factional conflict which dominated Court life during the last years of Elizabeth.

What is important is that libellous intentions were inferred from *1 Henry IV* and possibly from *2 Henry IV*, and that censorship beyond the state system was thus provoked. While of comparatively little interest in any discussion of the ideological bases of theatre censorship, the affair is indicative of the theatrical conditions of the times: the players had to accommodate not only the official censorship of the Master of the Revels, but arbitrary intervention from influential courtiers who were alert to real or perceived aspersions on their family name.

Controversy over the theatrical representation of Oldcastle was not settled by the recantation of the Chamberlain's company in the Epilogue to *2 Henry IV*. Late in 1599, the first (and only) part of *Sir John Oldcastle* was performed by the Admiral's Men. The dramatists who collaborated in the writing of this loose historical biography defend themselves in the Prologue against possible imputations of libel by a statement of dramatic intent; the audience is to see the true life of the martyr Oldcastle, whose name had suffered past abuse by 'forg'de invention':

> The doubtful Title (Gentlemen) prefixt
> Upon the Argument we have in hand,
> May breede suspence, and wrongfully disturbe
> The peacefull quiet of your setled thoughts:
> To stop which scruple, let this briefe suffise.
> It is no pamperd glutton we present,
> Nor aged Councellor to youthfull sinne,
> But one, whose vertue shone above the rest,
> A valiant Martyr, and a vertuous peere,
> In whose true faith and loyaltie exprest
> Unto his soveraigne, and his countries weale:
> We strive to pay that tribute of our Love,
> Your favours merite, let faire Truth be grac'te,
> Since forg'de invention former time defac'te.

The collaborators decisively rehabilitate the martyr while making few gestures towards historical authenticity: scenes are invented and chronology manipulated. Oldcastle is presented in unreserverdly heroic terms as a loyal subject of the Crown. Indeed, the play was printed the following year with a title page proclaiming the celebration of Cobham's ancestors: 'The first part of the true and honorable historie, of the life of Sir John Old-castle, the good Lord Cobham.'

Whether or not the Cobhams had anything to do with the commissioning and performance of *Sir John Oldcastle* is uncertain. On the occasion of the first performance in November 1599, ten shillings, over and above the initial ten pounds paid by Henslowe, were proffered 'for Mr. Mundaye and the Reste of the poets ... as a gefte'.[46] McKeen has suggested that Frances Howard, Lady Kildare, the Lord Admiral's daughter who had long been desirous of a match with Henry Brooke, now Lord Cobham, may have been responsible for the financial gift. As their patron's daughter she would certainly have been in a position to negotiate with the personnel of the Admiral's Men and to dictate the play's terms of reference. Munday and his fellows would thus have found themselves more than usually restricted in their choice and deployment of material. Sponsored drama produces its own constraints.

The Merry Wives of Windsor

If the Chamberlain's Men had been faced with accusations of intended libel over Falstaff's original name, the opening scene of *The Merry Wives of Windsor*, composed a few months after *1 Henry VI* in early 1597 in honour of the ceremony of the Knights of the Garter, would have appealed to audiences and players with a topical joke. Shallow, in conversation with his cousin Slender, accuses Falstaff of defamation:

> *Shal.* Sir Hugh, persuade me not; I will make a Star Chamber matter of it; if he were twenty Sir John Falstaffs, he shall not abuse Robert Shallow, Esquire.
> *Slen.* In the county of Gloucester, Justice of Peace, and Coram.
> *Shal.* Ay, cousin Slender, and Custalorum.
> *Slen.* Ay, and Ratolorum too; and a gentleman born, Master Parson, who writes himself 'Armigero' in any bill, warrant, quittance, or obligation – 'Armigero'.
> *Shal.* Ay, that I do; and have done any time these three hundred years.
> (I. i. 1–11)

Shallow's indignant reaction and comic exposition of his ancient lineage could conceivably have been written as a parody of the Brookes' reaction to the assumed slight upon their ancestry.

Curiously, mild satire of the Cobhams continues in *The Merry Wives*, appearing in the 1602 quarto but not in the folio. The death of William Brooke in 1597 may well have convinced Shakespeare that it was safe to take greater liberties; Henry Cobham, his heir, was well-connected at Court but, not being a member of the Privy Council, did not possess the same influence as his father. In the quarto, when the obsessively jealous Ford appears in disguise before Falstaff, he takes the name of Brook. Falstaff puns on the name when Brook is first announced, appropriately bearing a gift of sack: 'Call him in. Such Brooks are welcome to me, that o'erflows such liquor' (II. ii. 134–6). The word-play puts it beyond doubt that Shakespeare originally intended Ford to adopt the pseudonym Brook, and not Broome, as is printed in the folio. Several reasons have been advanced to explain the change made to Ford's alias and why it remained in its original form in the quarto. H. J. Oliver has suggested that 'Brook' stood in the play until 1604, when there was a Court performance, and that on this occasion an alteration was made because the inclusion of the name in the presence of the King would have been unwise.[47] George and Henry Brooke had participated in the Bye plot of 1603, a conspiracy to supplant James in favour of his cousin, Arabella Stuart, for which George Brooke was executed. Henry Brooke was also sentenced to death but, in a theatrical display of royal clemency, was spared on the scaffold. This hypothesis, however, seems to be unnecessarily complex. It could equally be suggested that if the Brookes were in disgrace, James would have taken no exception to the ridicule of the family name. Gary Taylor has argued that, following his marriage to Frances Howard, Henry Brooke used his enhanced position at Court to force textual alterations after numerous performances and the publication of the first quarto.[48] If this had been the case, one would expect an early reversion to 'Brook', which is comically effective, after Henry Brooke had been attainted in 1603. The House of Cobham was never to regain the prestige it had held throughout Elizabeth's reign. It would seem more probable that, when the play came before the Master of the Revels in 1597, he censored 'Brook' and substituted or left the players to substitute 'Broome'. The quarto is self-evidently a botched reconstruction of the play in performance. There is some evidence of actors' propensity to stray from their set-parts, and accordingly the players may well have considered that away from Court the suppression of 'Brook' was a piece of insignificant censorship which they could safely override so as not to lose the punning of Ford and Brook.[49]

Every Man Out of His Humour

Jonson's second humours play, *Every Man Out of His Humour*, seems better suited to the stage of the private theatre than to that of the Globe, where it was performed by the Chamberlain's Men in 1599. The play represents a radical break with popular comic tradition.

Jonson ignores familiar motifs and romantic intrigue and within the loose structure of the play concentrates on dissecting the follies and vices of socially heterogeneous characters. Yet at this particular time, Jonson is cautious in his mode of attack. He prudently distances himself from the thrust of the satire by making the play the composition of Asper. Although Cordatus, Asper's friend, describes the play as 'somewhat like Vetus Comoedia', resemblances between *Every Man Out of His Humour* and Aristophanic comedy are not marked. The play appropriates several of the devices of old comedy, but, no doubt because the same freedom enjoyed by its practitioners did not prevail for Jonson, its generalised mode of satire is removed from the transparent parody of Aristophanes.

Asper states his intention in the first Chorus, or Grex, of stripping 'the ragged follies of the time, Naked, as at their birth'. He is cautioned by Cordatus and later by Mitis, who warns him that 'the days are dangerous, full of exception, and men are growne impatient of reproofe'. Asper remains uncompromising in his purpose of exposing 'the times condition'. Yet the prudence counselled by Cordatus and Mitis serves to indicate that he was aware of possible reprisal, as does the manner in which they as 'censors', appointed by the author, anticipate any complaint which might attend Jonson's barbed social critique. The most telling use of such defensive devices follows the scene in which Fastidius Briske is boasting of his acquisition of courtly favour:

> There was a countesse gave me her hand to kisse to day, i'the presence: did me more good by that light, then – and yesternight sent her coach twise to my lodging, to intreat mee accompany her, and my sweet mistris, with some two, or three nameless ladies more: O, I have beene grac'd by 'hem beyond all aime of affection: this's her garter my dagger hangs in: and they doe so commend, and approve my apparell, with my judicious wearing of it, it's above wonder.   (II. vi. 19–27)

The citizen's wife, Fallace, is suitably impressed, and the scene closes with her plan to lock herself in her closet and 'thinke over all his good parts, one after another'. The discourse which follows between Mitis and Cordatus deserves particular attention for the way Jonson pre-empts any accusation of topical satire:

> *Mit.* Well, I doubt, this last *Scene* will endure some grievous torture.
> *Cor.* How? you feare 'twill be rackt, by some hard construction?
> *Mit.* Doe not you?
> *Cor.* No, in good faith: unlesse mine eyes could light mee beyond sense. I
>   see no reason, why this should be more liable to the racke, then the
>   rest: you'le say, perhaps, the city will not take it well, that the

D

marchant is made here to dote so perfectly upon his wife; and shee
againe, to bee so *Fastidiously* affected, as she is?

Mit. You have utter'd my thought, sir, indeed.

Cor. Why (by that proportion) the court might as wel take offence at him
we call the courtier, and with much more pretext, by how much the
place transcends, and goes before in dignitie and vertue: but can you
imagine that any noble, or true spirit in court (whose sinowie, and
altogether un-affected graces, very worthily expresse him a courtier)
will make any exception at the opening of such an emptie trunke, as
this BRISKE is! or thinke his owne worth empeacht, by holding his
motley inside?

Mit. No sir, I doe not.

Cor. No more, assure you, will any grave, wise citizen, or modest matron,
take the object of this folly in DELIRO, and his wife: but rather apply
it as the foile to their owne vertues. For that were to affirme, that a
man, writing of NERO, should meane all Emperors: or speaking of
MACHIAVEL, comprehend all States-men; or in our SORDIDO, all
Farmers; and so of the rest: then which, nothing can be utter'd more
malicious, or absurd. Indeed, there are a sort of these narrow-ey'd
decypherers, I confesse, that will extort strange, and abstruse meanings out of any subject, be it never so conspicuous and innocently
deliver'd.   (II. vi. 141–73)

The passage is an example of a text which acquires a satirical nuance
in performance. Cordatus's reference to the discrepancy between
Briske and 'any noble, or true spirit in court' would have to satisfy the
Master of the Revels reading the text; but in performance the line
would surely have been delivered with mocking intonation. The
indictment of 'narrow-eyed decypherers ... that will extort strange,
and abstruse meanings out of any subject' was, of course, to be
repeated in later plays. Here, however, Jonson's inbuilt defence seems
to have been successful in averting the censorship which affected his
later comical satires.

The finale of *Every Man Out of His Humour* did, however, suffer
censorship following a Globe performance, because it had dared to
represent the Queen on stage. Jonson's original epilogue had Macilente,
the envious, impoverished courtier, kneeling before Queen Elizabeth
and announcing his transformation at the sight of such majesty. In the
quarto, Macilente's change is abruptly effected and his address to the
Queen is printed as an appendix with a prefatory note in which Jonson
explains why he has been forced to alter the ending:

It had another *Catastrophe* or Conclusion, at the first Playing: which (Διὰ
τὸ τὴν βασίλισσαν προσψποποιεῖσθαι) many seem'd not to rellish it;
and therefore 'twas since alter'd: yet that a right-ei'd and solide *Reader* may
perceive it was not so great a part of the Heaven awry, as they would make
it; we request him but to looke downe upon these following Reasons.

Jonson proceeds to defend the decorum of the Queen's stage appearance: the monarch had previously appeared in plays and city pageants[50] and it was dramatically necessary in order to stress both the sycophancy of Macilente, who nurtures hopes of attendance on the Queen, and his metamorphosis. Jonson contends that he can see no cause for objection to such a personation, arguing that his imagination could not create 'a more Proper, Eminent, or worthie Figure', boldly but respectfully used 'to a Morall and Mysterious end'.[51] Nonetheless, those who took exception to a non-ritualistic, mimetic representation of the monarch were obviously successful in suppressing its appearance on the stage of the Globe in 1599. To have a boy actor playing the part of the Queen, apotheosised in contemporary discourse and iconography, would, in Sir Henry Wotton's comment on the 1613 production of *Henry VIII*, 'make greatness very familiar, if not ridiculous'.[52] The Master of the Revels would have approved the original epilogue for the more ritualised Court performance, with the Queen herself drawn into the play; but would have censored the audacious attempt at impersonation on the public stage.

Cynthia's Revels

Jonson's other two comical satires, *Cynthia's Revels* and *Poetaster*, were acted privately by the Children of the Chapel in 1600 and 1601 respectively. While *Cynthia's Revels* is somewhat disingenuously dedicated to the Court, addressed in the folio as 'a bountifull, and brave spring', the play delights in ridiculing that same 'speciall fountaine of manners'. Such satire was not performed unchecked, however, since plays produced in the private indoor theatres were also subject to authorisation by the Master of the Revels.[53]

Cynthia's Revels must have been one of the first plays in the repertoire of the revived company to come before Tilney. As an unsparing lampoon of the Queen's Court entourage, it might not be expected to emerge unscathed from its encounter with the censor. The existence of two distinct texts, the quarto of 1601 and the longer folio text, tends to support such a conjecture.

The crux of the matter is whether the additional material in the folio represents part of Jonson's original composition which was earlier suppressed or whether it was composed later prior to publication of the folio. Herford and Simpson accept the latter text as authoritative, comprising Jonson's final conception of the play, and suggest that he discreetly removed some of the passages before the Court performance in 1601 but drew on them again when he was later revising the play for publication.[54] Anne Barton refers to Jonson's 'conciliatory cuts', implying that self-censorship lies behind the omission.[55] There are modest indications in the quarto text that Jonson did have to modify his critique of Cynthia's court. In the opening dialogue between Cupid and Mercury, Cupid alludes to the 'Queene of these groves, DIANE', who has 'proclaim'd a solemne revells, which (her god-head put off) she will descend to grace'. The parenthesis is missing in the quarto, possibly because the idea of the Queen casting aside her divinity might detract from the compliment to Elizabeth as Diana/Cynthia. There is a further sign of external pressure on the quarto text in the attempt to modify an aspersion on the qualities of a typical courtier. In answer to Cupid's question as to whether Anaides is a courtier, Mercury rejects the idea, but comments damningly that 'he has two essentiall parts of the courtier, pride, and ignorance' (II. ii. 77–8). In the early version, there is a significant interpolation: 'I meane of such a Courtier, who is (indeed) but the *Zani* to an exact Courtier'. The addition is dropped in the folio text, its disappearance suggesting that it originated only in response to censorship.

Textual discrepancies between folio and quarto are elsewhere more substantial, ranging from the omission of short passages to serial changes. In the folio, in place of the announcement found in the quarto (IIII. v. 5–10) that Cynthia will preside at the evening's entertainment, Arete, the Queen's shrewd lady-in-waiting, tells the assembled courtiers that the 'sports' are to be postponed. This provokes Asotus, a would-be courtier, to express his chagrin at being denied the opportunity for self-promotion:

> *Aso.* What lucke is this, that our revels are dasht? Now was I beginning to glister, i' the very high way of preferment. And CYNTHIA had but seenne me dance a straine, or doe but one trick, I had beene kept in court, I should never have needed to looke towards my friends againe.   (IV. v. 76–81)

That Cynthia should favour a courtier because he could dance elegantly was not so fantastical: Sir Christopher Hatton, who became Lord Chancellor, had thus first attracted the Queen's attention. The omission of these lines may well have been forced upon Jonson: precisely because of its strain of truth, the satire has a dangerous edge in making not only the favourite, but implicitly also the royal patron, its target. The postponement of the Queen's revels in the folio text prompts Amorphus to devise an exhibition of the arts of courtship. The scenes depicting this risible entertainment (V. i–iv) expose the courtiers at their most absurd before they are outwitted in their fantastical game by Mercury. Whether this alternative dénouement comprised part of Jonson's original text which he was obliged to suppress or whether it represents later work is open to question. It seems likely, however, that the Master of the Revels would have taken exception to such a protracted representation of the excesses of the Court.

Equally trenchant in its exposure of court mores is the scene depicting the conversation of women of the court. Part of the episode in which the women fantasise on how they would wish to be transformed by Juno, is missing in the quarto (IIII. i. 136–214). Moira glosses her voyeurist fantasies of knowing 'what wer done behind the arras, what upon the staires, what i' the garden, what i' the *Nymphs* chamber, what by barge, and what by coach' as being the interests of a wise-woman. Philantia has autocratic ambitions: 'I would wish ... all the court were subject to my absolute becke, and all things in it depending on my looke; as if there were no other heaven, but in my smile, nor other hell, but in my frowne'. Phantaste would take on the shape and experience of women of different social status before becoming the unattainable woman toying with her many suitors. The power that the court ladies crave is associated with the authority exercised by the Queen, though shorn of its mystique. In reducing female power to trivial dimensions, Jonson was risking condemnation not only for exposing the petty ambitions of women who frequented the court, but also for suggesting the frailties of the Queen as protagonist of absolute female power. Such an interpretation of the scene could well have provoked its excision in the Elizabethan performance of the play, as embodied in the quarto text.

Significantly, Crites's scathing exposure of what Arete describes as 'the knot of spiders' at Cynthia's court (III. iiii) appears to have been modified in the quarto text. The honest Crites tells Arete that he has just witnessed 'the strangest pageant, fashion'd like a court'. The early text omits the portraits of the 'mincing marmoset made all of clothes, and face', of the traveller who has 'sceene the cringe of severall courts and courtiers' and of the bribe-taker who accepts 'the comming gold of insolent, and base ambition that hourely rubs his dry, and itchie palmes'. Again, the quarto version of the scene strongly suggests an attempt to remove such references to the most rebarbative traits of the habituées of the court.

Jonson's practice of revising his plays makes it impossible to state an unqualified view about censorship as the substantial reason for the different versions of *Cynthia's Revels*. The quarto text, lacking the tedious diversion of the courtship game in Act V, is certainly a more attractive stage version. Yet the additional folio passages and scenes do contain the play's most trenchant court satire, which may well have been censored by the Master of the Revels when he perused the play in readiness for a Court performance in January 1601.[56] It is equally possible that Jonson prepared his text in anticipation of censorial objections and restored the suspect passages in the next reign when it was safe to do so. The evidence is inconclusive, but whatever the precise reason for the divergent texts of *Cynthia's Revels*, it is at least clear that Jonson felt considerably less inhibited in the mid-Jacobean period in indulging his taste for court satire.

Poetaster

Jonson's awareness of the state's nervous attitude to dramatic satire and of the role played by informers in its detection, is conveyed in his next play for the Chapel Children, *Poetaster*, performed in 1601. The opening speech of Envy, who affects to be Prologue, but is also revealed as a predatory informer, shows him thwarted by one particular manoeuvre for eluding censorship, namely, the use of a foreign location to avoid the imputation of contemporary reference. Envy's expectations are foiled when he sees that the play does not have a local setting:

> ROME? ROME? and ROME? Cracke ey-strings, and your balles
> Drop into earth; let me be ever blind.
> I am prevented; all my hopes are crost,
> Checkt, and abated; ...
> What should I doe? ROME? ROME? O my vext soule,
> How might I force this to the present state?

After a third sounding the true Prologue enters, armed. He explains 'this forc't defence' on the grounds that:

> 'tis a dangerous age:
> Wherein, who writes, had need present his *Scenes*
> Fortie-fold proofe against the conjuring meanes
> Of base detractors, and illiterate apes,
> That fill up roomes in faire and formall shapes.

But the milieu of Augustan Rome, perceived as the repository of literary values, did not in the event deflect complaint against the satire of *Poetaster* and parts of the play were consequently suppressed. Moreover, Jonson's assiduously prepared reply to his critics in a final additional scene, the 'Apologeticall Dialogue', was itself disallowed both on the stage and in print.

The facts of the case emerge only in the folio text, specifically in the play's dedication to Richard Martin and in the 'Apologeticall Dialogue'. The latter comprises a conversation between the author and two dramatically extraneous characters, Nasutus and Polyposus. It is prefaced by an address to the reader, in which Jonson gives his reason for the inclusion of the Dialogue, 'which was only once spoken upon the stage': it is all the answer that he ever gave 'to sundry impotent libells' which discredited his intentions in the play. Anne Barton has suggested that Jonson himself took the part of the author in the 'Apologeticall Dialogue' in its sole performance on the Blackfriars stage in 1601.[57] If this was the case, the performance was even more of a defiant act and may well have contributed to the immediate suppression of the Dialogue. Jonson was determined to draw attention to its prohibition. In the Epilogue, which appears only in the 1602 quarto, he complains that both audience and reader have been deprived of the author's defence:

> HERE (Reader) in place of the Epilogue, was meant to thee an Apology from the Author, with his reasons for the publishing of this booke: but (since he is no lesse restrain'd, then thou depriv'd of it, by Authoritie) hee praies thee to think charitably of what thou hast read, till thou maist heare him speake what he hath written.

By the time of the publication of the folio text in 1616, however, changes in the preoccupations of censorship meant that Jonson was permitted greater licence or else took it for himself. The 'Apologeticall Dialogue' is appended to the text of the play in the folio. It conveys the author's profound sense of grievance at the clamour which had greeted his play. Nasutus's questions allow him to plead his case:

> *Nas.* I never saw this play bred all this tumult.
> What was there in it could so deeply offend?
> And stirre so many hornets?
> *Aut.* Shall I tell you?
> *Nas.* Yes, and ingenuously.
> *Aut.* Then, by the hope,
> Which I preferre unto all other objects,
> I can professe, I never writ that peece
> More innocent, or empty of offence.
> Some salt it had, but neyther tooth, nor gall,
> Nor was there in it any circumstance,
> Which, in the setting downe, I could suspect
> Might be perverted by an enemies tongue.
> Onely, it had the fault to be call'd mine.
> That was the crime. (ll. 69–81)

The two interlocutors supply further details. The multitudes claim that he has 'hit and hurt' and that his subsequent silence argues his libellous intentions; and, further, that he has 'tax'd the Law, and Lawyers; Captaines; and the Players by their particular names'. The latter is obviously a reference to Jonson's transparent satire of Dekker as Demetrius and Marston as Crispinius, both inferior poets in the play's hierarchical scale of judgment. But the author refutes the accusation, using Jonson's familiar denial of libel: 'My Bookes have still been taught/To spare the persons, and to speake the vices.' Warming to his defence, he asserts that his caustic comments on the law are to be found in Ovid's *Elegies* and argues, somewhat dis-ingenuously, that they cannot be applied 'unto our lawes or their just ministers', which he reveres. Finally, he defends the validity of satire, which some describe as 'meere rayling', on the grounds of its classical precedent:

Ha! If all the salt in the old *comoedy*
Should be so censur'd, or the sharper wit
Of the bold *satyre*, termed scolding rage,
What age could then compare with those, for buffons?
What should be sayd of ARISTOPHANES?
PERSIUS? or JUVENAL? whose names we now
So glorifie in schooles, at least pretend it.   (ll. 186–92)

Despite the valiant justification, it is unlikely that Jonson's case for the kind of freedom enjoyed by Aristophanic satire would have given the authorities pause for thought. Yet the allegations echoed by Nasutus and Polyposus show that the work of the satirist was vulnerable to repression in the interests of professions so diverse as players and lawyers, and not only at the hands of offended courtiers.

Not for the last time, Jonson was to be grateful for the intervention of a benefactor. In the folio text, he dedicates *Poetaster* to the lawyer Richard Martin, who prevented the complete suppression of the play when it was threatened by the 'ignorance, and malice of the times'. The dedicatory epistle reveals that Martin had protested the author's and the play's innocence to 'the greatest Justice of this kingdome'. The reference is probably to the Lord Chief Justice, although Herbert S. Mallory's suggestion that the case was referred to the Queen cannot be discounted.[58]

The outcry against *Poetaster* was of course subsequent to its official perusal by Tilney. Despite the accusations of libel, Martin's advocacy before the Lord Chief Justice saved the play, although not in its entirety. Passages are omitted in the quarto which reflect the com-plaints of some members of the audience who attended the first production at the Blackfriars. Either Jonson was entrusted with the task of self-censorship or, more probably, Tilney recalled the play and excised the offending parts. One such passage has Ovid senior attempting to force his son to abandon poetry and return to the law (I. ii. 98–136). The discourse closes with the cynical comments of Captain Tucca and the tribune Lupus on the easy practice and benefits of the legal profession:

> *Lupu.* Why, the *law* makes a man happy, without respecting any other merit: a simple scholer, or none at all may be a lawyer.
> *Tucc.* He tells thee true, my noble *Neophyte*; my little *Grammaticaster*, he do's: It shall never put thee to thy *Mathematiques*, *Metaphysiques*, *Philosophie*, and I know not what suppos'd sufficiencies; If thou canst but have the patience to plod inough, talke, and make noise inough, be impudent inough, and 'tis inough.
> *Lupu.* Three books will furnish you.
> *Tucc.* And the lesse arte, the better: Besides, when it shall be in the power of thy chev'rill conscience, to doe right, or wrong, at thy pleasure, my pretty ALCIBIADES.

Another passage missing in the quarto is that which has the flamboyant, wily Tucca, who has just received money from the player Histrio to commission an anti-Horace satire, describe the alleged infamies of certain actors:

> *Tucc.* I have stood up and defended you I, to gent'men, when you have beene said to prey upon pu'ness, and honest citizens, for socks, or buskins: or when they ha' call'd you usurers, or brokers, or said, you were able to helpe to a peace of flesh – I have sworne, I did not think so. Nor that you were the common retreats for punkes decai'd i' their practice. I cannot beleeve it of you.   (III. iv. 306–13)

From the 'Apologeticall Dialogue' we know that Jonson had 'tax'd' players and that they had contributed to the general tumult against *Poetaster*. Presumably, the removal of Tucca's slur on actors' behaviour was brought about by formal complaint from one of the adult companies rather than by particular individuals, since Jonson makes the point that they thought mistakenly that 'each mans vice belong'd to their whole tribe'. If so, it was a rare case of collaboration between the Master of the Revels and the players.

At the turn of the century, Chapman, in the 'Prologus' of *All Fools*, voiced his dissatisfaction with the current tendency of dramatists to exploit personal satire, to the detriment of true comedy:

> Who can show cause why th'ancient comic vein
> Of Eupolis and Cratinus (now reviv'd,
> Subject to personal application)
> Should be exploded by some bitter spleens,
> Yet merely comical and harmless jests
> (Though ne'er so witty) be esteem'd but toys,
> If void of th' other satirism's sauce?[59]   (ll. 13–19)

This is an ironical comment from a dramatist who was not averse to introducing topical satire into his early plays and, like Jonson, saw the playwrights' purpose in terms not of the construction of 'comical and harmless jests', but of moral instruction. Moreover, a number of Chapman's plays betray signs of censorship. The case for the censorship of *Sir Gyles Goosecappe*, Chapman's first play for the Children of the Chapel, rests on certain dramatic expectations which fail to materialise. Foulweather, in response to an enquiry by the knight Rudesby about Lady Furnifall's drinking habits, replies that she 'is never in any sociable vaine till she by typsie' (III. i. 180–1). Rudesby is promised a meeting with her at a supper to be held at Lord Furnifall's residence, at which she is expected to get drunk; but Lady Furnifall does not appear at the gathering. We are also led to expect the dupe Sir Giles to appear dressed as a fool; but, again, expectations are unfulfilled. Although the quarto text displays such traces of censorial interference, it does not appear to be based on a stage version of the play. This has prompted the play's latest editor to conclude that the copy underlying the printed text was prepared by Chapman to incorporate the revisions and deletions of the ecclesiastical licenser who perused the play in 1606.[60] The Stationers' Register entry stipulates that the play must be printed according to the approved copy, indicating that the text has been reformed by the licenser. But it would seem unlikely that the ecclesiastical censor judged to be offensive material which the Master of the Revels had earlier found to be unobjectionable, at a time when the satire was presumably more topical. The press licenser may well have endorsed excisions made by Tilney when the play was perused for the stage c. 1602. It is curious that there is no apparent effort to tidy up the dramatic anomalies. Chapman's *Byron* plays, later victims of censorship, were also published with a similar disregard for narrative consistency. Chapman may have seen in this refusal to adapt his plays to the altered context one of the few available means of protest.

The Old Joiner of Aldgate

The hypothesis that personal satire was woven into *Sir Gyles Goosecappe* is supported by certain evidence that in 1603 Chapman was consciously involved with the transmutation of real events into theatre and with the personation of living individuals under feigned names on the stage. The play in question, *The Old Joiner of Aldgate*, is lost; but the details of the affair surrounding it, which reached the Star Chamber, survive in contemporary documentation.[61] The events on which the play is based had an obvious piquancy and theatrical appeal in their projection of intrigue and duplicity. Seizing on the well-known experiences of the middle-class heiress Agnes Howe, Chapman dramatised her father's attempts to exploit her eligible status by encouraging rival suitors and the eventual out-manoeuvring of the three contenders by a preacher, Dr John Milward, who succeeded in marrying Agnes.

It appears that John Flaskett, one of the actual suitors, had taken his case to both Archbishop Whitgift and Bishop Bancroft and had asserted a claim of pre-contract, that is, of prior betrothal to Agnes Howe. Whilst the issue was under debate in the ecclesiastical courts, Flaskett, according to the Attorney General's bill in the Star Chamber, commissioned Chapman to write a stage play exposing the machinations of Milward. Chapman then sold the piece to Thomas Woodford and Edward Peers, who managed the Children of Paul's and with whom he had had professional dealings:

> a stage play should be made and was made by one George Chapman upon a plott given unto him concerning ... Agnes Howe ... (her cause and sutes then depending) and the same under coulorable and fayned names personated, so made and contryved was sold to Thomas Woodford and Edward Pearce for xx marks to be played upon the open stages in divers play houses within the citie of London.[62]

The play was duly performed in 1603. Shortly afterwards Milward raised objection to its contents, his complaint being corroborated by the evidence of his man, Edward Brampton, who had seen the production. The play was prohibited for four or five days and Chapman, Woodford and Peers were consequently arraigned in the Star Chamber.

The evidence against them, however, was at best tenuous: the persons involved in the actual case could not be identified by name with their stage counterparts and Chapman had treated his material with considerable dramatic licence. Flaskett, naturally enough, dismissed the stage matter as 'toys and jests such as are acted in other places'. Agnes's father, John Howe, was similarly disingenuous in his denial that he recognised himself in the character of Snipper Snapper, the barber, claiming that 'he had no reason to take it to himself for that kings had been presented on the stage and therefore Barbers might'. The three defendants were thus able plausibly to refute the charge of participation in a confederacy to represent living persons on the stage and they could not be convicted. Peers secured absolution from any responsibility by telling the court of his limited role in the theatrical partnership comprising the instruction of the children, which 'apperteyneth to his place and charge'. Woodford also gained his acquittal through his insistence that, by the time it came into his possession, the play book had already received the approval of the late Queen's Master of the Revels. Throughout the interrogation, Chapman continued to deny any allegation that he had been advised in his composition by persons who might have a vested interest in the Agnes Howe affair. He further maintained that 'he never sawe the same acted and plaied publiquely upon a stage'; and denied the charge that he had made any alterations or revisions to his original work since its first production. The authorities' suspicions that a play could be altered and thus be performed in a version materially different from that which had been approved by the Master of the Revels are implicit in Woodford's specific assurance that the play had not been reworked: 'he hath the booke itselfe without alteringe of it'. Chapman, in turn, claimed to have had no further access to the play book once it had been delivered out of his hands to Woodford. The questions asked of Chapman and Woodford about possible revisions of the text signify an awareness on the part of their accusers that the system of dramatic censorship might be thus overreached.

Chapman had beyond doubt capitalised on a local scandal and the authorities in their turn were well aware that real events lay behind *The Old Joiner of Aldgate*. Nevertheless, by comparison with other cases of alleged libel, the reaction of authority towards the play and its author was relatively mild. One reason for the defendant's immunity was, of course, the elusive nature of defamation and, more particularly, the difficulty of proving that any personal application was intended in the creation of character or situation. The apparent reluctance of the courts to take the case further may also in this instance be linked to the social status of the plaintiffs: a dramatist might remain relatively safe from reprisal following accusations of libel so long as he was depicting persons of no greater rank than Agnes Howe and John Milward.

The importance of sufficient status would seem to be borne out by a notable instance of government action against libels. On 10 May 1601, the Privy Council wrote to the Justices of the Peace in Middlesex complaining that they had heard of an unnamed company performing at the Curtain, who 'do represent upon the stage in their interludes the persons of some gentlemen of good desert and quallity that are yet alive under obscure manner, but yet in such sorte as all the hearers may take notice both of the matter and the persons that are meant thereby'.[63] It is implied that the players had transgressed in two respects: they had ignored the licensing procedure and they had performed a play which was liable to cause 'offence or scandal'. In consequence, the play was to be prohibited, the text examined and the players apprehended. There is no extant play which fits the description or the occasion of this case of Privy Council censorship. The directives are nonetheless of considerable significance in their explicit acknowledgment of a particular mischief which exercised the agents of theatrical censorship immediately before the Jacobean accession. Dramatic satire which relied upon personal identification was to be prohibited and more general criticism of professions and social groups was to be checked.

With the history play under increased surveillance and dramatic satire under threat of harsh reprisals, the years 1597–1603 appear as a period when playwrights were subjected to greater than ever incursions into their freedom. Apart from those which fell foul of the censor, the plays of the period are remarkable only for their orthodoxy and tameness. Semi-historical plays such as *Sir John Oldcastle*, *Alarum for London or The Siege of Antwerp* and *Sir Thomas Cromwell* steer away from controversial issues and avoid political debate. The Protestant propagandist Foxe's *Book of Martyres* replaces the much more balanced *Chronicles* of Holinshed as source. Interestingly, the plays in the repertoires of the Admiral's Men and Worcester's Men follow safe conventional themes, independent of the Catholic leanings of their patrons.[64] At a time when the authorities were not disposed to discriminate between the public and private faces of libel, and were likely to pounce upon any expression of the libellous impulse, playwrights had little scope for challenging the boundaries and every reason to entrench such privileges as they had. Just as the Court and country did, playwrights and men of the theatre awaited impatiently and with high expectations the advent of the new reign.

Notes

1 See Reavley Gair, *The Children of Paul's: the story of a theatre company, 1553–1608* (Cambridge, 1982), pp. 113–32 and Michael Shapiro, *Children of the Revels* (New York, 1977). Shapiro dates the revival of Paul's theatre company earlier c. 1597, pp. 17–21.

2 Chambers, *ES*, I, p. 214.

3 The Privy Council permitted the amalgamated company of Oxford's and Worcester's Men to play at the Boar's Head and 'nowhere else': Chambers, *ES*, II, p. 225.

4 See *Letters of King James VI and I*, ed. C. P. V. Akrigg (California, 1984), pp. 168–70.

5 Francis Cordale to Humphrey Galdelli or to Giuseppe Tusinga, Venice, *CSPD 1598–1601*, CCLXXI, pp. 251–2.

6 *Tudor Royal Proclamations*, III, pp. 233–4.

7 See Arber, *SR*, III, 677.
8 Richard A. McCabe, 'Elizabethan satire and the bishops' ban of 1599', *Yearbook of English Studies*, 11 (1981), 188–94.
9 *The Letters of John Chamberlain*, ed. N. E. McClure, (2 vols., Philadelphia, 1939), I, p. 70.
10 *CSPD 1598–1601*, CCLXXV, p. 452.
11 George Fenner to Giulio Piccioli, or Bernard Edlyno, Venice, *CSPD 1598–1601*, CCLXXI, p. 225.
12 *CSPD 1598–1601*, CCLXXIV, p. 404.
13 *CSPD 1598–1601*, CCLXXIV, p. 405 and CCLXXV, p. 449.
14 For Hayward's style of historiography, see S. L. Goldberg, 'Sir John Hayward, "politic" historian', *RES*, 6 (1955), pp. 233–45.
15 *CSPD 1598–1601*, CCLXXVIII, p. 555.
16 S. T. Bindoff, *Tudor England* (Harmondsworth, 1950), p. 303.
17 *CSPD 1598–1601*, CLLXXVIII, p. 567. In the same orders to the preachers, reference was again made to Hayward's history, 'wherein all the complaints and slanders which have been given out by seditious traitors against the Government, both in England and Ireland, are set down, and falsely attributed to those times, thereby cunningly insinuating that the same abuses being now in this realm that were in the days of Richard II, the like course might be taken for redress.'
18 *CSPD 1598–1601*, CCLXXVIII, p. 578.
19 *Censorship and Interpretation*, p. 17.
20 See below, pp. 127–31.
21 See Fredson Bowers, 'Essex's Rebellion and Dekker's *Old Fortunatus*', *RES*, 3 (1952), 365–66.
22 'Of Great Place', *Essays* (London, 1936), p. 31. The essay was written well after Essex's fall c. 1614.
23 *CSPD 1598–1601*, CCLXXIII, p. 365.
24 *Life of Sir Philip Sidney*, with an Introduction by Nowell Smith (Oxford, 1907), pp. 156–7.
25 'Invisible bullets' in *Shakespearean Negotiations: The Circulation of Social Energy in Renaissance England* (Oxford, 1988), p. 65.
26 *CSPD 1598–1601*, CCLXXIV, p. 404.
27 See L. L. Schücking, *Times Literary Supplement* (25 September 1930), p. 752; Alfred Hart, 'Was the second part of *King Henry the Fourth* censored?', *Shakespeare and the Homilies* (Melbourne, 1934), pp. 154–218; and George Walton Williams, 'The text of *2 Henry IV*: facts and problems', *Shakespeare Studies*, 9 (1976), 173–82.
28 See J. Nichols, *Progresses of Queen Elizabeth*, (2 vols., London, 1788), II, p. 41.
29 *Threshold of a Nation: A Study in English and Irish Drama* (Cambridge, 1979), p. 78.
30 'History and ideology: the instance of *Henry V*', *Alternative Shakespeares*, ed. John Drakakis (London, New York, 1985), p. 225.
31 Gary Taylor's 'We happy few: the 1600 abridgement', Stanley Wells and Gary Taylor, *Modernizing Shakespeare's Spelling with Three Studies in the Text of Henry V* (Oxford, 1979), pp. 72–117, has argued that the copy text of the quarto has been carefully prepared to accommodate a reduced cast of eleven actors. By the author's own admission, this does not

account for the absence of the Chorus throughout or the omission of the first scene of the play.

32 *Threshold of a Nation*, p. 74.

33 Gary Taylor, 'We happy few', p. 85.

34 On 21 July 1599, Francis Cordale, in correspondence with Humphrey Galdelli in Venice, wrote: 'I can send no news of the Irish wars, all advertisements thence being prohibited, and such news as comes to Council carefully concealed. I fear our part has had little success, lost many captains and whole companies, and has little hopes of prevailing.' (*CSPD 1598–1601*, CCLXXI, p. 251).

35 'History and ideology', p. 216.

36 'Strategies of state and political plays: *A Midsummer Night's Dream, Henry IV, Henry V, Henry VIII*', *Political Shakespeare: New Essays in Cultural Materialism* (Manchester, 1985), pp. 107–30.

37 See, for example, Howard Felperin, 'Shakespeare's *Henry VIII*: history as myth', *Studies in English Literature*, 6 (1966), 225–46; John D. Cox, '*Henry VIII* and the masque', *English Literary History*, 45 (1978), 390–409; William M. Baillie, '*Henry VIII*: a Jacobean history', *Shakespeare Studies*, 12 (1979), 247–66; and Janet Clare, 'Beneath pomp and circumstance in *Henry VIII*', *Shakespeare Studies* (Shakespeare Society of Japan), 21 (1985), 65–81.

38 *Comicall Satire and Shakespeare's 'Troilus and Cressida'* (San Marino, California, 1938), p. 1.

39 Quoted by Gary Taylor, 'William Shakespeare, Richard James and the House of Cobham', *RES*, 38 (1987), 334–54, at p. 335. See also David McKeen, *A Memory of Honour: The Life of William Brook, Lord Cobham*, 2 vols. (Salzburg, 1986), pp. 22–3.

40 Oldcastle had received hagiographic treatment by John Bale, *A brefe Chronycle concernynge The Examinacyon and death of the blessed martyr of Christ syr Johan Oldecastell the Lord Cobham* (1544) and by John Foxe in his immensely popular *Acts and Monuments* (1563), recounting the persecution of Protestants and their precursors. Sir John Oldcastle and Sir William Brooke did not in fact share the same ancestry. Oldcastle received the title of Lord Cobham through his wife, Joan de la Pole.

41 Taylor, 'William Shakespeare, Richard James and the House of Cobham', pp. 347–9 and Robert J. Fehrenbach, 'When Lord Cobham and Edmund Tilney "were att odds": Oldcastle, Falstaff, and the date of *1 Henry IV*', *Shakespeare Studies*, 18 (1986), 87–101, at pp. 95–6.

42 See *2 Henry IV*, ed. A. R. Humphreys (London, 1966), p. 186.

43 Allusions to Henry Cobham as Falstaff are cryptic. In February 1598, Essex wrote to Sir Robert Cecil asking him to tell Sir Alexander Ratcliffe that 'his sister is maryed to Sir John Falstaff'. Gossip later linked Ratcliffe's sister with Brooke. On 8 July 1599, Lady Southampton wrote to her husband in Ireland that 'Sir John Falstaff is by his Mistress dame Pintpot made father of a godly milers thum a boye thats all heade and veri litel body, but this is a secrit.' Cobham appears to have had no children. It may be, as McKeen suggested in his thesis, that the remark is allegorical, referring to the disappointment of someone's expectations of great things. Cobham was at this time unsuccessful in his ambition to become a member of the Privy Council. See McKeen, 'A memory of honour: a study

of the House of Cobham of Kent in Elizabeth I's reign' (doctoral dissertation, University of Birmingham, 1964), pp. 970–3.

44 *Shakespeare's Typological Satire: A Study of the Falstaff-Oldcastle Problem* (Athens, Ohio, 1979). The thesis advanced is an intriguing one; but it is difficult to accept the premiss that Shakespeare was consciously and consistently remoulding the medieval typological approach to history for the satiric purpose of mocking the Lollard-Puritan stance.

45 The only suggestion of this is Nashe's letter to William Cotton written between August and October 1596: 'when now the players as if they had writt another Christs tears, are piteously persecuted by the L. Maior and the aldermen, and however in there ol Lords tyme they thought there state setled, it is now so uncertayne they cannot build upon it' (*The Works of Thomas Nashe*, V, p. 194).

46 *Henslowe's Diary* eds. Foakes and Ricket, p. 126.

47 *The Merry Wives of Windsor*, ed. H. J. Oliver (London, 1971), p. lvii.

48 'William Shakespeare, Richard James and the House of Cobham', pp. 350–1.

49 See II. ii. 134–6, III. v. 121–2 and V. v. 231–2.

50 Of the 'divers Playes' in which the Queen was represented, Anne Barton comments that only *Histriomastix*, has survived: *Ben Jonson, Dramatist* (Cambridge, 1984), p. 67. Herford and Simpson, however, draw attention to Peele's *The Araygnement of Paris*, (printed 1584), *Ben Jonson*, IX, p. 481.

51 The apology offered by Jonson, affirming the inviolability of the Queen's image, makes an incongruous match for his comment to Drummond that 'Queen Elizabeth never saw her self after she became old in a true Glass' (*Ben Jonson*, I, pp. 141–2).

52 Sir Henry Wotton to Sir Edmund Bacon, 29 June 1613, in *The Life and Letters of Sir Henry Wotton*, ed. L. Pearsall Smith, (2 vols., London, 1907), II, p. 32.

53 The title pages of *Cynthia's Revels* and *Poetaster* in the 1640 folio refer to the allowance of the Master of the Revels.

54 *Ben Jonson*, IV, p. 17.

55 *Ben Jonson, Dramatist*, p. 80.

56 *Cynthia's Revels* has been identified with 'a showe with musycke and speciall songes prepared for the purpose', which is recorded in the Chamber accounts as performed at Court on 6 January 1601 and for which Nathanial Gyles, Master of the Children of the Chapel, was paid five pounds. The description of the play is supported by the long masque which dominates Act V of the quarto. See Chambers, *ES*, IV, p. 166 and III, p. 364.

57 *Ben Jonson, Dramatist*, p. 90.

58 *Poetaster*, ed. Herbert S. Mallory, *Yale Studies in English* (New York, 1905), p. 139.

59 See *All Fools*, ed. Frank Manley (London, 1968).

60 *Sir Gyles Goosecappe, Knight*, ed. John F. Hennedy, *The Plays of George Chapman: The Tragedies with Sir Gyles Goosecappe*, eds. Allan Holaday, G. Blakemore Evans and Thomas L. Berger (Cambridge, 1988), pp. 712–3.

61 See C. J. Sisson, *Lost Plays of Shakespeare's Age* (Cambridge, 1936), pp. 12–72. Sisson has assembled the documents relevant to the case.

Those which are recorded in *Proceedings of the Star Chamber* are of greatest importance for the reconstruction of the state response to satire.

62 *Lost Plays of Shakespeare's Age*, p. 58.
63 *APC 1600–1*, xxxi, p. 346.
64 See Andrew Gurr, 'Intertextuality at Windsor', *Shakespeare Quarterly*, 38 (1987), 189–200, at 194.

CHAPTER III

'Poore dismemberd poems':
the drama and the new regime,
1603–1608

Queen Elizabeth had a Camden, and King Charles a Clarendon, but poor
King James has had I think none but paltry scribblers.
(White Kennet, Bishop of Peterborough, 1718–28)

The players do not forbear to represent upon their stage the whole course of
this present time, not sparing either king, state, or religion, in so great
absurdity, and with such liberty, that anybody would be afraid to hear
them.   (George Calvert, Secretary of State, 1619–25)

It would be reasonable to surmise that the accession of James I would
have made little difference to the censorship of drama. The procedure
whereby the Master of the Revels perused all plays and licensed those
which gained his approval was well established by 1603. Tilney,
although increasingly aided by his deputy George Buc, remained in the
post until his death in 1610. Likewise, continuity in the Privy Council
and in the Church meant that the tone of government remained for the
time being Elizabethan. Robert Cecil, Elizabeth's chief minister, who
became Lord Salisbury in 1605, was appointed Secretary of State and
enjoyed his pre-eminence until his death in 1612. Together with Henry
Howard, Earl of Northampton, a former rival, and his friend Thomas
Sackville, Earl of Dorset, Cecil ensured that James's interests were
prosecuted.

Notwithstanding such continuities, the new dispensation did, however, bring immediate changes in both the preoccupations and the
operation of theatre censorship which were conditioned by the
character and experience of the monarch. James I was temperamentally
far removed from Elizabeth I. In contrast to Elizabeth, who had
assiduously fostered the cult of Gloriana, James was a man who cared
little for personal dignity. An episode in Edinburgh in 1599, recorded
by the presbyterian David Calderwood, encapsulates the King's indulgent attitude towards players who were reportedly making him a
figure of mirth. The company had been performing at Court and were

issued with a warrant instructing the bailiffs of the city to provide them with accommodation. The ministers of the Kirk, who had appropriated the right to license plays in 1575, objected on moral grounds to the players' presence in the city and in the Kirk sessions passed an Act prohibiting attendance at plays. Incensed at what he saw as the discharge of his warrant, the King directed them to annul their ordinance and demanded that the actors should have freedom to perform. In defence of their prohibition one of the ministers informed the King that he had heard that the players had dared to present 'secreit and indirect taunts and checkes' at James's expense and he concluded that 'there is not a man of honour in England would give such fellowes so much as their countenance'. The information evidently carried little weight with the King. After much debate in the Kirk sessions, the Act was rescinded.[1] In England, James was similarly to demonstrate his authority in countermanding decisions of the official stage licensers (not always to the players' advantage) but also to show indulgence when he was the object of dramatic satire. As is clear from the satirical features of plays performed or published immediately following the accession, the protection of the sovereign's mystique ceased to be one of the censor's priorities.

The King brought to government a new ethos and different national and international aspirations, which in time were to have an impact on the brief of the Master of the Revels. James's personal style of government practised in Scotland is reflected in the *ad hoc* operation of censorship during the early Jacobean period. Scottish government and bureaucracy were undeveloped and casual to a degree.[2] As King of Scotland, James was accustomed to treating with individuals and acquiring support through patronage rather than working through councils of state. In a famous speech to the English Parliament in 1607, the King claimed of Scotland: 'Here I sit and governe it with my Pen, I write and it is done, and by a Clearke of the councell I governe Scotland now, which others could not doe by the sword'.[3] Instances of literary censorship often arose from the King's personal disapproval of particular books, as distinct from the activities of either the Privy Council in England or, more commonly, the ecclesiastical licensers, who exercised control over the press on the claimed grounds of national interest. James had, for example, banned *The Faerie Queen* in Scotland because of Spenser's allegorical treatment of Mary Queen of Scots in Book V.[4] As King of England, James interposed his will to prevent the performance of certain plays and the circulation of provocative books. As will become apparent, the most controversial cases of censorship during the early Jacobean period were those which suffered royal intervention after the play had been licensed and performed.

Sir Robert Wilbraham's astute comparison of Queen Elizabeth and King James in the year of the accession is pertinent to their different responses to the drama: 'The Quene slow to resolucion, and seldome to be retracted: his majestie quick in concluding and more variable in subsistinge'.[5] James, as we shall see, was often prepared to countenance plays which many considered indecorous and libellous in their satire; but when the critique touched on issues which he cherished, such as the projected union between England and Scotland, he was irascible and quick to act. He was equally quick to relent or to forgive: there is nothing in Jacobean times to compare with the reprisals taken against the London theatres following *The Isle of Dogs* in 1597.

The theatre was amongst the immediate beneficiaries of the King's liberality, which was greeted as a welcome contrast with Elizabeth's parsimony. Following his arrival from Scotland, James's gesture of elevating the Chamberlain's Men to the King's Men and installing them as Grooms of the Chamber and members of the royal household promised well for the players' future protection. The words of the royal patent bespeak his generosity as a literary patron: local officials are to allow the players to perform without 'hindrances or molestacions', to aid and assist them 'if anie wronge be to them offered, And to allowe them such former Curtesies as hath bene given to men of theire place and quallitie'.[6] The decree omits the proviso embodied in earlier patents granted to all other companies that their plays must first be licensed by the Master of the Revels. The omission of the reference to the censor may suggest no more than an initial unfamiliarity with the pre-existing structure of dramatic censorship. We have no evidence, however, before 1606 that the Master of the Revels was licensing plays performed by the King's Men. It may well have been that there was a short interval in which the King's Men enjoyed the same freedom from restraint favoured by James in 1599, when the English actors appeared in Scotland.

James's consort, Anne of Denmark, and his son Prince Henry also honoured the existing companies. The Queen in 1604 gave her patronage to the Children of the Chapel – one of the companies of child actors under the management of Edward Kirkham – as well as to the adult company which had formerly borne the ensign of the Earl of Worcester. She had a progressive taste in the arts; through her predilection for the masque, she advanced the careers of Jonson and Daniel and stimulated within her household the genre which was to become the dominant literary expression of the Stuart Court.[7] Similarly, when the Admiral's Men were taken over by Prince Henry in 1603 and became servants of the Prince, Chapman and Drayton, who were associated with the company, also enjoyed Henry's favour. The Queen's patronage of the children's company produced a situation which undermined the prerogative of the Master of the Revels as sole licenser of plays for performance. The patent awarded to the Children of the Queen's Revels in 1604 disregarded Tilney's Office and, apparently as a result of the Queen's direct intervention, entrusted the licensing of the company's plays to Samuel Daniel, who was in her service as a Groom of the Privy Chamber:

> Provided allwaies that noe such Playes or Shewes shalbee presented before the said Queene our wief by the said Children or by them any where publiquelie acted but by the approbacion and allowaunce of Samuell Danyell, whome her pleasure is to appoynt for that purpose.[8]

His short term spent working in an official capacity seems to have been an unfortunate one for Daniel, largely because of his apparent inability or disinclination to check the scurrilous and satirical plays of the Queen's company.

It has been suggested that royal patronage constituted a more effective means of control than the enforcement of play censorship by the Revels Office because the interests of the Crown and the players were so inextricably linked.[9] But, as Jonathan Goldberg has pointed out, plays performed at Court were always drawn from the public repertory and we have no instance of a Jacobean play originally commissioned for the Court.[10] The support of the companies and their dramatists by the heads of the royal households was to lead to a diversification of interests and attitude, depending on the patron. Thus the Queen's reported presence at plays where, according to the French ambassador, she enjoyed a 'laugh against her husband' reflects the acrimony which sometimes prevailed between the households and the absence of any common working brief for the censors. In another respect too, the new conditions made censorship less uniform and monolithic under James. The royal households supported elaborate networks of patronage which enabled playwrights to exploit their Court connections.[11] The Bedchamber, staffed mainly by Scots, was now to become as, if not more, politically significant as the formal and ceremonial institution of the Privy Council.[12] Through a royal favourite, dramatists who had disregarded the authority of the Master of the Revels might appeal for clemency to the King or Queen. A notable case is the controversy over *Eastward Ho*, when Jonson and Chapman solicited the favourites of James and Anne to intervene on their behalf.

In one respect, however, as we have seen, the power of the Revels Office was extended during the period. From 1606 George Buc, who had been granted the reversion of the Office on 23 June 1603, appears to have appropriated the power of licensing plays for print in his own right. From 16 November 1606, his name begins to appear frequently in the Stationers' Register. Entries recording plays licensed by the then Master of the Revels or his deputy continue for thirty years until 1637, when a Star Chamber decree tightened official controls over publication. W. W. Greg has argued that Buc's position as press licenser was analagous to that of other professionals, such as churchmen, schoolmasters, and even the French ambassador, each mentioned in the Registers, whose imprimatur the wardens were prepared to accept as persuasive that a play contained no dangerous matter.[13] On the other hand, Elias Schwartz has questioned Greg's suggestion that Buc's status as licenser of books was merely advisory, drawing attention to the letter written by Chapman to Buc in 1608 after the latter had refused to allow the publication of *The Conspiracy* and *The Tragedy of Charles Duke Byron*.[14] While it must be acknowledged that there is no record of any formal arrangement or delegation of power between the ecclesiastics and the Revels Office, the tone of Chapman's letter indicates that Buc possessed and exercised effective authority over the printing of plays.

The names of Tilney, Buc, Astley and Herbert appear in the Register as regular licensers of plays for print during the period 1606–37. It might be deduced from this development that the wardens now formally accepted the stage licence as sufficient warrant for the entry of a play and that more plays printed after 1606 would be closer textually to their stage versions. In straightforward cases, where publication followed soon after performance, this may well have been the case. But there were obvious exceptions. A number of plays were licensed for publication by Buc which must previously have been licensed for the stage by Tilney. In the case of Herbert, Greg has calculated that, out of nearly eighty plays licensed by him or his deputies for publication, nine pre-dated his time as Master of the Revels and must have had their original prompt books perused by Tilney or Buc. In these instances, two separate licences for performance and publications must be inferred, as also on these occasions when the playwright revised his work for publication or released a different version of the text from that which had been performed. It is probable that in the vast number of cases when a play was re-submitted to the Master of the Revels, prior to publication, it was not perused a second time; but that in a situation where the play had caused some controversy, as was the case with Chapman's *Byron* plays, it was re-checked and further reformed.

The 'Acte to restraine Abuses of Players'

As has been noted, Buc's appropriation of the authority to license plays for publication marks a further stage in the demise of ecclesiastical control of drama. The 'Acte to restraine Abuses of Players'[15] of 1606, however, shows the influence of parliamentary puritans in promoting legislation which banned from the stage the more familiar use of 'the holy Name of God or of Christ Jesus, or of the Holy Ghoste or of the Trinitie', such usages being a legacy of the Catholic drama. The prohibition refers to the performance of plays, not to their publication, and since prosecution was to be upon complaints laid before the Justices, Greg has proposed that, on the whole, the Act may have had minimal impact.[16] Nevertheless, evidence in manuscripts and in post-1606 editions of plays suggests that dramatists, playhouse book-keepers or the Master of the Revels did in fact censor texts in deference to the terms of the Act. Moreover, there are indications that after 1606 objections were taken to controversial doctrinal references not expressly outlawed by the Act, which had previously been spoken with impunity.

The expurgation of oaths by the Master of the Revels or by a play-house scribe is evident in most extant Jacobean and, following revival, Elizabethan manuscripts. The excision of profanity in *Woodstock* clearly points to production after 1606. In the manuscript of *The Second Maiden's Tragedy*, licensed for the stage by Buc in 1611, some, but not all, oaths have been deleted. The oaths which the dramatist had drawn upon to colour the speech idioms of the soldiers and Votarius are limited to the single words 'life' and 'heart'. Buc, who licensed the play in 1611, has either missed or allowed three occurrences of the former, but deleted the latter expletive. 'By th' mass' (IV. iii. 92), the strongest oath in the play, has been excised by a different hand. Again, Herbert's licence of 1624 is present on the manuscript of *The Honest Man's Fortune*. Here the playhouse scribe was careful to modify the authors' use of oaths before he submitted the abridged transcript of the play – the full version of which is printed in the 1647 folio – to the Master of the Revels. At one point the scribe has originally transcribed 'God wot', but has later inserted 'o' in 'God', deleted 'wot' and interlined 'sooth'. The manuscript has 'Heaven' on eight occasions where the later folio prints 'God'; it must follow, therefore, that the scribe made certain judicious alterations as he prepared the manuscript for stage use.[17] The same care to remove profanity can be detected in the private transcript of *Demetrius and Enanthe* prepared for Sir Kenelm Digby by Ralph Crane: in the 1647 folio version of the play, now entitled *The Humorous Lieutenant*, of non-theatrical provenance, expletives which presumably formed part of the original composition by Beaumont and Fletcher are retained.[18]

A comparison of certain pre-1606 editions of plays with later editions, whose copy texts are derived from theatrical revivals, illustrates how prompt books were reformed prior to such revivals. Details in pre- and post-1606 editions respectively of *Much Ado About Nothing*, *Richard III* and *Doctor Faustus* exemplify the effects of the new regulations. In *Much Ado About Nothing*, the folio omits Dogberry's comically pedantic instruction to the sexton: 'Write down that they hope they serve God; and write God first, for God defend but God should go before such villains!' (IV. ii. 16–9). Expurgation in the folio text of *Richard III* similarly dilutes the comic effect. In the earlier quarto texts, Buckingham's use of 'zounds' produces an ironic reproof from Gloucester:

> *Buck.* Come Citizens, zounds ile intreat no more.
> *Glo.* O do not sweare my Lord Buckingham (H2v).

The folio merely prints: 'Come Citizens, we will entreat no more' and Gloucester's rejoinder, now of course redundant, is omitted. An earlier warning of the Last Judgment by Clarence in the quarto, reminding his murderers of the damnable quality of their deed, has been modified in the folio text. The quarto prints: 'I charge you as you hope to have redemption,/ By Christs deare bloud shed for our grievous sinnes,/ That you depart and lay no hands on me' (D2v). The folio omits the doctrinal references. Clarence's plea is thus more bluntly stated: 'I charge you, as you hope for any goodnesse,/ That you depart, and lay no hands on me' (p. 535).

Doctor Faustus

The textual changes noted above (together with other expurgations in the texts of Jonson's folio of 1616 and Shakespeare's of 1623) are limited in scope. Perhaps the play which was most thoroughly censored in consequence of the 1606 Act is the 1616 'B' text of *Doctor Faustus*, based on a Jacobean revival with some additional material. That such later productions suffered from censorship in deference to the Act is hardly surprising, considering the eschatological dimension of the tragedy. There are instances, similar to those found in other

Jacobean texts, of the deletion of common oaths and substitutions, such as that of 'heaven' for 'God'. In the 'A' text, Mephostophilis informs Faustus that the 'shortest cut' for conjuring is to abjure the Trinitie (l. 298). In the 'B' text, the specific Christian terminology has been changed and Faustus is instructed to renounce 'godlinesse'. Faustus's arrogation that a sound magician is a 'mighty god' (l. 92) in the 1604 text is modified to 'demi-god' in the later version. Once more, as the hour of reckoning draws near, one of the scholars urges Faustus to 'looke up to heaven, remember gods mercies are infinite' (ll. 1400–1). In the 'B' text, Faustus is merely reminded that 'mercy is infinite'. Faustus implores, 'My God, my God, looke not so fierce on me' in the 1604 version of his final soliloquy. This has been changed in the 'B' text to 'O mercy heaven, looke not so fierce on me'.

Censorship of the copy text of the 1616 edition of the play, however, goes beyond the strict prohibition of utterances taken as blasphemous and fastens upon several of the doctrinal allusions in the play. Faustus's rejection of divinity as the basest form of learning, 'unpleasant, harsh, contemptible and vilde' (l. 142), which by its presumption precipitates his fall from grace, has been omitted in the 'B' text, apparently to satisfy or forestall censorship, since his dismissal of the other scholastic disciplines remains. The omission of further short passages and lines in the 1616 text can reasonably be attributed to censorship in deference to the Act. In the 'A' text, intimidated by the presence of Lucifer, Beelzebub, and Mephostophilis, the infernal Trinity, Faustus makes his diabolic vow to Lucifer: 'Never to name God, or to pray to him,/To burne his Scriptures, slay his Ministers,/ and make my spirites pull his churches downe.' (ll. 726–8). Again the lines are missing in the 'B' text, even though the rest of the scene follows the 'A' text closely; consequently, Lucifer's rejoinder that the triad will highly gratify Faustus seems unwarranted in the 'B' version of the dialogue. In the 'A' text but not the 'B', following Robin's conjurations which bring him from Constantinople, Mephostophilis utters his vivid apostrophe to Lucifer: 'Monarch of hel,/under whose blacke survey/Great Potentates do kneele with awful feare,/Upon whose altars thousand soules do lie' (ll. 1023–5). The two texts are not closely parallel at this juncture, so we cannot say certainly that the evocation of demonic influence in the state was censored; but the idolatrous implication that kings are in thrall to the devil makes it possible. Without the accent of the diabolic invocation, the dramatic effect of the 'B' text is certainly weaker.

The muting of the doctrinal allusions is, however, most obvious in Faustus's last agonised soliloquy. Faustus calls on Christ's blood in both versions; but in the 1616 text he does not evoke the image of its streaming in the firmament. The sacrificial context of grace and reconciliation is again modified in 'B' by the omission of the line which contains Faustus's plea: 'Yet for Christs sake, whose bloud hath ransomd me'. An earlier 'B' text omission is similarly significant, that of the Old Man's gentle reminder of Christ's atonement: 'But mercie Faustus of thy Saviour sweete/ Whose bloud alone must wash away thy guilt' (1312–14). Faustus's intensely realised apprehension of Heaven and Hell in the final soliloquy has undoubtedly been blunted as a result of censorship. In the 'A' text he imagines God: 'And see where God stretcheth out his arme, And bends his irefull browes' (ll. 1468–9). In the later edition God's presence is less immediate: 'And see a threatening arme, an angry Brow' (l. 2053). While, formerly, Reformation censorship had suppressed the appearance of the divinity on stage, now it seems that even iconographic references were judged blasphemous.

The manuscript underlying the 1616 edition of *Doctor Faustus* has, therefore, suffered thoroughgoing censorship in accordance with Jacobean legislation, to the extent that the theological context is less explicit and incisive. Greg was surely wrong to regard the copy text of the 'B' version of the play as primarily authorial papers edited in the printing house without any relation to performance.[19] The extent and nature of the censorship of the 'B' text – beyond simple expurgation of oaths – suggest that, when the play was revived, revised and augmented with the Rowley and Bird 'adycions' recorded by Henslowe, it was regarded as a new play, re-submitted to the Master of the Revels, and censored in accordance with recent legislation and what seems to be a more pronounced anti-Catholic attitude towards doctrinal issues and sacred reference on the stage. Its fate suggests a further narrowing of the permitted religious boundaries of the drama after 1606. The 'A' text displays a potent doctrinal context, whereas the 'B' text is less intense in its intellectual dramatisation of Christian reference.[20] As we have seen, the 1606 'Acte to restraine Abuses of Players' is itself relatively limited in scope; but it would seem on the basis of the censorship of the 'B' text of *Doctor Faustus* that it could be invoked to sabotage plays which dealt liberally and critically with matters of scripture or doctrine.

Playwrights varied in the degree to which they heeded the strictures of the Act. Their level of compliance could be an interesting indicator of how far they were prepared to acknowledge the conditions imposed by authority in other areas of the drama. The number of oaths in the Beaumont and Fletcher Folio, containing texts of non-theatrical provenance, demonstrates that the pair made little attempt to comply with the Act. Shakespeare on the other hand, evidently attempted to comply with the legislation. Frances A. Shirley has shown that there is a considerable drop in the number of oaths used in Shakespeare's plays after 1606, noting that they are most prevalent in the history plays and the earlier non-Roman tragedies.[21] In *Macbeth*, however, written after the enactment, there are only about a dozen oaths. Whether the Act had any more far-reaching effect on Shakespeare's choice of dramatic material is extremely doubtful; Frances Shirley's suggestion that Shakespeare's use of pagan settings may have been partly influenced by the need to circumvent its restrictions must be treated with some scepticism. Throughout his work Shakespeare used doctrinal reference suggestively and figuratively and it may be assumed that he would not have regarded the Act as an absolute bar to material which would otherwise have engaged his interest.

The Duke of Guise's contemptuous remark in *Bussy D'Amboise* that he likes not the Court of the English 'making Semi-gods/ of their great Nobles; and of their old Queene/ An ever-yoong, and most immortall Goddesse' (I.ii. 10–3) is an unambiguous example of a remark which obviously could not have been uttered on the stage during Elizabeth's lifetime. As we have seen, the ageing Queen was accustomed to being apotheosised in plays such as *Old Fortunatus*, *Every Man Out of His Humour*, *Cynthia's Revels* and *Histriomastix*. James showed no inclination to perpetuate the cult of the sovereign he had long flattered; the death of Elizabeth and the end of the Tudor dynasty made censorship less proscriptive towards more recent historical events. The two parts of Heywood's play *If You Know Not Me, You Know Nobody*, depict Elizabeth's early life under duress and culminate in the defeat of the Armada in 1588. Rowley and the Admiral's Men in *When You See Me You Know Me* (1604) similarly capitalised on the liberation of Tudor material in their ahistorical depiction of Henry VIII mingling with the Tudor underworld and being mistakenly imprisoned. The titles of these plays alone convey a familiarity and lack of inhibition regarding quasi-historical drama on a Tudor theme. Dekker and Webster turned to the reign of Mary Tudor, the claims to the crown of Lady Jane Grey and the projected Spanish marriage leading to Wyatt's rebellion, to furnish material for *Sir Thomas Wyatt*. The lapse of a decade before Shakespeare chose to handle the Tudor past in *Henry VIII*, in part a corrective to Rowley's recently revived account, implies a degree of caution towards the dramatisation of the turbulent events which preceded the birth of Elizabeth. Dekker's *The Whore of Babylon*, which dramatises in thinly disguised fashion

Catholic intrigues during the Queen's reign, is another play which is unlikely to have been performed at the time of its composition in the same form as it appears in the printed text of 1607.[22]

Even where texts of plays remain constant, their meanings may undergo change in different contexts. Within the compass of James's accession certain dramatic references acquired new significance and associations and consequently became liable to censorship. Such cases are not numerous and textual changes so caused are comparatively insignificant; but they do illustrate a constant surveillance of texts regardless of authorial intention. Lines omitted from the 1605 quarto of *Hamlet* (II.ii. 238–68), for instance, include Hamlet's reference, in conversation with Rosencrantz and Guildenstern, to Denmark as a prison, which no doubt might have invited imputations of an affront to the Queen, Anne of Denmark. The copy text of the second quarto is held to be Shakespeare's autograph, with some playhouse annotations made before the preparation of the prompt book. This suggests that in all probability it was Shakespeare himself who applied expedient self-censorship to the text. *Richard III* was obviously scrutinised at some time during the later Jacobean period and a passage, present in six earlier quartos, was probably removed because of derogatory inferences concerning the contemporary Duke of Buckingham.[23] As has been noted, moreover, the deletion of oaths in the manuscript of *Woodstock* provides evidence that the play was censored prior to a Jacobean revival. Another textual excision seems to have been made at the same time. On taking possession of the kingdom, Richard claims to be 'Superior Lord of Scotland' (II.ii. 109). A pencil cross, redefined in ink, which is similar to those made in other manuscripts licensed by Buc, is present in the margin and the line is deleted. A reminder that Scottish kings had formerly paid homage to an English monarch, whilst satisfying the English sense of nationalism, would have been inapposite in the context of a Scottish occupant of the throne.

James identified himself with and was represented in comtemporary eulogy as the Emperor Augustus, protector of the arts and agent of peace.[24] The Augustus of Jonson's *Poetaster* is a generous literary patron who sees satire as therapeutic in the state and refuses to heed the detractions of inferior poets against Horace. The fostering of the Augustan image may indeed have induced or flattered James into tolerating the satirical thrust of the drama early in his reign; but other instances of his behaviour show that he was far from an advocate of liberty of expression. As we have seen, Spenser's allegorical treatment of the trial and execution of Mary Queen of Scots in Book V of *The Faerie Queen* had led to the banning of the poem in Scotland. James's demand that it should also be suppressed in England and its author arrested and punished went unheeded. Typically, once he was established on the throne and the allegory no longer undermined any claim to the succession, James made no attempt to suppress the 1609 folio of Spenser's works when he was in a position to do so.[25]

Discourse which ran contrary to the King's absolutist views was quickly suppressed. The works of George Buchanan, his former tutor, which advocated the limitation of the King's prerogative and resistance to tyrannical rulers were suppressed in Scotland and England, although continental imports circulated. When the French historian, Jacques-Auguste de Thou, was planning to extend his *History of His Own Time* to the arrival of Mary Stuart in Scotland and the events of her unfortunate reign, James used all his powers of coercion to prevent him using the unsympathetic Buchanan as source and, then, when this strategy failed, to amend what he had written.[26] Subsequent events reveal the convoluted pattern of the King's tactics to secure his ends. Political pressure was put upon William Camden – who was already known to have treated Scottish affairs circumspectly in the 1609 edition of *Britannia* – to resume work on his *Annals of Great Britain in the Reign of Elizabeth*, begun in the Queen's reign. The intention was that the *Annals* would then be consulted by de Thou in place of Buchanan's *History of Scotland*. A copy of Camden's completed manuscript after it had been censored either by the King or by his Privy Councillor, the Earl of Northampton, was duly sent to him.[27] Despite courteous correspondence with Camden, de Thou was unwilling to comply with James's strictures and, rather than be constrained into presenting what he saw as a selective version of events, chose not to publish the remaining books of his *History*. Camden, for his part, published the first part of his *Annals* in 1615; but, like de Thou, preferred not to encourage publication of their sequel. He submitted the latter part to James with a resignedly weary address: 'to his Majesty's judicious censure, whether it please him that they should be suppressed or published, for I am indifferent'. Evidently, James chose not to promote publication, since the works were first published only in Leiden in 1625. The affair well illustrates James's uneasy relationship with historians and did nothing to dispel Camden's judgement, expressed in a letter to de Thou, that he lived in 'an age of lying and intolerance'.[28]

James's absolutist vision of monarchy nevertheless impinged only slightly on the early Jacobean drama and its censorship. What, however, rapidly surfaced in the drama which was to shape subsequent censorship was popular dissatisfaction with the King, his

Court and his cherished objective of union with Scotland. James was perceived as being negligent in his approach to government, prodigal with his favours and lacking judgment in his promotion of rapacious courtiers. The degree to which these issues were the subject of dramatic censorship will be discussed in the following chapter. It is notable that the majority of plays to be discussed – *Sejanus, The Malcontent, The Dutch Courtesan, Eastward Ho, The Isle of Gulls, Philotas,* and *The Conspiracy* and *The Tragedy of Charles Duke of Byron* – were staged before their performance was suppressed or censored, a reflection of the uncertainty surrounding the practice of censorship with the change of dispensation.

Charlemagne or the distracted Emperor

The only early Jacobean play to have survived in manuscript is that of the anonymous *Charlemagne or the Distracted Emperor*. We know nothing of its stage history or even of its precise date.[29] Although the manuscript bears some slight evidence of Buc's hand, it has not suffered any substantial interference; yet it is of interest to our analysis in that it shows precisely what the censor was initially prepared to allow as the new reign established itself. Charlemagne, bewitched by his devious Empress Theodora, is here satirised as an absurdly uxorious figure who, on Theodora's death, transfers his doting affections to Bishop Turpin and the foolish La Fue. La Busse, the honest son of the wily Ganelon, exposes corruption in terms which evoke quite specifically contemporary abuses at James's Court: 'offyces are like huntinge breakfaste, gott/hurlye, burlye; snatcht with like greedynes,/ I and allmost disjested toe assoone' (ll. 665–7). Yet there are no signs that the censor has objected to such indictments of the Emperor and his favourites.

A number of passages have been marked for omission, apparently by a stage reviser abridging the play for performance. Unlike playhouse excisions in other dramatic manuscripts, the content of these passages does not suggest that the prevailing concerns of censorship dictated their removal although it may be significant that in several deleted passages, Orlando, Charlemagne's nephew, bewails his lost rights of succession. So soon after James's accession, it may have been considered inexpedient to draw attention to the frustrated claims of his rivals for the throne.

Buc's intervention is limited. Curiously, while he has accepted all the court satire, he has registered his disapproval at a generalised comment on episcopal greed. The besotted Charlemagne advises

Bishop Turpin to choose for himself 'a fytt rewarde' from all the Emperor's 'domynions and aucthoryties'. Richard, the late Empress's lover, comments that, being a 'worthy reverend prellatt', the Bishop is not possessed by such desires. La Busse retorts 'sfotte man let hym be ten thousand reverend prellatte a will styll wante somethynge' (ll. 1420–1). Two square crosses, one in pencil, the smaller in ink, are recognisable from later manuscripts as Buc's; the scoring through of 'reverend prellate', the substitution of 'preists' and the marginal note 'Read preists' unequivocally demonstrate the censor's objections. Also marked for omission on the same page by a bracket and scribbling is Charlemagne's fawning address to Bishop Turpin:

Oh nowe religion teache me to beleive
another god; or I must forfayte heaven
and worshypp what I see, thys happye creature
nowe courtyers flatterye cannot keepe my sence
from knowinge what I feele, for I am weake
tys all my comforte nowe, to thynke on thee ...   (ll. 1401–6)

Buc may have demanded this cut, since the colour of the ink and the style of the excisions are not immediately recognisable as the stage reviser's. Whoever was responsible, the blasphemous content of the lines would seem to have brought about their removal. Two other lines spoken later in the play may also owe their exclusion to Buc. For the sake of La Busse, Charlemagne agrees to pardon Ganelon despite his conduct: 'Thy father houlde as muche unwortynes/ as may excusse tyrranye in a prynce' (ll. 2673–4). The excision of these lines suggests a literal-minded reaction to an unpalatable concept without heed to the dramatic context.

There is accordingly little positive evidence of censorship in *Charlemagne*. An examination of the manuscript enables us to say with confidence, only that whilst the censor still judged explicit criticism of the Anglican episcopacy to be unacceptable, he either failed to make the associations invited by the satire or acquiesced in the lampoons of the sovereign and the objects of his favours.

Sejanus

One of the first plays performed (late 1603) by the newly promoted King's Men at the Globe was Jonson's political tragedy *Sejanus*. Jonson had stated his intention in the 'Apologeticall Dialogue' of *Poetaster* of turning his attention away from comical satire to tragedy in the hope that the change of genre would render his work less liable to misinterpretation: 'There's something come into my thought,/ That must, and shall be sung, high, and aloofe,/ Safe from the wolves black jaw, and the dull asses hoofe.' Ironically enough, the tragedy excited censure and censorship: not only did it fail to appeal to its popular audience, but it caused Jonson to be arraigned for treason before the Privy Council.

Jonson dedicated the 1616 folio text to one of his earliest patrons, Esmé Stuart, Lord Aubigny, a Gentleman of the King's Bedchamber and brother of the King's favourite, the Duke of Lennox. In his address, Jonson refers to the harsh reception given to *Sejanus* and expresses his gratitude to Aubigny for the benefits he has received. Exploiting the analogy with Sejanus's fate at the hands of the mob, Jonson refers to the reaction of 'our people here' as one of 'violence' and 'malice'. It is usually assumed that Jonson is referring exclusively to the response of the Globe audience and to Aubigny's defence of the play in the face of hostile criticism. But there appears to be more than merely a general indictment of popular philistinism encoded in the dedication. The opening allusion to the text as a 'ruin' alerts the reader to the possibility of censorship. To describe the reaction to *Sejanus* as one of 'malice' is curious in the context of the public response to the play. It makes more sense, however, if we read the complaint as an oblique allusion to those members of the Privy Council who opposed the play and infer that Jonson's gratitude to Aubigny stems from influence exerted on his behalf.

We know that some time after the first performance of *Sejanus*, Jonson was ordered to appear before the Privy Council to answer charges of treason. Evidence that he was questioned about his dramatic intentions consists solely of a rather cryptic comment recorded by Drummond from his conversation with Jonson: 'Northampton was his mortall enimie for brauling on a St Georges day one of his attenders, he was called befor the Councell for his Sejanus and accused both of popperie and treason by him'.[30] Fleay makes the reasonable conjecture that Jonson's reputed fracas with Northampton's attendant on St George's Day occurred in 1605, when Northampton was made Knight of the Garter.[31] Since Jonson's appearance before the Council was subsequent to this incident, he must have been examined just before the publication of the play late in 1605. The reason for the indictment of treason is not evident from the text, which as we know from the address to the reader 'is not the same with that which was acted on the publike Stage'. One editor, Jonas A. Barish, has suggested that the official investigation was instigated because of parallels perceived between the careers of Sejanus and the Earl of Essex, both of which epitomise the downfall and execution of a powerful favourite

who aspired to unseat the monarch he served.[32] Annabel Patterson
has pointed out that Jonson chose as his source Tacitus, a historian
known for his republican sympathies and as a champion of free
speech, of whom Jonson had remarked to Drummond that he 'wrott
the secrets of the Councill and Senate', and that both the historical
context and the Tacitean bias would have alerted a receptive audience
that Jonson's interests might not be entirely confined to imperial
Rome.[33] That Essex and his supporters were known to be fervent
admirers of Tacitus, Patterson takes as a clear indication that the
original *Sejanus* was in some way connected with Essex's conspiracy.
The idea of any Essex parallel implies, however, that Jonson had either
lost his apparent early admiration for Essex[34] or that he was obliged
to refashion his portrayal of Sejanus between the play's first performance in 1603 and its publication in 1605, since the flawed
character who inhabits the play would hardly have reflected honour
upon his supposed *alter ego*. But Jonson's portrayal of the crafty and
murderous Sejanus is consistent with Tacitus's portrayal of the upstart
favourite. There is no contemporary corroboration that the play was
perceived as a mirror of the tragedy of Essex, as there is in the case of
Daniel's *Philotas* in 1605. In the absence of any specific parallels
between the personalities of Essex and Sejanus, therefore, it seems
more plausible to find the origins of the treason charge in the
animosity of Northampton towards Jonson, although alleged echoes
of Essex's rebellion may indeed have provided a pretext for the case.

Northampton, through his alliance with Cecil, had risen to power
with the Jacobean accession. He had been a crypto-Catholic who had
expediently changed his faith, the better to harmonise with the new
order.[35] Jonson, on the other hand, was known to be a Catholic and in
January 1606 was examined in the Consistory Court of London, the
diocesan court acting in its more overtly theological function, to
answer charges of recusancy brought against him and his wife.[36] As a
means of deflecting suspicion from himself, Northampton may have
attacked Jonson, both for his adherence to Catholicism and for his
satirical treatment of political machinations in *Sejanus*. As Herford
and Simpson say: 'It was no doubt hard to believe that the poet who
had just used the Court of Augustus as a vehicle for unmeasured
personal ridicule of his contemporaries, had portrayed the Court of
Tiberius in the guileless spirit of a scholar bent only on the historical
accuracy of his play'.[37] An ascendant courtier like Northampton no
doubt felt uneasy at Jonson's unrelenting exposure of a world where
the public interest was so cynically sacrificed to personal advancement. The importance of *Sejanus* is precisely the fact that it was

vulnerable to arbitrary interference from individuals with specific personal grievances and that the temporary instability of the censorship at a time of transition facilitated such politicking.

That Jonson felt compelled to stress the politically orthodox premiss of his play is suggested by the closing statement of 'The Argument' in the quarto text:

> This do we advance as a marke of Terror to all *Traytors*, and *Treasons*; to shewe how just the *Heavens* are in powring and thundring downe a weighty vengeance on their unnaturall intents, even to the worst *Princes*: Much more to those, for guard of whose Piety and Vertue, the *Angels* are in continuall watch, and *God* himself miraculously working.

Here Jonson's diatribe on the heinousness of tyrannicide could pass for the sentiments of King James, but it appears to have more to do with expediency than with political conviction. It is notably omitted from the folio text. Presumably once the Privy Council's interest in *Sejanus* had receded, Jonson felt it no longer necessary to impose an acceptable ideological gloss on the play.

If the Privy Council were ready to interpret *Sejanus* as a satire on the contemporary political scene, it is more than likely that Jacobean audiences recognised that the social and political satires which predominated in the children's companies were fuelled by disenchantment with the new regime. Familiar critiques, particularly those excoriating the sudden rise of favourites, the dissolute ruler and the decline of courtly decorum, are encoded in foreign settings; but the frequency with which these same abuses are satirised makes the source of their inspiration unmistakable. Yet there was an uncertainty about the conditions of censorship which encouraged certain playwrights, at least initially, to take risks. Of these, the most audacious was Marston.

The Malcontent

The Malcontent, Marston's first Jacobean play, was written for the children at Blackfriars. It is not known whether the company had by then obtained Queen Anne's patronage or, accordingly, whether the play was licensed by Daniel; but the freedom with which Marston attacked political and social conditions suggests that he took advantage of the uncertain state of the Revels Office. In the play, state corruption is localised in the court of the Duke of Genoa. In the disguise of the malcontent Malevole, the former Duke is able to assume the role of satiric commentatior. This 'affected strain', as he calls his imposture, gives him the licence of a fool; he has that which 'kings do seldom hear or great men use – Free speech'. Marston, of course, is using the same strategy of concealment: the play's distance in time and place deflects the imputation that the satire is contemporary and immediate.

The pugnacious Prologue indicates that Marston anticipated the charges of political and personal associations that would attend such an uncompromising account of the abuses of power. He evokes, as Jonson did, the ideal of the Golden Age and its supposed artistic freedom. The same point is taken up in the Induction, composed by John Webster. Sly's comment that only the wealthy can afford the luxury of 'censure' is countered by Burbage with the question: 'Why should we not enjoy the ancient freedom of poesy?' But from the address to the reader, in all three editions of 1604,[38] it appears that the play had aroused suspicions of topicality and discrepancies between the printed texts demonstrate that the Golden Age had not arrived.

Marston informs the reader in the lengthy address that some detractors have been 'most unadvisedly over-cunning' in their mis-constructions and 'with subtlety (as deep as hell) have maliciously spread ill rumours'. The evidence of press censorship further suggests that the play was considered provocative theatre. Certain textual excisions are to be found in one or more of the three quartos. The first instance relates to Malevole's cynical statement in reply to Pietro's question, that he comes 'from the public place of much dissimulation, the church'. 'The church' has been variously removed in a number of surviving copies of the different quartos, the methods of excision ranging from the closing of type on some corrected sheets to a violation of the page itself by cutting away the offending words. G. K. Hunter suggests that the publisher was responsible for the textual interference.[39] If so, he must surely have been acting on the orders of a higher authority; he was presumably following either a deletion in the manuscript made by the ecclesiastical licenser, who had passed the play on 5 June 1604, or an earlier stage-cut. We know from the address to the reader that Marston was more than usually involved in overseeing publication and he no doubt fought to maintain the integrity of his text against the incursions of censorship.[40] There are, moreover, further signs of conflicting pressures brought to bear on the printers. In the first quarto, a pointed reference to current religious opportunism is omitted. This occurs as Malevole sporadically mocks various courtiers for their doctrinal persuasions. Bilioso, the old marshal, is asked what religion he will adopt, now that the dukedom has apparently changed hands; his retort – 'of the Duke's religion, when I know what it is' (IV. v. 94) – has been cut. The topical allusion to both king and courtier is obvious: some ambiguity surrounded James's doctrinal leanings and, as we have seen, men such as Northampton and Southampton were affecting conversions to advance or preserve their positions. Again, an innuendo was apparently sensed in Bianca's sly observation about one of the newly preferred courtiers – 'And is not Signior St. Andrew Jaques a gallant fellow now?' (V. v. 24) – since the character is omitted in the first two editions.

Of far greater interest is the censorship of a passage which undermines the absolutist ideology espoused by the King. In the dénouement, Malevole dwells upon popular responses towards the ruler and delivers a warning about the fate of kings who fail in their obligations:

> O, I have seen strange accidents of state:
> The flatterer, like the ivy, clip the oak,
> And waste it to the heart; lust so confirmed,
> That the black act of sin itself not shamed
> To be termed courtship.
> O, they that are as great as be their sins,
> Let them remember that th'inconstant people
> Love many princes merely for their faces
> And outward shows; and they do covet more
> To have a sight of these than of their virtues.
> Yet this much let the great ones still conceit
> When they observe not Heaven's imposed conditions,
> They are no kings, but forfeit their commissions   (V.vi. 137–49

Malevole's critique of absolutism, with its assumption that authority is derived not from any divine right but from a commission which can be withdrawn if neglectfully performed, is all the more subversive of Stuart ideology because he is speaking in his true persona as Duke Altofronto. The passage is present only in the third quarto and in some copies it exists in an alternative state: the more innocuous 'men' is substituted for 'prince' and 'kings', thus avoiding direct reference to royal authority and, more specifically, what amounts to a legitimisation of the dethronement of monarchs. G. K. Hunter numbers this passage amongst the additions to the text as it was acted by the King's Men. But the lines do not fit into either of the two categories he sees as defining the additions: namely, certain passages enlarging the situation already developed in the earlier form of the play and others entirely in prose, offering an expansion which Hunter suggests was undertaken for Robert Armin, clown with the company.[41] The tone and substance of Altofronto's speech are entirely congruent with Malevole's earlier denunciations of the vices of the times and it provides a much more incisive moral conclusion. In view of the content of the passage, there would seem to be a stronger case for its censorship in the texts underlying the first two quartos – in which there is evidence of other censorship – and for its partial restoration in the third quarto than there is for regarding it as an addition which has no dramatic function. The argument for censorship is strengthened by the omission of further lines which immediately follow Altofronto's caution: Maquerelle's complaint that, after being in attendance at court for twenty years, she now sees 'old courtiers' despised and 'thrust to the wall like apricocks'. The lines are open to ready interpretation as an indictment of the new Jacobean regime and of the scramble for favours by new men.

The texts of *The Malcontent* show obvious signs of censorship; but it is far from clear when this took place or who was responsible. It is likely that during printing Marston exerted pressure on the publisher to restore lines which had previously been excised, whether as a result of press or theatrical censorship. That he was able to do so in itself suggests a relaxation of earlier restraints. Evidently neither playwright nor the officers of censorship had yet any clear idea about the relationship between satire and the new order. This uncertainty about the permissible limits of satire seems to have facilitated the uncensored performances of two other early Queen's Revels' satires by Marston, *The Fawn* and *The Dutch Courtesan*, although a certain notoriety appears to have attached to them. The portrayal of King Gonzago in *The Fawn*, as it has been argued, links the play with the production of 14 June 1604 referred to by the French ambassador, in which the King was burlesqued on the stage to the delight of the Queen: 'Consider for pity's sake what must be the state and condition of a prince, whom the preachers publicly assail, whom the comedians of the metropolis bring upon the stage, whose wife attends these representations in order to enjoy the laugh against her husband'.[42] Anne of Denmark, whose relationship with her husband was sometimes fractious,[43] no doubt took pleasure in the depiction of familiar traits shared by the character of Gonzago and by James. Gonzago is characterised by his claim to worldly wisdom, his sententious speech and a conviction of his own invulnerability. His utterances are self-opinionated and replete with scholastic jargon. As James was prone to do, he parades his learning in a thicket of elaborate rhetoric. In the circumstances, Marston's Prologue – in which he contends that 'here no rude disgraces shall taint a public or a private name' – is one of the most disingenuous of its kind. Knowing that he had the Queen's approval and hence Daniel's licence, Marston presumably felt confident that his play could be performed and published with impunity.

In the case of *The Dutch Courtesan*, however, there is an equivocal reference in a contemporary treatise which suggests that the play was the subject of some controversy and that attempts may have been made to suppress it. Anthony Nixon in *The Black Year*, published in 1606, writes critically of prevailing social mores. Referring to the diminishing returns of the book trade, he decries those playwrights who censure other men's works when 'their own are sacrificed in Paules Churchyard for bringing in *The Dutch Curtezan* to corrupt English conditions, and sent away *Westward* for carping both at Court, Cittie and country'.[44] The reference is obviously to Marston, and to both his composition of *The Dutch Courtesan* and his part in *Eastward Ho*, for which, unlike his collaborators Jonson and Chapman, he seems to have escaped imprisonment. The expression 'sent away Westward' could be an oblique allusion to execution at Tyburn, popularly known as going westward, or it could suggest that Marston fled the City to escape the fate which befell Jonson and Chapman. The controversy over the anti-Scots satire of *Eastward Ho* is a *cause célèbre* of theatrical censorship. Nixon's coupling of the plays implies that *The Dutch Courtesan* also caused a stir in some circles; on what account we can only guess. The main targets of Marston's satire in the latter play are the puritan Mulligrubs, whose head of the family aspires to be an alderman of the City (II.iii. 77–8). It is possible that this scenario drew reaction from members of the City council, who may also have taken exception to the profusion of blasphemies in the play; and it may be that Paul's churchyard, the centre of the book trade, subsequently witnessed the seizure and destruction of copies of the work.

Eastward Ho

Eastward Ho was first performed in 1605, by which time many were familiar with the conditions described by Arthur Wilson in his *Life and Reign of James I*, published in 1653:

> Many of the Gentry that came out of *Scotland* with the king were advanced to Honours, as well as those he found here, to shew the Northern Soil as fruitful that way as the Southern: But knights swarmed in each Corner ... This Airy Title blew up many a fair Estate. The *Scots* naturally by long Converse, affecting the French Vanity, drew on a Garb of Gallantry, (meeting with plentiful Soil, and an open handed Prince).[45]

Much of the play's satire is directed against the rapacity and ambition of the Jacobean parvenu. The newly invested but still impoverished knight who is both sycophantic and pretentious is ridiculed in the character of Sir Petronel Flash. The play relentlessly mocks the affectations of the upwardly mobile, represented by his future wife, Gertrude, in her adoption of French fashion and her social aspirations: 'O sister Mill, though my father be a low-capt tradsman, yet I must be a Lady: and I praise God my mother must call me Medam' (I.ii. 3–6). The vacuousness of Gertrude's pretensions is exposed in her journey from the 'Bow-bell' in Cheapside to her knight's 'Eastward Castle' which he has 'built with air' to satisfy her desire to bury her mercantile origins. That Sir Petronel is a parody of the spurious Jacobean gentlemen who flocked to Court is evident from the conversation between the two gentlemen on the Isle of Dogs, where he has been washed ashore from his abortive sea voyage. The pair argue the provenance of his knighthood:

> 1 Gent. I ken the man weel, hee's one of my thirty pound knights.
> 2 Gent. No no, this is he that stole his knighthood o'the grand day, for
> *foure pound*, giving to a Page all the money in's purse I wot well. (IV.i.
> 178–81)

As editors have noted, the hints of Scottish dialect here were surely meant to evoke King James; the exchange provides the actors with scope for mimicry and the satire would have been broadened in performance. As we shall see, however, it was not only these lines which provoked the King's anger and the punishment of Jonson and Chapman, as recorded in Drummond's notes of his conversation with Jonson and in the letters Jonson and Chapman wrote from prison appealing for their release.

The King's informant was Sir James Murray, one of the newly created knights. This we know from Drummond, who was told by Jonson that 'he was delated by Sir James Murray to the king for writting something against the Scots in a play Eastward hoe and voluntarly Imprissonned himself with Chapman and Marston, who had written it amongst them. The report was that they should then had their ears cutt and noses'.[46] Jonson may have been embellishing his version of the experience whilst reminiscing with Drummond, since from the details in his own and Chapman's letters it would seem that Marston escaped punishment and that Jonson's imprisonment was far from voluntary. The case is well documented through the survival of their letters appealing to the King, the Earl of Suffolk, the Lord Chamberlain, the Earl of Salisbury and to James's favourite, Philip Herbert, Earl of Montgomery. Further letters of appeal were addressed to Jonson's patrons Aubigny, Lucy Countess of Bedford and the Earl of Pembroke, also a favourite of the Queen.[47] In their supplication to favourites of both King and Queen, moreover, the letters provide unwitting testimony to the nature of the relationship between patron and client and to the power of the patronage system, as well as revealing the standard defence employed by dramatists in response to libel charges.

In his letter to the King, written on behalf of himself and Jonson, Chapman appeals to James's 'Cesar-like Bountie (who Conquerd still to spare the Conquerd: and was glad of offences that he might forgive)', whilst casting the blame on Marston. The play's offence, he maintains, is comprised in 'two Clawses, and both of them not our owne'. There is a similarly aggrieved tone in Jonson's more expansive communications. To Salisbury, he describes Chapman as 'a learned and honest Man' with whom he shares an unjust punishment for a play against which 'no Man can justly complayne'. Exempting himself from purposing any offence, he pleads: 'If others have transgressed, let not me bee entitled to theyre Follyes'. From the style of the play's most provocative passages, editors have indeed accredited them to Marston. But there is no evidence that the King or Privy Council were ultimately inclined to pursue further investigations. The King had demonstrated that dramatic satirists were not immune from retribution and the reprisal seems to have appeased his anger.

The playwrights had exacerbated their satirical indiscretions by side-stepping the licensing procedure. Chapman's letter to the Lord Chamberlain opens with an apology for his failure to submit the play for proper licence, followed by his excuses: 'your Person so farr remov'd from our requirde attendance; Our Play so much importun'de, And our cleere opinions, that nothinge it contain'd could worthely be held offensive'. The supplication to Suffolk raises the problem of Daniel's authority as licenser for the Children of the Queen's Revels. No mention is made of him; Chapman assumes deferentially that the necessary permission for theatrical performance must be granted by the Lord Chamberlain. It may have been that after Daniel had been interrogated by the Privy Council, early in 1605, about his motivation for writing *Philotas*,[48] his standing was irreparably damaged. Or the extremity of the circumstances may have warranted a direct appeal to the state official under whose auspices all Court entertainment lay. A similar appeal to Daniel, in possession of no real power, would have availed him little.

The letters present a dual defence: not only are the dramatists innocent of any involvement in the composition of particular passages, but their intentions have in any event been misconstrued. Jonson, in his letter to Salisbury, argues that he has been maligned and asserts that he has modified his style since his 'first Error', an allusion to his part in the writing of *The Isle of Dogs*. His self-exculpation has a familiar Jonsonian theme: he may have shown 'generall vice', but 'it hath alwayes bene with a reguard, and sparing of perticular persons'. The defence is incontestable, as is his earlier assertion that 'no Man can justly complayne, that hath the vertue to thinke but favorably of himselfe'. The would-be complainant finds satire an elusive offence; to identify its target is to admit of its recognisable truth. Jonson knew well how to exploit the gap between perception and articulation of the satirist's intentions. The argument is reiterated in a letter, probably to his patron the Countess of Bedford, a close friend of Queen Anne, in which he describes the response to *Eastward Ho* as 'so mistaken, so misconstrued, so misapplied, as I do wonder whether their Ignorance, or Impudence be most, who are our adversaries'. Chapman addresses a similar argument to King James. He should be judged, he claims, according to general actions which are of 'loyall and most dutifull order' and not by particular deeds which are not antagonistic but 'lie subject to construction'. Both Jonson's and Chapman's words suggest that complaints had been directed at more passages than the Scots satire alone, which of itself is hardly very prominent. But as we shall see from examination of the text of *Eastward Ho*, it appears that Jonson's casual reference, as reported by Drummond, to 'writting something against the Scots' inadequately reflects the extent of the play's satire and of its subsequent censorship.

The repercussions of *Eastward Ho* illustrate the importance of patronage to the dramatist. The release of Jonson and Chapman reprieved from the appointed sentence for libel – namely, the slitting of ears and noses – can, no doubt, be ascribed to their connections at Court and to their awareness of who in turn enjoyed favour, as well as to the King's short but recoverable temper. Although he recognised Salisbury's unreliability as a patron, informing Drummond that the Earl 'never cared for any man longer nor he could make use of him',[49] Jonson was not averse to professing in his letter the flattery of a client towards his hoped-for patron. If Salisbury will secure his liberty, Jonson writes, he will undertake another form of captivity, binding his muse to the 'thankfull honoring' of the Earl and his descendants. Jonson's other letters to patrons from prison are less supplicatory in tone, since the reciprocal relationship of patron and client was more firmly established. Aubigny had previously defended the integrity of *Sejanus* and, as has been said, may have intervened in Jonson's defence when he was called before the Privy Council. Jonson's connection with Lucy, Countess of Bedford, had been forged in the reign of Elizabeth, when he seems to have relied on her to promote his interests at

Court.[50] Pembroke was similarly known to Jonson as a generous benefactor and patron. If Jonson had an enemy in high place, in the Earl of Northampton, he also had influential friends, who helped to secure his release some time before November 1605, at which time he was peripherally involved with the investigations into the Gunpowder Plot.[51]

The arbitrariness of Jacobean censorship is borne out by the fact that *Eastward Ho* was published and twice reprinted in 1605. Indeed, its licensing and entry into Stationers' Register on 4 September 1605 may even have occurred before the dramatists' release.[52] The controversy did, however, give rise to some interference with the text, albeit rather belatedly. In the first issue of the earliest edition of the play, Seagull, a sea captain, extols the merits of Virginia, and in so doing makes a sly indictment of the universal preponderance of the Scots:

> And then you shal live freely there, without Sergeants, or Courtiers, or Lawyers, or Intelligencers – onely a few industrious Scots perhaps, who indeed are disperst over the face of the whole earth. But as for them , there are no greater friends to English-men and *England*, when they are out an't, in the world, then they are. And for my part, I would a hundred thousand of 'hem were there, for wee are all one Countreymen now, yee know; and wee shoulde finde ten times more comfort of them there, than wee do heere.
>
> (III.iii. 40–8).

The passage articulates the English dislike of the Scottish newcomers and reflects dissatisfaction with the patronage and perquisites which James lavished on the many Scotsmen he had brought south. The omission of these lines from the second issue of the first quarto and from the two successive editions printed the same year demonstrates that it was this passage, rather than the First Gentleman's imitation of the Scottish accent in Act IV, which caused the greatest offence.

There is further evidence that satirical references to the Scots and the Court had been more prominent in the play's early performances. J. Q. Adams and Herford and Simpson have drawn attention to certain bibliographical anomalies in the first edition of *Eastward Ho* which point to the omission of passages.[53] On certain pages, the use of wide slugs between speeches suggests that those pages were reset during the process of printing to accommodate the removal of offending lines. These features are first noted in Act I scene ii, lines 21–51 (A4v), in a scene which satirises Gertrude's impatience to be rid of her citizen origins and to display her new-found social status in her imitation of French and Scottish fashion. The detailed stage direction prepares for the visually comical impact of Poldavy, a tailor who enters 'with a faire gowne, Scotch Varthingall, and French fall in his armes', and of Gertrude 'in a French head attire and Cittizens gowne', followed by the leading in of a monkey by Gertrude's waiting woman. But little is made of the satirical potential of these stage properties, apart from Gertrude's pun on the common qualities of the Scottish farthingale and the miserly Scot: 'Now (Ladyes my comfort) what a prophane Ape's here! Tailer, *Poldavis*, prethee fit it, fit it: is this a right Scot? Does it clip close? and beare up round?' (I.ii. 47–50) Taking into account the blank spaces and the printing of Gertrude's speech in short, five-word lines, Herford and Simpson estimate that nine lines have been excised from the text, including three from Gertrude's speech. The obvious inference is that the gibe against the Scottish has been curtailed. There are several literary allusions to the slavishly imitative behaviour of apes and it is probable that in an original direction the ape made some lewd gesture at the reference to the Scot.[54] There is also, notably, a wide space before Mildred's cautionary speech (ll. 31–41) in which she warns her sister against being dazzled by titles which 'presume to thrust before fit meanes to second them'. The critiques of the common desire for honours and titles are unmistakably topical and it is probable that more damning indictments of such social ambitions and the indiscriminate promotions of the new regime were cut from the original.

A further omission must account for the wide spacing and fewer lines on C1v and C2 of the quarto.[55] Here, Quicksilver, Touchstone's apprentice, aided by Touchstone's mistress Sindefy, is preparing to run away from his master in search of more illustrious positions. He will, he announces airily, be maintained at court or perhaps become a merchant. Sindefy offers gratuitous advice on the perils of the court and describes the irksomeness of sycophancy to powerful courtiers:

> Well *Francke*, well; the Seas you say are uncertaine: But hee that sayles in your Court Seas, shall finde 'hem tenne times fuller of hazzard: wherin to see what is to bee seene, is torment more then a free Spirite can indure; But when you come to suffer, howe many injuries swallowe you? What care and devotion must you use, to humour an imperious Lord? proportion your lookes to his lookes? (your) smiles to his smiles? fit your sayles to the winde of his breath? (II.ii. 69–77)

Blank lines and generous word distribution along one line indicate that in all probability a more sustained attack on court life had been uttered in the original performance. When the play came to be printed, however, there were presumably last minute attempts to censor it and the printers removed the more provocative parts of the text. It seems unlikely that such censorship in the printing house was undertaken solely on the printers' initiative, as Herford and Simpson have suggested. It would have been in the interests of the printers to produce an undoctored text and they would be unlikely to play the role of unofficial censor. The inconvenience of re-setting the type and cancelling sheets invites the conclusion that they were implementing orders to remove the specific references which had incensed the King, rather than that they had adopted a cautious policy on their own behalf.

The failure of the players and playwrights to have *Eastward Ho* licensed, the role played by an informer in its suppression, and the last minute censorship of the text, point again to the vagaries of censorship during the early Jacobean period. But the virulence of the reaction to the play would have been a clear signal to authors that they could not bank on a lenient response to unbridled dramatic satire.

The Isle of Gulls

Sometime between late 1605 and early 1606, the Children of the Queen's Revels were deprived of royal patronage: on the title page of the Blackfriars play *The Isle of Gulls* by John Day, published in 1606, the company is simply referred to as the 'Children of the Revels'.[56] There is no contemporary reference to account for the rupture, which must presmably have deprived Daniel of his office as licenser of the company, since this privilege had been granted in its royal patent. We can only conjecture either that in the wake of the commotion over *Eastward Ho* the King's sanction extended not only to depriving the writers of their liberty and censoring the play, but also to divesting the company of the Queen's association; or that the controversy aroused by *The Isle of Gulls* during its early Blackfriars production strained to breaking point the King's toleration of topical satire.

The Isle of Gulls certainly contributed to the Blackfriars reputation for staging audacious contemporary satire. The title alone, with its echo of the notorious *Isle of Dogs*, would have induced audiences to expect more than a glance at current affairs. Day both exploits and denies the connotation in the Induction. The First Gentleman questions the Prologue about the author: 'But why doth he call his play *The Ile of Gulls*? it begets much expectation'. The Prologue rejects the notion that the author has any political motive – 'Not out of any dogged disposition, nor that it figures anie certaine state or private government' – and argues that the story can be found in Sidney's *Arcadia*. But the First Gentleman is not convinced, replying drily, 'Out a question he hath promised thee some fee, thou pleadest so hard for him' and, pursuing his line of enquiry, 'Is there any great mans life charactred int?'. In response, the Prologue concedes only general satire in the impersonation of Dametas, who is not 'of true-borne gentilitie', and who 'expresses to the life the monstrous and deformed shape of vice.' Again, we are alerted to the targets of Day's satire. Indeed, those in the audience familiar with *Arcadia* would soon see in the play's derisive tones a distortion of Sidney's courtly romance.

Despite the Prologue's asseverations of the author's innocent intentions, it is evident that much of the original appeal of *The Isle of Gulls* would have come from its sharp satirical gibes at contemporary affairs. The Duke and Duchess, Basilius and Gynetia, were originally designated king and queen, as in the new *Arcadia*, since 'queen' still remains in two places in the text, but their status has been diminished. In the first scene, Basilius replies to Gynetia as his 'faire Queene' (A3v) and later, besotted by Lisander disguised as an Amazon, he promises to make her 'Queene over the most submisse Captive that ever love tooke prisoner' (FVr). The scene in which both Basilius and Gynetia are gulled into an abortive assignation with the Amazon is partly composed in rhyming couplets; here, we have 'Duke' rhyming with 'spring' and 'sings' (H1r). The confusion may stem from the differing rank of Basilius between the old and the new *Arcadia*; it is also possible, however, that the crude purpose of such a change in the text of *The Isle of Gulls* was to deflect the obvious association with James. There are certainly resemblances between Basilius and James. In *Arcadia* it is the worthy Kalander who is presented as enjoying the hunt, whereas in the play Basilius hails its pleasures in euphoric tones (C2v). James's fondness for hunting, reputedly to the detriment of matters of state, was well known. The Venetian ambassador's comment that James 'seems to have forgotten that he is a king except in his kingly pursuit of stags to which he is foolishly devoted'[57] was a common complaint. Day touches obliquely upon the popular animosity felt towards the Scots and other national grievances. There is an obvious parallel between Basilius's domains of Arcadia and Lacedemon and James's two kingdoms which is at its most explicit in the meeting of the Lacedemonians, Julio and Aminter, with the Duke. The two disguised suitors for the King's daughters present an extensive list of abuses arising from the King's absence from Lacedemon:

Duk. What grevances oppresse them? briefly speake.
Ami. Marchandise (my Ledge) through the avarice of purchasing Officers, is rackt with such unmercifull Impost, that the very name of Traffique growes odious even to the professor.

Julio. Townes so opprest for want of wonted and naturall libertie, as that
the native Inhabitants seeme Slaves, and the Forrayners free Denizens.
Amin. Offices so bought and sould, that before the purchaser can be sayd
to be placed in his Office, he is againe by his covetous Patrone
displac't   (E2v)

Apart from the allusions to the avarice of the customs officers and to
the buying and selling of offices, the passage does not contain matter
which can be related specifically to complaints against the new regime;
but it does reflect a prevalent fear that England might, in time, be
absorbed into Scotland. In his cursory dealings with the Lacedemonians'
grievances there is more than a hint of James's notorious apathy
towards the business of government.

The Prologue's words in the Induction anticipate the satire of
Basilius's favourite, Dametas, scorned by Basilius's daughters as a man
who acts only for 'profit and preferment'. In *Arcadia* Dametas is
presented as a boorish clown who is unwarrantably esteemed by the
king. To some extent, the play follows the source, but the captains'
account of the rise to favour of the Duke's minion contains nuances of
the way James sponsored his favourites, lavishing honours and gifts
upon them. The two captains speak disparagingly of the ignoble
Dametas:

1 *Cap.* What doe you think of *Dametas.*
2 *Cap.* As of a little hillock, made great with others ruines ... How did he
first stumble on the Princes favour?
1 *Cap.* As some doe upon offices, by fortune and flatterie, or as truth saies,
the Prince having one day lost his way, wandring in the woods found
the *Dametas*, affected his discourse, tooke him along to the Court, and
like great men in love with their own dooings, countenanct his defects,
gave him offices, titles, and all the additions that goe to the making up
of a man worshipfull.   (B1r)

Chambers's specific identification of Dametas with Robert Carr has
to be rejected on the grounds of date: Carr seems to have first attracted
the King's attention in 1607, some time after the composition,
performance and printing of the play.[58] George Hone, Earl of Dunbar,
who came south with the King, is a possible candidate, as is James
Hay; but no exact identification is necessary, since the King's predilections were sufficiently notorious for the thrust of the satire to be
appreciated on the Blackfriars stage.

The Isle of Gulls is amongst a small number of plays for which there
exists some record of the state response. In his letter to Sir Thomas
Edmondes of 7 March 1606, Sir Edward Hoby conveys the news that
in the preceding month the play had been much discussed in the

Commons and that some of the actors were subsequently imprisoned in Bridewell: 'At this time was much speech of a play in the Black Friars, where, in the "Isle of the Gulls", from the highest to the lowest, all men's parts were acted of two divers nations: as I understand sundry were committed to Bridewell.'[59]

The interest the play aroused in Parliament and the reprisals which followed, together with some possible censoring of the text before publication and the loss of the company's royal patronage, suggest a widespread feeling that the licence of the satirist should not be permitted to develop unchecked. It was apprehended that the liberty of playwrights and actors was contributing to a general sense of disenchantment with the new regime and furthering disrespect for the King, his Court, and his government. In so doing, it had trespassed beyond the bounds of the permissible.

Philotas

In the context of the displeasure Daniel must have caused through his indulgent attitude towards topical satire, the reaction of the Privy Council to his own play, *Philotas*, marks these years as a singularly unfortunate period for him. The play was performed before the King, by the Children of the Queen's Revels in January 1605, with the sanction of either Buc or Tilney and it was printed the same year.[60] It is an untheatrical piece; its use of the Chorus makes it reminiscent of closet drama, seemingly designed for a specialised audience. The events it describes are dramatic commonplaces: the downfall of Philotas, favourite and commander in the army of Alexander the Great, who through failing to publicise his knowledge of a plot against Alexander and the intrigues of envious courtiers is arraigned, found guilty of treason, tortured and executed. As with Jonson's *Sejanus*, however, its scholarly use of classical material failed to deflect interest in its topicality as policitical drama. In the dedication to Prince Henry – an inducement to secure royal protection – we learn that Daniel had been 'tax'd for wishing well'. No names are mentioned: but from extant letters to Robert Cecil, now Viscount Cranborne, and to the Earl of Devonshire and in the 'Apology' appended to the 1623 text, it becomes apparent that the Privy Council detected sympathetic allusions to the rebellion and trial of Essex and Daniel was brought before them to answer charges.[61]

In Daniel's letter to Cecil, dated simply 1605, there is no reference to the specific cause of the allegations against him; but he vindicates himself on the grounds that, since history is repetitive, correspondences are inevitable and inadvertent: 'There is nothing new under the Sunne, nothing in theas tymes that is not in bookes, nor in bookes that is not in theas tymes.' This is a claim which, as Brents Stirling has pointed out, ran contrary to Daniel's declaration in the 'Epistle Dedicatorie' to his poem *The Civil Wars*, in which he stresses the didactic nature of history.[62] In the rest of his letter, Daniel is concerned with his reputation and anxious not to draw further attention to the play. In contrast to Jonson's spirited ripostes to his critics, he presents no strongly worded defence of his intentions. He offers to leave the Court, taking his book with him, 'pretending some other occasion, so that the suppressing it by autoritie might not make the world to imagin other matters in it then there is'. 'Withdrawing the booke' must, of course, refer to the play manuscript which, considering Daniel's close connection with the Children of the Queen's Revels, would have served as the play book. Daniel's further request that either Cecil or Northampton might supply him with some 'viaticum' to aid him during his proposed exile from Court is an interesting one in the context of Northampton's earlier involvement with the accusation of treason against Jonson for *Sejanus*. Cecil and Northampton had formed an alliance in Privy Council and it may have been that the Earl was again responsible for drawing the Council's attention towards a play which he construed as having a referentiality beyond its source material.

Daniel's defence on his appearance before the Privy Council emerges in his undated letter to the Earl of Devonshire, formerly Lord Mountjoy, in which he repeats his case as he had apparently presented it before 'the Lordes'. In response to allegations that he had intended some representation of Essex's career, he affirmed that he had written the first three acts of the tragedy 'the Christmas before my L. of Essex troubles, as divers in the cittie could witnes'. Moreover, the Master of the Revels had perused the play. (Even though *Philotas* was a Queen's Revels play, Daniel presumably could not license his own work.) It appears from the letter that Devonshire had heard part of the tragedy and had then found nothing objectionable in it, but had later reacted against being implicated in the affair. Daniel stresses that he had not cited him in support of the decision to perform the play; at the time when he had read part of it to the Earl, that had been far from his purpose. But evidently Devonshire, who had been with Essex in Ireland and had participated in his rebellion, resented Daniel's appeal to him and feared a revival of interest in Essex's exploits, which might undermine his own rehabilitation and influence in the Privy Council.

In his concluding reiteration of loyalty to Devonshire, Daniel's rueful acknowledgment that his only error has been 'indiscreation, and misunderstanding of the tyme' is revealing. The implication is that he had wrongly gauged the climate of censorship and interpretation. The point is repeated in the 'Apology': 'And withall taking a subject that lay (as I thought) so farre from the time, and so remote a stranger from the climate of our present courses. I could not imagine that Envy or ignorance could possibly have made it, to take any particular acquaintance with us.' The time which had elapsed since Essex's disgrace and the advent of what seemed to be a less repressive regime had presumably encouraged Daniel to think that there was no longer any need to be as circumspect towards certain dramatic material as his friend Fulke Greville had been in the previous reign when he had consigned his tragedy of Antony and Cleopatra to the flames.

Daniel's lengthy defence of his intentions in *Philotas* as contained in the 'Apology' was significantly first printed in 1623 as an appendix to the text in the *Whole Works*, edited by John Daniel, the poet's brother. Again, Daniel employs the commonplace nature of the theme in his defence. He repeats the circumstances of composition: the play was begun before the 'unhappy disorder of Essex's rebellion', with the intention of its being performed 'as a private recreation'; writing was interrupted when he was called upon to make additions to his *Civil Wars* and the play was laid aside; to supplement his income he later resumed work on his tragedy, thinking it would compare favourably with 'the idle fictions, and grosse follies' of the contemporary stage. The fact that the 'Apology', with its specific rebuttal of the Essex connection, was not printed until eighteen years after the play's initial publication suggests that Daniel's asseverations of innocence did not allay all suspicions about his motives.

Whether the fall of Essex did affect the way Daniel shaped and interpreted events in the last two acts of *Philotas* is debatable. Brents Stirling has argued that Daniel has at particular moments departed from his sources, referred to in the 'Argument' as Plutarch and Quintus Curtius, so that the events of the play parallel the arraignment of Essex; and that the change in the source location from an encampment to the court deepens the analogy. Laurence Michel also accepts that the fate of Essex inspired the final two acts of the play, particularly in relation to the prosecution of Philotas and the personal animus of his prosecutors. He suggests that Daniel was concerned in the first three acts with the threat to the state of the overmighty subject, but that in the latter two, written later, he became pre-occupied with the workings of tyranny rather than 'the dangers of insubordination'.[63] Daniel's known sympathies for Essex and his faction tend to corroborate the internal evidence. He had praised Essex in his *Civil Wars* (although he had cautiously excised the relevant stanzas from the 1601 edition); he addressed a poem of sympathy to Essex's closest supporter, the Earl of Southampton, on his release and, of course, Mountjoy was his patron. It is highly probable that, as Daniel moved to complete his tragedy, he was conscious that recent events well exemplified the argument of the play and suggested a more sympathetic treatment of Philotas.

The significant question arising from the charges against Daniel is why the Privy Council felt it necessary to interfere at this time with a play which had already been perused, on Daniel's word, by the Master of the Revels, on the grounds that it had associations with a conspiracy to cause insurrection. Daniel can hardly be considered insensitive to the times in his judgment that, with the new dynasty established, he could deal safely with events which might have had a bearing in the previous reign but scarcely impinged on the present. Reasons can only be conjectured. Any play judged sympathetic to Essex's cause, and which suggested that Essex's enemies, the King's ministers, had played as large a part in his ruin as did his own ambition, would have been seen as potentially seditious by Cecil, who had been involved in managing the outcome of the Earl's arraignment. In the play, Philotas's downfall is engineered by his chief opponent Craterus. The comments about Craterus made particularly by the Chorus, as Brents Stirling notes, mirror the claims made by Essex and his supporters at the trial, namely, that the outcome was fixed and that private animosities were being masked and prosecuted behind the façade of public interest. The Privy Council's reaction, or perhaps more specifically that of Cecil and his ally Northampton, may have sprung more from their concern that Daniel was exposing on the stage Cecil's wily and self-serving conduct at the time of Essex's indictment rather than from any fear that *Philotas* might foster a revival of interest in the defeated cause. It is surely significant, that in his 'Apology' Daniel feels it prudent to include a reference to Craterus as one who 'wisely pursued this businesse [and] is deemed to have beene one of the most honest men that ever followed *Alexander* in all his actions, and one that was true unto him even after his death'. Contemporary commentators drawing upon the history of Alexander saw Craterus in this light[64]; but it is a view which in no way reflects the envious and scheming counsellor of the play.

The text of *Philotas* exemplifies what Annabel Patterson describes as the functional ambiguity of works composed under the conditions of censorship.[65] The final Chorus is ambivalent in its comment on the intemperate wrath of kings, which may be justified but which may merely serve to provoke further insurgency. Throughout, the Chorus elicits sympathy for Philotas and, following the third act, exposes the motives of his accusers: 'SE how these great men cloath their private hate/ In those faire colours of the publike good;/ And to effect their ends, pretend the State,/ As if the State by their affections stood.'

Yet Daniel, in the 'Argument' prefacing all editions of the play, distances himself from the judgment of the Chorus, 'who vulgarly (according to their affections, carried rather with compassion on Great-mens misfortunes, then with the consideration of the cause) frame their imaginations by that square, and censure what is done.' It is probable that Daniel's denigration of the Chorus was composed once the play had been performed and after his appearance before the Privy Council. Michel has suggested that certain lines of the 'Argument', which stress the preservation of the state above the tragedy of Philotas, were a later addition because they correspond to parts of the 'Apology'. He does not, however, include Daniel's gloss on the Chorus within the suggested additions. But since this immediately follows the proposed new material and since it also serves to shift the disposition of the play against Philotas, it seems likely that Daniel inserted the comment in response to allegations that he was seeking to rehabilitate Essex and expose the motivations of his adversaries. Nevertheless, despite the disclaimers advanced in the dedication, 'Argument' and 'Apology', the Chorus's judgments are consistent with the dramatic representation of Alexander and Craterus and allow for the ambiguity surrounding Philotas's connection with the plot against Alexander. The defence mounted by the 'Argument' may have appeased certain members of the Privy Council, but the play itself retained its more complex perspective.

King Lear

So far the discussion of early Jacobean censorship has focused on plays which provoked interference after their performances. In almost all of these cases, censorship has been transmitted to the text following performance and prior to publication and it is not always possible to discover the extent of the censor's intervention. With *King Lear* we are in a different position. There are two substantially different texts, the 1608 quarto and the folio, which bibliographers have analysed as independent texts of equal authority.[66] There is some consensus that the folio is a revision of the quarto undertaken entirely or in part by Shakespeare. Its copy text is recognised as having playhouse affiliations and as such we might expect it to incorporate the censorship of the Master of the Revels. Less certainty attends the provenance of the quarto, whose copy text has been seen as a transcript of the play in performance and as based on authorial foul papers. But it contains few marks of performance and recent editors and bibliographers have been inclined to see a more direct association with Shakespeare's manuscript.[67] These hypotheses, however, appear to be in conflict with the publication details of the play. The unusually informative entry in the Stationers' Register of 26 November 1607 would lead one to expect that the quarto would be based on a carefully prepared text, representative of the play as it had been performed before King James after it had received Buc's approval:

> *Nathaniel Butter.* Entred for their copie under th [e h] andes of
> *John Busby.* Sir GEORGE BUCK knight and Th [e] wardens A booke
> called. Master WILLIAM SHAKESPEARE *his 'historye of Kinge
> LEAR' as it was played before the kinges majestie at Whitehall uppon
> Saint Stephens night at christmas Last by his majesties servantes
> playinge usually at the 'Globe' on the Banksyde*[68]

But, as has been noted, the features of the quarto, published in 1608, bear no relation to a carefully prepared theatrical prompt book. The wardens may have seen such a copy bearing the theatrical licence of Buc; the unusual reference in the entry to the performance and its date suggests that this would have been a licence for performance rather than publication. But the edition published by Butter and Busby over a year later had a different provenance. It is the folio text which seems closer to the play in performance and bears signs of Buc's interference.

When we investigate the variants between the two texts in the context of censorship, we enter an area of some controversy. In the main, those textual critics who dismiss the idea of an arch-text in favour of the theory that there were two different versions of the play have paid little heed to or rejected censorship as a reason for the texts' divergences.[69] This view has been challenged by Annabel Patterson, who argues that *King Lear* was one of the most topical of plays to be performed in the public theatre in its oblique contribution to the debate over the union of England and Scotland; and that such obliquity and multivalency of meaning, whereby Lear appears as both type and anti-type of James, are the consequence of the artist working under considerable restraints.[70] Professor Patterson is not concerned directly with the transmission of censorship to the text and does not therefore confront the question whether certain textual variants are due to censorship or, as has been argued, artistic second thoughts.[71] But her contention for the play's immediate socio-political relevance

, makes the assumption that such an historically allusive text would have been of particular concern to the censor.

In order to test the argument for the censor's direct intervention, or for self-censorship as distinct merely from artistic revision, certain passages and lines which appear only in the quarto text and which bear upon contemporary political issues need to be examined. First of all, part of a dialogue between the Fool and the King had been omitted in the folio text. In the quarto, in response to Lear's request that he should teach him the difference between a bitter and a sweet fool, the Fool comments pointedly:

> *Foole.* That Lord that counsail'd thee to give away thy land,
> Come place him heere by mee, doe thou for him stand,
> The sweete and bitter foole will presently appeare,
> The one in motley here, the other found out there.
> *Lear.* Do'st thou call mee foole boy?
> *Foole.* All thy other Titles thou hast given away, that thou wast borne with.
> *Kent.* This is not altogether foole my Lord.
> *Foole.* No faith, Lords and great men will not let me, if I had a monopolie out, they would have part an't, and Ladies too, they will not let me have all the foole to my selfe, they'l be snatching.   (C4v-D)

The text of the folio resumes with the Fool's riddle about the egg and the two crowns. The satire which the folio omits is wide-ranging, from the King judged as a fool for his impolitic actions to the greed of influential men and women who grasp at monopolies. Lear's Fool goes beyond the liberties of the 'all-licensed' fool in his acerbic gibes and his railing at particular abuses of power. The topical critique is unmistakable. Throughout the reign James's practice of granting monopolies to courtiers to supplement the royal income was a contentious issue. Such privileges had been ruled contrary to the common interest in the courts in 1602 and remained an abiding source of resentment to those who were excluded from them.[72] A reference to the giving away of titles readily evokes the image of King James, as does the Fool's dismissal of Lear as a fool: James was known as the 'wisest fool in Christendom'.[73] The satire is so overt that there is some consensus amongst editors and bibliographers that the passage must have been cut by the censor. Another passage which, particularly in the context of a Court performance, would contain disturbing nuances and which is omitted in the folio, is Edmund's account to Edgar of how current events are fulfilling a recent prediction:

> unnaturalnesse betweene the child and the parent, death, dearth, dissolutions of ancient amities; divisions in state, menaces and maledictions against King and nobles; needles diffidences, banishment of friends, dissipation of Cohorts, nuptial breaches, and I know not what   (C2v)

All we have in the folio text is Edmund's first comment: 'I promise you the effects he writes of, succeede unhappily'; which without further elaboration is effectively meaningless and cannot, therefore, owe its truncated form to dramatic deliberation. Whilst accepting that Edmund's earlier reference to eclipses is inspired by the remarkably juxtaposed eclipses of September and October 1605 and that these phenomena alone would have given the quarto passage a topicality 'which certainly might have led the censor to scrutinize it carefully', Gary Taylor rejects the interference of Buc as the reason for omission, on the grounds that the passage is too general to cause offence.[74] But censors cut rather than prune, as evidence in the theatrical manuscripts bearing traces of the censor's own hand shows. If there were grounds for Buc's interference in the first place – and allusions to 'dissolutions of ancient amities, divisions in state, menaces and maledictions against King and nobles' suggest matters more immediate than power struggles in pagan Britain – then it is probable that he decided to remove the whole speech so as to prevent the actors reviving any of its parts.

One clear serial change in the folio relates to the presentation of internal division and the intervention of the French. In the text underlying the folio a deliberate attempt seems to have been made to cut lines which relate to the French invasion of Britain. The first such excision is of part of a speech by Goneril, in which she denounces Albany for his lack of martial aggression in opposing the French:

> Wher's thy drum? *France* spreads his banners in our noyseles land,
> With plumed helme, thy state begins thereat
> Whil'st thou a morall foole sits still and cries
> Alack why does he so?   (H4r)

The entire scene in the French camp near Dover (IV. iii), with its reference to the return of the King of France to confront internal dissent, has been omitted in the folio, as has an exchange between Kent and the Gentleman at the end of the fourth act which tells of rumours of foreign activity. A further cut has expunged several of Albany's lines spoken in the English camp when, with misgivings, he accepts that he must oppose the French invasion:

> Where I could not be honest
> I never yet was valiant, for this busines
> It touches us, as *France* invades our land.
> Not bolds the King, with others whome I feare,
> Most just and heavy causes make oppose.   (K3)

The divergent accounts which comprise part of the scene between Kent and the Gentleman (III.i) suggest that the main emphasis of the

original lines which the folio rejects was on the advantage gained by
the French as a result of civil unrest in Britain. It is illuminating to
compare the two versions of the political situation as recounted by
Kent. The quarto prints:

> there is division,
> Although as yet the face of it be cover'd,
> With mutuall cunning, twixt *Albany* and *Cornwall*
> But true it is, from *France* there comes a power
> Into this scattered kingdome, who alreadie wise in our negligence,
> Have secret feet in some of our best Ports,
> And are at point to shew their open banner,
> Now to you, if on my credit you are build so farre,
> To make you speed to Dover.   (F3v)

The folio version of Kent's speech does not, however, depict the
French as preparing to invade the country at all. Instead Kent reports
that the French King's spies are aware of internal disputes and the
harsh treatment delivered to Lear:

> There is division
> (Although as yet the face of it is cover'd
> With mutuall cunning) 'twixt Albany and Cornwall:
> Who have, as who have not, that their great Starres
> Thron'd and set high; Servants, who seeme no lesse,
> Which are to France the Spies and Speculations,
> Intelligent of our State. What hath bin seene,
> either in snuffes, and packings of the Dukes,
> or the hard Reine which both of them hath borne
> Against the old kinde King; or something deeper,
> Whereof (perchance) these are but furnishings.   (p. 804)

The folio speech thus offers no more than an oblique suggestion that
France may profit from internal dissension.

Attention to stage directions similarly reveals a purposeful change in
dramatic intent. The directives of the battle in the folio do not mention
the source of Cordelia's army: 'Alarum within. Enter with Drumme
and Colours, Lear, Cordelia, and Souldiers, over the Stage, and
Exeunt' (p. 814). In the quarto the international situation is more
explicit: 'Alarum. Enter the powers of France over the stage, Cordelia
with her father in her hand' (K3v).

The two texts, then, present different perspectives of the foreign
invasion. In the quarto, Cordelia and the King of France invade with
the intention of claiming Cordelia's portion of the kingdom. Cordelia
persuades her husband to change his purpose (IV. iv. 25–9) to a quest
to avenge the treatment of Lear. The King, however, retires to France
to settle his own internal disputes and Cordelia is left with the foreign

army. The folio, as Gary Taylor points out, systematically removes 'verbal and visual reminders of the French presence, so that Cordelia seems to lead not an invasion but a rebellion'.[75] There is no internal inconsistency in either of the two texts; but the obvious question is what prompted the re-modelling of the invasion in the folio. Gary Taylor rejects ideas first offered tentatively by Chambers and Madeleine Doran, that the folio copy text could have been tampered with by the censor, and argues for a revision on purely artistic grounds. Taylor comments that: 'Jacobean censorship of references to foreign powers always involves *negative* portrayal of *contemporary* figures' and concludes that 'censorship seems, on the historical evidence, extremely unlikely'.[76] But the premiss may require expansion in so far as it implies that more generalised views of national character or international conflict were not also likely to cause the censor disquiet. It is reasonable to suggest that the tradition of Franco-Scottish friendship and James's policy of rapprochement would have made a reminder of past hostilities discordant and unwelcome. Certainly, we may suppose that scenes depicting the successful invasion of Britain by a French army in a play which touched directly on matters of current political debate would have been unwelcome to James; and in perusing plays to be performed before the King and, no doubt, foreign ambassadors, Buc would have been alert to those issues which lay at the heart of James's policies. Accordingly, the King's 'aversion to mixing himself up in wars, even in the guise of aid'[77] is likely to have shaped Buc's attitude to the idea of Cordelia bringing succour to her father with the aid of France and its army. It is not, of course, suggested that Buc was responsible for the re-working of the text; but that pressure was brought to bear on Shakespeare to alter the perspective of an invasion and to remove the French army from the stage. This theory presupposes that the revisions of *King Lear*, which produced the folio text, followed very closely the play's original composition, pre-dating the 1606 performance before the King, and that such revisions were in part determined by the strictures of the Master of the Revels. The hypothesis does not militate against the 'two texts' theory currently favoured by textual critics; but it does propose that the demands of censorship determined the nature of the folio text to a greater extent than is generally allowed.

Macbeth

The absence of a text of *Macbeth* earlier than that of the folio means that there is no positive evidence to corroborate a suggestion by F. P.

Wilson that the extreme brevity of the play could be accounted for by theatrical censorship.[78] Since editors and commentators generally accept that the play was one of three performed by the King's Men before James and Christian of Denmark, during the summer of 1606, it is indeed probable that the play suffered some interference from the Master of the Revels prior to the Court performance.[79] The various issues with which the play engages: witchcraft, the Scottish context, the healing touch to cure the 'King's Evil' in Act IV scene iii and, most significantly, regicide, would have spurred the censor to pay close attention to their deployment.

There are no obvious lacunae in the text, but Nevill Coghill has drawn attention to one dramatic episode which is notably under-developed. The scene is that located in the English court. Coghill argues that Shakespeare's original intention was to present Edward the Confessor in the act of touching the sick and miraculously healing them of scrofula, as celebrated by Holinshed.[80] In spite of the groundwork being prepared for Edward's appearance – namely, by the doctor's announcement in Act IV scene iii that the King who is with 'a crew of wretched souls, that stay his cure' will soon enter to join Malcolm and Macduff – audience expectations remain unfulfilled. There is a sense of incompleteness which could be attributed to lines excised from the text. In so relating Edward, Shakespeare was treading on delicate ground. Despite his absolutist claims, James adopted a sceptical attitude towards the magical healing ritualised by Edward, declaring that miracles had now ceased and that the practice of healing was idolatrous.[81] Had such a scene been presented before the King, it would have created an embarrassing contrast between the sacerdotal Edward, reputedly endowed with the divine power of healing, and the learned but pedantic James I. It may also be significant that Buc, in his royal panegyric *Daphnis Polystephanos* (1605), had presented the alliance between Malcolm and Edward as prefiguring the union of England and Scotland.[82] If Buc had perused the play, he would have been sensitive to the ideological implications of any dramatic encounters between the monarchs: and in deference to James may well have censored any scene which indulged English nationalism by depicting Malcolm paying homage to Edward.

In the absence of comparative texts, theories of censorship by Tilney or Buc of the text underlying the folio must remain speculative. The constraints of censorship, however, help to account for several of the changes Shakespeare made to his source material and for the circum-vention of controversial issues. In the *Chronicles*, Banquo is described as an accomplice to Macbeth: Shakespeare makes him innocent and an honourable man, no doubt because Banquo was regarded as an ancestor of the Stuart line.[83] Again, in the source, Duncan's murder is an act of open political assassination, in contrast to the off-stage, closet murder in the play. The King's perpetual fear of regicide may have conditioned this redaction. Indeed, in writing a play which depicted the assassination of a Scottish king followed by the justifiable deposition of a tyrant, Shakespeare was walking a tightrope. James expressly denounced tyrants, but he asserted unequivocally a doctrine of non-resistance.[84] There is a tension between the doctrine of tyrannicide and, in Malcolm's claim to the throne, the law of primogeniture which is not resolved, with the effect that the former is subsumed beneath the latter.

As we have seen, Buchanan's recent history of Scotland had been banned in England for its advocacy of elective monarchies and for its defence of the right of oppressed subjects to depose their king. Although he had trimmed Buchanan's exposition of the merits of a monarchy based on rationalist principles, the editor of the second edition of Holinshed's *Chronicles* in 1587 had drawn upon Buchanan's version of Scottish events to bring the narrative up to date. As David Norbrook has cogently argued, *Macbeth* embodies a major revision of the political assumptions implicit in the sources.[85] Although the historical figure of Macbeth was condemned by both conservative writers and also Buchanan, his career evoked latent associations with constitutionalist issues. Shakespeare side-steps such matters. Fortune and chance are as active in Macbeth's election as are the nobility. The ten years during which Macbeth ruled justly are omitted, leaving the impression that misrule is the consequence of the reign's illegitimacy. The central issue in debates about the Scottish monarchy – namely the sovereign's accountability to the people – is ignored. In a sense, Shakespeare manages to de-politicise his material. Four years after the performance of *Macbeth*, James issued his proclamation against Dr Cowell's *Interpreter*, castigating men who waded 'in all the deepest mysteries that belong to the persons or State of Kings or Princes, that are gods upon Earth' and meddled 'with things above their capacitie'. Shakespeare's circumspect redaction of his sources and the play's silence on those ideological issues which were anathema to James may well have sprung from judicious self-censorship.

The Conspiracy and Tragedy of Charles Duke of Byron

Chapman's two plays on the life of the French Duke of Byron were the first of several Jacobean plays whose dramatic deployment of near-contemporary events elicited the interference of the authorities with performance and publication. In the main, the plays, involved as they are with factional intrigue at the court of Henri IV, are untypical of the dramatic output of the children's company, who produced them at Blackfriars early in 1608. The introduction of a now lost scene of low comedy, however, more in keeping with audience expectations of the mode of Blackfriars productions, cost the company their venue and led to increased restraints on the use of history as source.

There is nothing to suggest that the plays were not initially licensed in the ordinary way by the Master of the Revels. There is certain evidence, however, that the dramatisation of recent turbulent events in France brought about the intervention of the French ambassador, Antoine Lefèvre de la Boderie, which resulted in a prohibition on their further performance. No doubt the spectacle of the boy actors playing the French King and nobility was perceived as aggravating the affront. Accounts of La Boderie's action, the actors' attempts to circumvent official curbs, the playing of the lost scene satirising the French court and La Boderie's further strategies to have the plays suppressed are all communicated in the ambassador's despatch of 8 April 1608 to the French Secretary of State, Pierre Brulart de Puisieux.[86] Following the suppression of the plays at La Boderie's instigation, in the same way as *Eastward Ho*, they were nevertheless revived when the King and Court were out of London. The players' audacity was compounded by the presentation of a new scene in which the Queen boxed Henri's mistress, Mademoiselle de Verneuil, on the ears. La Boderie complained to Salisbury that the company had not only flouted the official ban but had added material which, according to the ambassador, was baseless and had nothing to do with the Duke of Byron. The three actors who could be rounded up were imprisoned, but this time Chapman was able to escape and avoid incarceration. La Boderie would seem to have worked with some wily indirection, for which he was later commended by Puisieux, to arouse the anger of a rather lethargic King against Chapman and the Children of Blackfriars. He tells Puisieux that in yet another play the comedians had satirised the King and his favourite and, in cipher (here in italics), he reveals how he had exploited this offence in his strategy of retaliation:

One or two days before that they had depicted the King his Scottish demeanour and all his favourites in a very strange manner *for after having made him rage against the heavens on the flight of a bird and made him beat a gentleman for having turned loose his dogs they represented him drunk at least once a day. This I have been informed of, I thought he would be sufficiently angry against the said comedians without my encouragement of*

his anger and it was preferable to refer their chastisement to the irreverence
which they had formulated against him rather than what they might have
said of the ladies. Hence I resolved not to mention the subject again and not
to give it any more attention. When the said King was here he showed
extreme irritation against these rascals and commanded they should be
punished and especially that there should be diligence in finding the author.

We also learn from La Boderie's *communiqué* that, as a further
consequence of the King's displeasure, all playing was forbidden
within the City of London: an order which was apparently rescinded
when the companies agreed not to represent any modern history or
make topical references on the stage. Ostensibly the players were
punished not for their performance of a prohibited play about French
politics and sexual intrigue, but for their explicit mockery of the King.
Although it is difficult to estimate how significant the *Byron* plays
were in cautioning playwrights to avoid current politics, the undertaking extracted from the theatre companies, regarding the non-
performance of foreign and topical affairs, must have had a substantial bearing on subsequent drama. It is certainly true that Chapman
did not again attempt to dramatise contemporary material. It is not
until 1619, when Fletcher and Massinger turned to recent events in the
Netherlands, that we again encounter a surviving play in which
foreign affairs are quarried for theatrical material.

The other play to which La Boderie refers, as containing a parody of
James, his irascibility and his entourage of favourites, bears evident
resemblances to such plays as *The Fawn* and *The Isle of Gulls* which
also satirise the recognisable weaknesses of the King. The play itself is
lost, but there is further documentation which refers to it and the
consternation it aroused. On 3 April 1608 the Florentine agent in
London, Ottaviano Lotti, in one of his weekly despatches home, wrote
in cipher of a recent play ridiculing 'the new fashion found in
Scotland', which he expected to cause the banishment of the players.
He adds that 'the author of the play has run off in fear of losing his
life, probably because he mingled ideas that were too wicked, in which
so much was concealed.'[87] Although the connection has not previously been made, these details correspond with La Boderie's longer
communiqué five days later. There is further mention of the *Byron*
plays and of the King's anger provoked by the lost satire in a letter
from Sir Thomas Lake, who was then attending the King at Thetford,
to Salisbury:

His Majesty was well pleased with that which your lordship advertiseth
concerning the committing of the players that have offended in the matters
of France, and commanded me to signifye to your lordship that for the

others who have offended in the matter of the Mynes and other lewd words, which is the children of the blackfriars, That though he had signified his mynde to your lordship, by my lord of Mountgommery yet I should repeate it again, That his Grace had vowed they should never play more, but should first begg their bred and he wold have his vow performed, And therefore my lord chamberlain by himselfe or your lordships at the table should take order to dissolve them, and to punish the maker besides.[88]

Chambers has conjectured that the satire which caused the dissolution of the Blackfriars company was by Marston, who was summoned before the Privy Council on 8 June 1608 for some unspecified offence, and that Lake's reference to 'the matter of the Mynes' is a reference to a Scottish silvermine whose working had been an unsuccessful royal enterprise. Marston has also been regarded by Hillebrand and Finkel-pearl as the author of the notorious satire, which effectively may have closed his career as a dramatist satirist.[89]

The controversy did not in the long term adversely affect the careers of Chapman or the actors in his play. To escape the kind of reprisal which had followed *Eastward Ho*, Chapman lodged secretly with the Duke of Lennox, cousin and favourite of the King and companion of Prince Henry. In an undated letter to Crane, Lennox's secretary, clearly intended for the Duke, he expresses gratitude for the protection he has been given, but some impatience at his continued professional exile now that 'the matter is disperst'.[90] The patronage of Prince Henry and Lennox no doubt prevented any lasting damage to Chapman's career as poet and playwright. The King's ire against the Blackfriars Children was similarly shortlived. They were forced to vacate their indoor theatre, thus facilitating the course of theatrical history by allowing the King's Men to take over the lease; but they were performing at Court once more during the Christmas season. In 1610, the former members of the children formed a newly amalgamated company based at Whitefriars. Earlier indiscretions did not prevent the company becoming once again by royal patent the Children of the Queen's Revels.

Despite indications of royal forgiveness, Chapman encountered considerable opposition when he attempted to publish his plays. The difficulties which he experienced on publication are described in an undated letter to an unnamed person, almost certainly Buc, who did eventually license the plays. Chapman's letter is a crucial document in view of all that it tells us about dramatic licensing for the stage and for publication in the early Jacobean period and because of the allusion it makes to both the author's and the censor's lack of control over the text once it becomes the property of actors. It is thus quoted in full:

Sir — I have not deserv'd what I suffer by your austeritie; if the two or three lynes you crost were spoken; my uttermost to suppresse them was enough for my discharge: To more then which no promysse can be rackt by reason; I see not myne owne Plaies; nor carrie the Actors Tongues in my mouthe; The action of the mynde is performance sufficient of any dewtie, before the greatest authoritie. wherein I have quitted all your former favors, And made them more worthie then any you bestowe on outward observers; if the thrice allowance of the Counsaile for the Presentment gave not weight enoughe to drawe yours after for the presse, my Breath is a hopeles adition; if you say (for your Reason) you know not if more then was spoken be now written no, no; nor can you know that, if you had bothe the Copies, not seeing the first at all: Or if you had seene it presented your Memorie could hardly confer with it so strictly in the Revisall to discerne the Adition; My short reason therefore can not sounde your severitie: Whosoever it were that first plaid the bitter Informer before the french Ambassador for a matter so far from offence; And of so much honor for his maister as those two partes containe, perform'd it with the Gall of a Wulff, and not of a man: and, theise hautie and secrett vengeances taken for Crost, and officious humors are more Politique than Christian; which he that hates will one day discover in the open ruyne of their Auctors; and though they be trifles he yet laies them in Ballance (as they concern Justice, and bewray Appetites to the greatest Tyrannye) with the greatest; But how safely soever Illiterate Aucthoritie setts up his Bristles against Poverty, methinkes yours (being accompanied with learning) should rebate the pointes of them, and soften the fiercenes of those rude manners; you know Sir, They are sparkes of the lowest fier in Nature that fly out uppon weaknes with every puffe of Power; I desier not you should drenche your hand in the least daunger for mee: And therefore (with entreatie of my Papers returne) I cease ever to trouble you, By the poore subject of your office for the present.[91]

From Chapman's letter it is clear that Buc had originally licensed the plays for performance and that in the wake of the difficulties they had produced, he was now somewhat audaciously attempting to secure a further licence for publication. What is unclear is the sequence of events connecting theatre and press censorship. Is Chapman writing after the production which incorporated the additional scene of the quarrel between the Queen of France and the royal mistress and does his reference to the actors speaking censored lines therefore include this scene? Or, as John Gabel has argued, was the letter written in the the interval between the ambassador's first complaint resulting in the plays' prohibition and their revival with new material previously unseen by the censor?[92] The evidence is inconclusive. Gabel points out that La Boderie twice mentions the actors performing new material and argues that the scene of female confrontation, as it appears in the text, is dramatically extraneous and therefore must have been a later addition. But if the actors had recovered material censored by Buc, then as far as La Boderie's appreciation of the performance was concerned, this would have been tantamount to an addition. From textual evidence, all we can say for sure is that the scene was integrated into Chapman's own copy of the play, which is the provenance of the printed text, and it could not therefore have been improvised by the actors.

The plays were entered into the Stationers' Register in June 1608 and published the same month.[93] That publication should be so immediate upon the controversial stage production is yet another indication of the unpredictability of early Jacobean censorship. It is also, of course, an indication of the different parameters governing stage and literary censorship: the presentation upon the stage of prime movers in contemporary events was far more likely to incur the intervention of the censor than their appearance in print.

Chapman dedicated his *Byron* plays to Sir Thomas Walsingham and his son. Walsingham may have gained status as a patron from the fact that his wife was an intimate of Queen Anne, although there is no recognition in the dedication that the plays received any support from him when they were under official scrutiny. It is clear, however, that Walsingham had seen and admired them: '(having heard your approbation of these in their presentment) I could not but prescribe them with your name'. In terms which recall Jonson's allusion to the text of *Sejanus*, in his dedication to Aubigny, as a ruin, Chapman refers to the depredations of censorship and speaks of 'these poore dismemberd Poems'. Textual details substantiate the notion that Buc suppressed a number of passages before he licensed the plays. It is a reasonable conjecture that the plays were censored on two occasions; but there is no evidence to determine whether particular cuts were made prior to publication or to performance. Censorship of the copy text can be detected in Act IV of *The Conspiracy*, which describes Byron's mission to England, and Act II of *The Tragedy*, which contains remnants of the fracas between Queen and mistress. Byron's visit to the Court of Elizabeth I in 1601 was fully described in Chapman's sources.[94] In *The Conspiracy*, however, the 'schooling' of the marechal is not dramatically presented but merely reported, in a tedious and protracted scene (IV. i.) between the two noblemen, Crequi and D'Aumont. In the final scene of *The Tragedy*, Byron refers back to his audience with Elizabeth and her discourse on the Earl of Essex, whose fate Byron recognises as prefiguring his own. Yet any such adumbration is missing in the nobles' report of the encounter between Elizabeth and Byron. The formal presentation of the Queen on the stage and, as the later reference implies, the sympathetic interpretation of Essex's acts, were most probably suppressed before the play was performed. Further signs of censorship are evident in the exceptionally short second act of *The Tragedy*; this contains a masque performed before the French court, in which Cupid recounts an end to recent 'effeminate warre' between Sophrosyne, or Chastity, and Dapsyle, or Liberality, in harmony with the Peace promoted by Henri. Unless we assume the deliberate excision in the copy text of a scene which realised the confrontation between the two rivals for the King's affections, the meaning of the allegory is lost and there is little sense in Henri's words at the close of the divertissement: 'This show hath pleased me well, for that it figures/ The reconcilement of my Queene and Mistris'. Presumably Buc had excised the offending scene and Chapman deliberately chose to leave the loose ends trailing as signs of external interference.

Direct government intervention following the performance of the *Byron* plays and the lost royal satire mark the King's decreasing toleration of satirical licence and a tightening of official control over dramatic output. These developments also compelled significant modifications of genre and correspondingly of dramatic preoccupations. With the promise extracted from the acting companies that they would not in future represent any modern history or treat of current affairs, further major restrictions were imposed on the choice of dramatic material.

How then is the impact of the new dispensation on the drama to be assessed? Philip J. Finkelpearl has argued that Jacobean censorship was lax and that 'libelous activity in the Jacobean theatre was treated with remarkable leniency'.[95] In comparison with the repressive policy of the late Elizabethan years, this would certainly seem to be true. The period of relative relaxation in the censorship exercised by Tilney and Buc in the Revels Office and by Daniel as licenser for the Queen's Revels synchronised, however, with instances of direct government intervention and the persecution of playwrights and actors following the performance of offensive works. The King's reaction to performances of *Eastward Ho* and *The Conspiracy* and *Tragedy of Byron* indicates that playwrights could not rely on royal indifference to provocative drama and the response of the Privy Council to *Sejanus* and *Philotas* demonstrates the continual difficulty of handling political material which was vulnerable to factional interpretation. Moreover, in these instances the integrity of the extant texts has been damaged by the censor. The fact that playwrights were often not able to restore the provocative lines later suggests that censorship was not as lenient as it would appear.

In support of Finkelpearl's argument, contemporary reports do suggest a disinclination or inability to check the satirical thrust of drama. George Calvert's comment to Ralph Winwood in 1606, used as an epigraph to this chapter, that the players were treating King, state and religion with great irreverence, is well known. Foreign ambassadors, as has been seen, remarked with some bemusement on the popularity of audacious dramatic satire. The Queen's reported presence at such performances does indeed suggest not only a demystification of royal authority, dissipating the aura which was so central to the cult of Elizabeth's Court, but that playwrights and actors felt confident enough to produce, without fear of reprisal, satirical performances which impugned the King's own reputation. Yet, as Kevin Sharpe comments, ambassadors depended upon information, even rumours, from courtiers and newsmongers and their *communiqués* inevitably represent a partisan view.[96] In 1608, moreover, the Florentine agent's account of the reaction to the lost satirical play, in which 'much was concealed', and whose author had to flee for his life, conveys a somewhat different state of affairs. These diverse reports suggest a situation of flux and arbitrary sanctions, not one of certainty in which playwrights knew the boundaries of permissible expression. Whether this unstable relationship between the theatrical profession and the censor was to continue throughout the Jacobean period will be explored in the final chapter.

Notes

1 David Calderwood, *Historie of the Kirk of Scotland* (1628), Chambers,*ES*, II, pp. 267–8. See also *The Plays and Poems of William Shakespeare By the Late E. Malone*, ed. J. Boswell (21 vols., London, 1821), III, pp. 450–62.

2 See Jenny Wormald, *Court, Kirk and Community: Scotland 1470–1625* (London, 1981), pp. 150–2 and her article 'James VI and I: two kings or one?', *History*, 68 (1983), 187–209. In the latter she quotes from a letter written by an irate King when officials failed to turn up at his summons: 'I hae been Fryday, Setterday and this day waithing upon the direction of my affairs, and never man comand. ... Quhat is spokin this nicht is forgot the morne' (p. 193).

3 *The Political Works of James I*, ed. C. H. McIlwain (London, 1918), p. 301.

4 See Richard A. McCabe, 'The Masks of Duessa: Spenser, Mary Queen of Scots, and James VI' *English Literary Renaissance*, 17 (1987), pp. 224–42.

5 'Journal of Sir Robert Wilbraham', Robert Ashton, *James I By His Contemporaries* (London, 1969), pp. 6–7.

6 Chambers, *ES*, II, pp. 208–9.

7 See Graham Parry, *The Golden Age Restored: The Culture of the Stuart Court, 1603–42* (Manchester,1981), pp. 41–2.

8 Chambers, *ES*, II, p. 49.
9 Glynne Wickham, *Early English Stages, 1300–1660*, (London, 1963), II, pt.I, pp. 90–5.
10 Jonathan Goldberg, *James I and the Politics of Literature* (Baltimore, London, 1983), p. 231.
11 This point is developed in a forthcoming study of dramatic censorship by Richard Dutton. I am grateful to Dr Dutton for summarising his perspective on Jacobean censorship for my benefit.
12 See Neil Cuddy, 'The revival of the entourage: the bedchamber of James I, 1603–1625', *The English Court*, ed. David Starkey (London, 1987), pp. 173–226.
13 W. W. Greg, 'Entrance, licence, and publication', *The Library*, Fourth Series, 25 (1944), 1–22 at p. 13.
14 Elias Schwartz, 'Sir George Buc's authority as licenser for the press', *Shakespeare Quarterly*, 12 (1961), 467–8. Chapman's letter is quoted on p. 142.
15 3 Jac. 1. c.21, *Statutes of the Realm*, IV, p. 1097.
16 *The Shakespeare First Folio* (Oxford, 1955), p. 150 note.
17 See R. C. Bald, *Bibliographical Studies in the Beaumont and Fletcher Folio of 1647* (Oxford, 1938), p. 71.
18 See F. P. Wilson, 'Ralph Crane, scrivener to the King's Players', *The Library*, Fourth Series, 7 (1927), 194–215, at 206.
19 See *Doctor Faustus: Parallel Texts*, pp. 63–85
20 From a different premiss this point is argued by Michael J. Warren, '*Doctor Faustus*: The old man and the text', *English Literary Renaissance*, 11 (1981), 111–47.
21 Frances A. Shirley, *Swearing and Perjury in Shakespeare's Plays* (London, 1979), p. 131.
22 Whether the play is to be identified with *Truth's Supplication to Candle-light*, for which Henslowe was paying Dekker in January 1600, is open to question. If this were so, Bowers observes that there must have been considerable revision since it is inconceivable that the political and personal references in the printed play would have been permitted under Elizabeth. See *The Dramatic Works of Thomas Dekker*, ed. Fredson Bowers (Cambridge, 1955), II, p. 494.
23 See below, pp. 199–200.
24 See Goldberg, *James I and the Politics of Literature*, pp. 43–50.
25 See McCabe, 'The Masks of Duessa', p. 224
26 See Hugh Trevor-Roper, 'Queen Elizabeth's first historian: William Camden' in *Renaissance Essays* (London, 1985), 121–48, at 125–34.
27 A draft of the *Annals* was deposited with Sir Robert Cotton before it was sent to the King. De Thou for some time believed the work to be by Cotton. When Camden saw the transcript, it was 'full of mutilations and gaps and certain words had been effaced by the effrontery of the copyist' (quoted by Trevor-Roper, p. 131).
28 De Thou replied: 'We struggle in the same sea ... the same baleful stars look down on us, the same tides and storms drive us up and down, towards rock and reef,' (quoted by Trevor-Roper, pp. 132–3). James's distrust of historians is further illustrated by his dissolution of Camden's Society of Antiquaries as being a potential subversive body (see Trevor-Roper, p. 125).

29 J. H. Walter in the *Malone Society Reprint* (Oxford, 1938) conjectures that the play was composed 1604 and draws attention to the reference to 'coronatyon day' (1745) which suggests that a coronation was sufficiently recent to be topical. If he is right, then Buc began to license plays for the stage rather earlier than had been previously surmised. See below p. 204, note 1. Quotations are from the Malone Society edition.
30 *Ben Jonson*, I, p. 141.
31 See *Ben Jonson*, I, p. 166.
32 *Sejanus*, ed. Jonas Barish (New Haven, London, 1965), p. 16. Barish does, however, accept that the charge against Jonson may not have been as specific as this and conjectures that perhaps more objectionable to the authorities would be 'the depiction of a government tyranny establishing itself through the use of informers'. See, also, B. N. de Luna, *Jonson's Romish Plot* (Oxford, 1967), p. 109.
33 See *Censorship and Interpretation* (Wisconsin, 1984), pp. 50–6.
34 Patterson interprets I.ii. 82–3 of *Cynthia's Revels* as a cautious apology for Essex. Her conjecture that in the wake of the gunpowder plot Jonson became disturbed by the memory of Essex's rebellion rests on the uncertain premiss that Jonson later lost some confidence in the judgement of Tacitus the historian. But this begs the question of whether Jonson had conceived such a negative view of the Earl by the time the play was composed.
35 The change in allegiance was noted by the Venetian ambassador: 'Old Howard, who has lately been appointed to the Council, and Southampton, who are both Catholics, declare that God has touched their hearts, and that the example of their King has more weight with them than the disputes of theologians. They have become Protestants, and go to church in the train of the King.' (Quoted by L. L. Peck, *Northampton: Patronage and Policy at the Court of James I* (London, 1982), p. 55).
36 *Ben Jonson*, I. p. 220.
37 *Ben Jonson*, I, p. 36. For an incisive analysis of Jonson's political satire in *Sejanus* see Geoffrey Hill, 'The world's proportion: Jonson's dramatic poetry in *Sejanus* and *Catiline*', *Jacobean Theatre*, Stratford-upon-Avon Studies (London, 1960), I, pp. 113–33.
38 The publication of three separate editions in one year is, of course, most unusual. The third quarto incorporated additions composed for the King's Men, but there is no ready explanation for the two earlier quartos. See *The Malcontent*, ed. G. K. Hunter (Manchester, 1975), p. xxvi. It is probable that the play was in such great demand because of its notoriety.
39 *The Malcontent*, ed. Hunter, p. xxix.
40 Marston writes: 'I have myself therefore set forth this Comedy; but so, that my enforced absence must much rely upon the printer's discretion; but I shall entreat slight errors in orthography may be as slightly overpassed.' Hunter notes that a number of press corrections in the first quarto suggest a 'more concerned and author-like view of the play' (p. xxxiii).
41 Hunter, pp. xlviii–xlix.
42 F. von Raumer, *History of the Sixteenth and Seventeenth Centuries, Illustrated by Original Documents*, (2 vols., London, 1835), II. p. 206. The identification of Gonzago with James was first made by Bullen in 1887 (*Works of John Marston*, I, p. xliii). It was accepted by Alexander

W. Upton, 'Allusions to James I and his court in Marston's *Fawn* and Beaumont's *Woman Hater*', *PMLA*, 44 (1929), 1048–65 and more recently by Philip J. Finkelpearl, *John Marston of the Middle Temple* (Cambridge, Massachusetts, 1969), pp. 220–2. David Blostein accepts the argument with some reservation in his Revels edition (Manchester, 1979), pp. 31–2.

43 On 16 June 1603, for example, Sir Thomas Edmondes, writing to the Earl of Shrewsbury, reported the King's discontent at the Queen's conduct. The cause is unspecified, but we learn that the Queen was refusing to admit James's nominees to her Privy Chamber. See *James I By His Contemporaries*, pp. 92–3.

44 *The Blacke Yeare* (London, 1606), sig. B2r.

45 See *James I By His Contemporaries*, pp. 6–7.

46 *Ben Jonson*, I, p. 140.

47 The dramatists' letters are all printed in *Eastward Ho*, ed. R. W. van Fossen (Manchester, 1979), pp. 218–25. I have used the modernised forms of characters' names from this edition.

48 See below, pp. 127–8.

49 *Ben Jonson*, I, p. 142.

50 See *The Golden Age Restor'd*, p. 174. In 1601, Jonson had inscribed a copy of *Cynthia's Revels* to her.

51 *Ben Jonson*, I. pp. 40–1.

52 There is no record of the duration of their imprisonment. All we know is that Jonson's letters to the Earl of Salisbury and the Earl of Montgomery could not have been written before May 1605, when the two earldoms were created by the King, and that on 9 October Jonson was a guest at a party given by Robert Catesby (see van Fossen, *Eastward Ho*, p. 5).

53 See J. Q. Adams, '*Eastward Hoe* and its satire against the Scots', *Studies in Philology*, 28 (1931), 689–701 and *Ben Jonson*, IV, pp. 495–500.

54 Herford and Simpson draw attention to the popularity of such tricks. They quote Jonson in the Induction to *Bartholomew Fair* in which there is a reference to a juggler with 'a wel-educated Ape' that will 'sit still on his arse for the *Pope*, and the *King* of *Spaine*' (*Ben Jonson*, IV, p. 496).

55 *Ben Jonson*, IV, pp. 508–14: Herford and Simpson provide a type-facsimile of the relevant pages of the 1605 quarto.

56 See the *Ile of Gulls*, with an Introduction by G. B. Harrison, Shakespeare Association (London, 1936).

57 Quoted by D. Harris Willson, *King James VI and I* (London, 1956), pp. 179–80.

58 Chambers, *ES*, III, p. 286. Carr had returned to England in 1607 after a sojourn in France. He came to the King's notice after a fall from his horse in that year (*King James VI and I*, pp. 336–7).

59 In Thomas Birch, *The Court and Times of James the First*, (2 vols., London, 1848), I, pp. 60–1.

60 See *Philotas*, ed. Lawrence Michel (New Haven, Connecticut, 1970; first published 1949), p. 36. As Michel says, the acting of the play can only be inferred; but Daniel had been paid for an interlude to be performed before the King by the Queen's Majesty's Children of the Revels on New Year's Day 1604 (old style). In a letter to the Earl of Devonshire (see below, p. 128), Daniel refers to the licence of the Master of the Revels.

61 Both letters are printed in Michel's edition, pp. 37–9.

62 Brents Stirling, 'Daniel's *Philotas* and the Essex case', *Modern Language Quarterly*, 3 (1942), 583–95, at 587–8.

63 *Philotas*, ed. Michel, p. 63.

64 John Thornborough, Bishop of Bristol, referred to Craterus in his pro-Union pamplet, *Joiefull and Blessed Reuniting the two mighty and famous kingdoms*: 'Let our strife rather be like that of Ephestion and Craterus, who contended whither should love their King Alexander most; in so much that Alexander was enforced to decide the controversie, adjudging that Ephestion loved the king best, and Craterus Alexander best' (quoted in *Censorship and Interpretation*, p. 68).

65 *Censorship and Interpretation*, p. 18. Annabel Patterson makes only passing reference to *Philotas*.

66 For a useful summary of recent work relating to the texts of *King Lear*, see E. A. J. Honigmann, 'Shakespeare's revised plays: *King Lear* and *Othello*', *The Library*, Sixth Series, 4 (1982), 142–73.

67 See Stanley Wells and Gary Taylor, *William Shakespeare: A Textual Companion* (Oxford, 1987), p. 510.

68 Arber. *SR*, III, 366.

69 In recent studies of the text of King Lear, only Gary Taylor has given serious attention to censorship; but he sees its impact on the folio text as minimal. See 'Monopolies, show trials, disaster, and invasion: *King Lear* and censorship', *The Division of the Kingdoms*, eds. Gary Taylor and Michael Warren (Oxford, 1983), pp. 75–117.

70 *Censorship and Interpretation*, pp. 58–64.

71 This argument is developed notably by Steven Urkowitz in *Shakespeare's Revision of King Lear* (Princeton, New Jersey, 1980).

72 See Roger Lockyer, *'The Early Stuarts: A Political History of England 1603–1642* (London, 1989), pp. 190–6.

73 The remark has been attributed to Henri IV; but Jenny Wormald affirms that the tag can be traced to the minor household official Anthony Weldon, whose acerbic *The Court and Character of King James* has done much to taint James's reputation. See 'James VI and I: two kings or one?', p. 191. If the term originated with Weldon, it post-dates an early performance of *King Lear*; but, presumably, it reflects a common perception of the King.

74 'Monopolies, show trials, disaster, and invasion', pp. 81–3.

75 See 'The war in *King Lear*', *Shakespeare Survey*, 33 (1980), 27–34 at 31.

76 'Monopolies, show trials, disaster, and invasion', p. 80–1.

77 This remark on King James's foreign policy is recorded in a despatch of 1610 from the Venetian ambassador in England to the Doge and Senate (*CSP Venetian 1607–10*, p. 426).

78 Wilson's hypothesis that 'cutting may have been necessitated by objections taken by the censor to a play in which awkward political implications were likely to be discovered' was first mentioned in a note in W. W. Greg's *The Editorial Problem in Shakespeare* (Oxford, 1942), p. 147.

79 See Henry N. Paul, *The Royal Play of Macbeth* (New York, 1948), p. 41. The King's Men acted on three occasions before the two Kings in mid-1606.

80 Nevill Coghill, 'Have we lost some part of the scene at the Court of

King Edward the Confessor?' in *The Triple Bond*, ed. Joseph G. Price (Pennsylvania, London, 1975), pp. 230–4.

81 The King's attitude is recorded in the letter of an annonymous papal spy quoted by Coghill, *ibid.*, p. 301. See also Keith Thomas, *Religion and the Decline of Magic* (Harmondsworth, 1973), p. 228.

82 See David Norbrook, '*Macbeth* and the politics of historiography',*Politics of Discourse: The Literature and History of Seventeenth Century England* (Berkeley, Los Angeles, 1987), p. 96. Buc followed James's ancestry through the English line back to Edward. An audience, however, would surely be more likely to identify James with Malcolm.

83 See *Macbeth*, ed. Kenneth Muir (London, 1951), p. xxxviii.

84 Citing Saul, Nebuchednezzar and Nero as examples of despots, idolators and usurpers, James argued that it was a people's duty to eschew and fly the fury of unlawful tyrants 'without resistance, but by sobbes and teares to God, according to that sentence used in the primitive Church in the time of persecution', in 'The True Lawe of free Monarchies: or the Reciprock and Mutual Dutie Betwixt a free King, and his naturall subjectes' in *Minor Proseworks of King James VI and I*, ed. James Craigie (Edinburgh, 1982), p. 69.

85 Norbrook, '*Macbeth* and the politics of historiography', pp. 78–96.

86 The full French text of La Boderie's letter is included in J. J. Jusserand's 'Ambassador La Boderie and the compositer of the Byron plays', *Modern Language Review*, 6 (1911), 203–5.

87 See John Orrell, 'The London stage in the Florentine correspondence, 1604–1618' *Theatre Research International*, 3 (1977–78), 157–76, at 164.

88 *State Papers Domestic, James I*, XXXI, p. 73.

89 See Chambers, *ES*, II, pp. 53–5, H. Newcomb Hillebrand, *The Child Actors* (Urbana, 1926), II p. 200 and Finkelpearl, *John Marston of the Middle Temple*, pp. 256–7. Hillebrand notes the problem raised by Lake's letter, which seems to imply that it was not the children performing at Blackfriars who had caused offence by presenting 'matters of France'. But, as Hillebrand says, the Byron plays were published as played 'at the Blackfriars'; it is probable, then, that Lake was not certain of the details.

90 This letter was printed by Bertram Dobell, 'Newly discovered documents of the Elizabethan and Jacobean periods: letters and documents by George Chapman', *The Athanaeum*, 3832, 6 April 1901, p. 433.

91 Dobell, p. 433.

92 See '*The Conspiracie and Tragedie of Charles Duke of Byron Marshall of France*', ed. John B. Gabel, *The Plays of George Chapman: The Tragedies with Sir Gyles Goosecappe*, eds. Allan Holaday, *et al.*, pp. 267–9 and Gabel's article 'The original version of Chapman's *Tragedy of Byron*', *Journal of English and Germanic Philology*, 63 (1964), 433–40, where he has argued in detail that the stage quarrel was a non-authorial interpolation made after the initial prohibition. John Margeson in the Revels edition (Manchester, 1988), rejects this view on the grounds that Chapman printed the masque as his own (p. 12).

93 See *The Conspiracie and Tragedie of Byron*, ed. Gabel, p. 269.

94 Chiefly Edward Grimeston's *A General Inventorie of the History of France* (1607), p. 945.

95 '"The Comedians' Liberty"': censorship of the Jacobean stage reconsidered',
   English Literary Renaissance, 16 (1986), 123–38, at 129.
96 *Faction and Parliament: Essays on Early Stuart History*, ed. Kevin Sharpe
   (Oxford, 1987), p. 13.

CHAPTER IV

'Too sawcie in censuring princes': drama and censorship, 1608–24

who-so-ever in writing a moderne Historie, shall follow truth too neare the heeles, it may happily strike out his teeth. There is no Mistresse or Guide that hath led her followers and servants into greater miseries
(Walter Raleigh, Preface, *The History of the World*, 1614)

Symon   Weele see first, the King shall after supper
Glover   I Commend your worships wisdome in that Mr Maior
Symon   Nay tis a point of Justice and be well examined not to offer the King worse than Ile see my selfe; for a play may be dangerous, I have knowne a greate man poysond in a play.
(Thomas Middleton, *Hengist, King of Kent*, c. 1616–20)

By the time George Buc assumed total control of the Revels Office, after Tilney's death in 1610,[1] the vogue for dramatic satire which dominated the early years of James's reign seems to have been arrested; although, as will become apparent, the satiric purpose became subsumed in other genres. The decline of topical satirical comedy can be attributed, in part, to the series of reprisals suffered by several dramatists in the wake of audacious plays and, in part, to the return to a centralised system of censorship under a new Master of the Revels. Buc was in a position to develop a form of theatrical censorship appropriate to the particular interests of the Jacobean regime, unhampered by precedents of the previous reign. The matters dominating theatrical censorship during the mid- to late-Jacobean period were those on which King and country were divided. In particular, the King's policy of pacification in Europe drew widespread opposition which he attempted to silence. Other material which ventured either explicitly or obliquely to question royal absolutism was also likely to incur the censor's disapproval.

Cases of non-dramatic censorship demonstrate the nature of the constraints which playwrights might encounter. In 1610, following the assassination of Henri IV, the publication of works on French affairs was prohibited. On 14 May, Thomas Wilson, an author whom Salisbury had employed as a foreign intelligencer, wrote to Warden Waterson of the Stationers' Company, ordering him to 'suffer nothing to be imprinted concerning the death of the late french King' and to 'stopp such as to ther own damage shall goe about to putt to press those things which after they shall not be suffred to utter'.[2] Apparently the injunction went unheeded: a French treatise to be translated into English was entered on the same day and on the following day a ballad, 'The wofull complaynt of Ffraunce for the deathe of the late kinge HENRY the Ffowrth', also appears in the Register.[3] It is evident that the wardens acted recalcitrantly and refused to heed Wilson's strictures unless they received direct communication from Salisbury himself. The Lord Treasurer duly wrote to Waterson on 15 May forbidding the publication of reports of the King's death until the government should sponsor an official account.[4] His orders, reflecting James's fear of widespread dissemination of the news, seem to have been obeyed, for there is no record of further accounts of the event appearing in print.

During the final years of the reign, when James's self-image of the European peacemaker was being undermined from all sides, there were increased restrictions on discussion of foreign policy. The years 1619–22 were particularly repressive. The King strove to suppress expressions of support for his son-in-law Frederick, the Palsgrave, in the latter's defence of the Palatinate against the Habsburgs; Frederick, against James's advice, had accepted the crown of Bohemia in 1619. On 22 September, for example, Joseph Hall wrote to Dudley Carleton that he had been censured for his zeal in praying for the Queen of Bohemia.[5] Popular protest against the projected Spanish marriage and preaching on the proposed alliance generally were similarly stifled. Hearing that negotiations with Spain were being denounced from the pulpit, the King issued orders in December 1620, through the Bishop of London, that the clergy were not to 'meddle in their sermons with the Spanish match nor any other matter of state'.[6] When Thomas Scot, a clergyman who later became a preacher to the English garrison at Utrecht, sought to gratify anti-Spanish sentiment in his pamphlet Vox Populi (1620) reprisals were swift.[7] Although the satirical tract was published anonymously in the Netherlands, in order to elude censorship, it was eagerly sought by English stationers striving to meet a popular demand. In 1621, an unnamed publisher was charged with unlawfully circulating the work and escaped punishment only by incriminating Scot, who had by then escaped to the Netherlands.[8] Again, debate on foreign policy was prohibited in the Parliament of

1621.[9] Hostility against Spain was at its height when Prince Charles and the then royal favourite, the Duke of Buckingham, returned from Spain late in 1623 from their abortive expedition to negotiate the marriage of the Prince with the Infanta. In the Parliament of the following year there was a clamorous demand for war. Thomas Locke reported to Dudley Carleton on 29 February 1624 that: 'The Upper House cry out for war, especially the bishops. The Bishop of Durham was so excited that he declared he would lay aside his rochet and gird on a sword, if the king would take that course'.[10] Against a background of fierce nationalism and the Crown's pursuit of deeply unpopular policies, dramatic censorship can be seen operating to contain the expression of such restiveness. Despite the fact that plays dealing with foreign relations would have attracted wide audiences, in this restrictive climate few playwrights dared to tackle the issues. All the plays that did and of which we are aware – *Philaster, The Marquis d'Ancre, Sir John van Olden Barnavelt, A Game at Chess* and *The Duchess of Suffolk* – either suffered from censorship or were suppressed altogether.

Neither did even oblique criticism of James and his pacifist policies always elude detection. In 1614, Raleigh's *The History of the World* was called in by James's express orders despite the fact that the work had been duly licensed. According to Chamberlain in his letter to Carleton, the reason for its suppression was that it had been 'too sawcie in censuring princes'.[11] Raleigh had presented several portraits of weak or dissolute rulers, but one in particular came a little too close to common perceptions of the King. The parallel between James and Ninias, who succeeded the magnificent Queen Semiramis and who was 'esteemed no man of warre at all, but altogether feminine, and subjected to ease and delicacie', is unmistakable.[12] Unwisely, Raleigh had compared the early years of James's sovereignty unfavourably with the reign of Elizabeth.

Playwrights also set forth their indictments of the age. The decaying standards of the Jacobean Court, presided over by a King who was seen as prodigal, indulgent towards favourites, pretentious and despotic in his vapourings on the prerogative, preoccupied dramatists such as Webster, Tourneur, Middleton, Beaumont and Fletcher, who concealed their broadsides beneath ingenious metaphor and artifice. It was difficult, of course, for the Master of the Revels to censor such references outright, for that would have implied an awareness of the shortcomings of the King and of his social and courtly milieu. Nevertheless, in the censorship of *Mustapha, The Maid's Tragedy* and *The Second Maiden's Tragedy* (all by Buc) and of *The Honest Man's*

Fortune (by Herbert), there is evidence of the censor attempting to shore up royal authority by suppressing the more explicit critiques of the Court and of the King's absolutist ideology.

Mustapha

The life and work of Fulke Greville, Lord Brooke, illustrate the caution which writers engaged in political discourse were compelled to exercise. As has been noted, Greville decided near the end of Elizabeth's reign to burn his tragedy of Anthony and Cleopatra for fear of its being associated with the fall of Essex. When he applied at the beginning of the new reign to Robert Cecil for access to state papers in order to write a history of the times of Queen Elizabeth, he was discouraged by Cecil, who, according to Greville, thought that he might 'cleerly deliver many things done in that time, which might perchance be construed to the prejudice of this'.[13] He abandoned the project rather than submit to censorship, which he stigmatised as 'a world of alterations as in the end the worke it selfe would have proved a story of other mens writing'.[14] Greville's former association with Essex and his 'Elizabethanism' continued to fuel Cecil's mistrust and he was barred from public office until after the Lord Treasurer's death in 1612.[15]

Greville's two surviving tragedies, *Mustapha* and *Alaham*, were, as the author says in his *Life of Sidney*, 'no Plaies for the Stage'. Buc's censorship of *Mustapha* for the press in 1608 – a decade after its composition[16] – does, however, provide some evidence of the limits on ideological debate under James. Indeed, Greville was well aware of the new means and associations which a work might evoke years after its composition. In the context of his discussion of his own plays in the final chapter of the *Life of Sidney*, Greville had encouraged the reader to be aware of the political referentiality of drama even when such meanings were not specifically intended by the author: 'for every part he may perchance find a Player, and for every Line, (it may be) an instance of life, beyond the Authors intention, or application, the vices of former Ages being so like to these of this Age, as it will be easie to find out some affinity, or resemblance between them.'[17] The location of *Mustapha*, the court of the formidable sixteenth century Turkish ruler Soliman II, and the story of his infamous murder of his son Mustapha seem far removed from Jacobean politics. But when Buc perused *Mustapha*, it would appear that he was conscious of connections between the discourse on sovereignty in the play and the ideological debates which dominated political thought in Jacobean England.

The concerns of Buc's censorship can be deduced from the variants between an early manuscript of *Mustapha* and the quarto of 1609, which Buc had licensed for publication the previous year. There are a number of omissions in the printed text which would seem to have been caused by Buc's intervention. The first consists of Soliman's words to Rossa, in response to her insinuations that Mustapha is a threat to Soliman and his throne: 'Kings life kept but in flesh, and easily pierc'd;/Kinges Crownes no higher than private armes may reach' (I.i. 80–1). Two further lines in which Soliman denounces the belief 'That Princes Thrones are like enchanted fires,/Mighty to see, and easie to passe over' (II.ii. 55–6) are also absent in the quarto. Professor Bullough in his edition has suggested that either Greville or the publisher Butter, or indeed Buc himself, deleted the lines as potentially offensive.[18] It seems unlikely that Butter would have assumed the responsibility of censoring the copy for his edition and it is most improbable that Greville would have removed lines which, taken in the context of their argument and dramatic situation, are not as provocative as they may seem in isolation. In the first instance, Soliman is seeking to reassure Rossa that he values love above all his possessions and the omitted lines are merely a restatement of the commonplace that kings are mortal. The second passage actually serves to reject as fallacious the view that the sovereign's grasp of power is vulnerable: princes' thrones are only perceived as 'easie to passe over' when seen in 'false Glasses'. Nevertheless, out of context the lines may be interpreted as antagonistic to the Jacobean celebration of absolutism and divine right and Buc, acting with the literal-mindedness of the censor, may have taken exception to them.

Comparison of the two early versions of *Mustapha* reveals that the quarto contains an incomplete text. It ends abruptly with Rossa crazed by the death of her son Zanger, whose suicide follows his horrified discovery of his mother's schemes, and seeking solace in madness. In the manuscript, on the other hand, the narrative is further developed to show the public consequences of Soliman's despotism. The people rebel against the tyrant and the final scene depicts the dilemma of the good counsellor Achmat, as he grapples with the intractable problem of whether it is proper to support them in their uprising or whether he should leave the judgement to God: 'shame in obedience wronge in doeinge righte/ dutye a thornye path to infamye'.[19] Swayed by Rosten's argument that by supporting the rebellion he is endangering the state, Achmat finally decides on obedience, but not before he wills the people to 'teare downe the throanes of Tyrantes' and 'revive the olde equallitye of nature'. Geoffrey Bullough does not consider censorship as a possible cause of the abrupt ending of the quarto text, believing that the quarto was set up from a manuscript which lacked several leaves and whose last page was mutilated. In view of the subversive ideology expressed if not endorsed in the scene, however, it is extremely likely that Buc reacted against the last act, which admits considerable sympathy for the popular insurgency against Soliman. Although in his final speech Achmat acknowledges that 'thoughe princes swerve ... God onlye Judge. hee knowes what they deserve', the rest of the scene focuses on his exposition of conflicting attitudes towards resistance to a tyrant. He argues initially that duties to kings are conditional, that 'when they from god, then wee from them maye fall' and that the oppressed people are justified in rebellion when obedience 'nursethe Tyrannyc'. His conclusion that rebellion must nevertheless be eschewed for the greater good of the state is given perfunctory treatment and does not carry the moral and political impact of his earlier argument. Buc would surely have objected to such a balanced exposition of a dichotomy which, as the King's prohibition of Buchanan's works had demonstrated, should to James's mind have received an unequivocal answer.

Some time between the publication of *Mustapha* in 1609 and his death in 1628, Greville revised the play. The later version appears in manuscript and also in the folio edition of Greville's *Workes*, published in 1633. In the revised edition, political comment acquires greater prominence. Choruses are introduced which further expose Soliman's tyranny and reveal the corruption of religious and state institutions. The debate between a priest and Mustapha (III.v in the early manuscript and 1609 quarto; IV.iv in the revised text) has been enlarged in the later text and sharpened: Mustapha rejects the argument for rebellion, affirming of kings, 'Our Gods they are, their God remains above/To *thinke against annoynted Power is death*', whilst the Priest counters forcefully, 'To worship Tyrants is no worke of faith'. Greville appears to have revised this scene, so that the political issues, and in particular the argument about active or passive responses to the abuse of power, are made more explicit. The fact that the revised edition of *Mustapha* was published posthumously in 1633 may be significant.[20] Although there is arguably little change in the political perspective of the later text, its more pronounced condemnation of tyranny and its more extensive rehearsal of the debate would have made it vulnerable to the attentions of the Jacobean censor; the fact that the play had once received a licence may have facilitated the licensing of the later text along with previously unpublished works.[21]

The Second Maiden's Tragedy

In 1611 the King's Men brought an anonymous, untitled play, also concerned with a tyrannous regime, before Buc for stage licence. Buc devised a title for the play, *The Second Maiden's Tragedy*, probably because he discerned similarities with Beaumont and Fletcher's *The Maid's Tragedy*, and permitted its performance with the proviso, written on the final folio, that his reformations were observed: 'This second Maydens tragedy (for it hath no name inscribed) may with the reformations bee acted publikely. 31 October 1611. G. Buc'.[22] The manuscript handled by the censor is, in fact, the only version of the play; there is no evidence until 1653 of intended publication.[23] It is an invaluable document for what it tells us both about the concerns of mid-Jacobean theatre censorship and about the methods employed by the Master of the Revels.

From the licence inscription on the final leaf, it is clear that Buc used a slightly darker ink than that of either the scribe or later annotators. It is, of course, possible that he used a different ink when perusing the manuscript on another occasion. There is, in any event, irrefutable evidence of Buc's hand throughout the manuscript. He deleted oaths, took out provocative words and phrases and interlined substitute wording. To signify his disapproval of certain passages, he drew large cruciform marks in the margin. In certain instances these ink crosses are superimposed on larger pencil crosses, which has led T. H. Howard-Hill to the reasonable conjecture that Buc used pencil as an informal working tool, during his initial perusal of the manuscript, to mark passages which he thought needed further consideration.[24]

Some of the manuscript excisions and alterations are quite obviously in a different hand and in a different ink from that used by Buc. The dramatic content of those lines accompanied by such markings is, however, remarkably similar to the material to which Buc had objected, providing clear evidence that plays were censored in the playhouse, either in anticipation of the censor's objections or in response to his verbal instructions. Buc has, for example, struck out a number of oaths in the manuscript, but the specifically Catholic oath 'By th' mass' (IV.iii.92) uttered by the Tyrant, has been deleted by a different hand. The Master has also excised a number of critical remarks directed at the Court and prevailing sexual mores. When the Lady's father Helvetius, acting as pander for the Tyrant, attempts to force his daughter to prostitute herself, he tells her to 'talk like a courtier, girl, not like a fool!'. Buc has made a cross in the margin, deleted 'courtier' and interlined 'woman' (II.i. 76). At the point where the Lady, faced with the prospect of rape by the Tyrant, says that she 'scorns death/As much as great men fear it' (III. 160–1), Buc has drawn a pencil cross and interlined 'some' before 'great men'. 'Great' has been deleted by a different hand. Moments later, Govianus contrasts the nobility of the Lady's suicide with the lasciviousness of other women: 'Twas a strange trick of her. Few of your ladies/In ord'nary will believe it. They abhor it./ They'll sooner kill themselves with lust than for it' (II. 219–21). Marginal crosses in pencil and ink and the heavy scoring of the lines convey Buc's objections to the sweeping indictment. On internal evidence, other excisions and amendments would suggest Buc's intervention, but external evidence shows that this is not always the case. Coerced by Anselmus into the role of seducer to test his wife's fidelity, Votarius remarks 'I must put on/A courtier's face and do't; mine own will shame me' (I.ii. 164–5). 'Courtier's' has been deleted and replaced by 'brazen'; but the inter-lineation is not, apparently, by Buc.

The first passage in the play to be marked for omission contains a sustained attack on the ascendant courtiers of the Tyrant's reign. The deposed Govianus scornfully denounces one of the noblemen for his ignorance and ill-treatment of his tenants:

> I knew you one and twenty and a lord
> When your discretion sucked; is't come from nurse yet?
> You scorn to be a scholar; you were born better.
> You have good lands; that's the best grounds of learning.
> If you can construe but your doctor's bill,
> Pierce your wife's waiting women, and decline your tenants
> Till they're all beggars, with new fines and rackings,
> Y'are scholar good enough, for a lady's son
> That's born to living.   (I.i. 82–90)

A wavy line alongside the passage signifies its removal, although again the colour of the ink does not link the instruction directly with Buc. The nature of the attack, however, as with other passages marked for exclusion, implies that there existed a degree of collaboration between the censor and the playhouse bookkeeper.

Censorship, either by the Revels Office or in the playhouse, is most in evidence in the scenes depicting the Tyrant's projected sexual relationship with the Lady and Helvetius's attempts to persuade his daughter to acquiesce in the Tyrant's demands. At the point where Helvetius, referring to the King, requests the Lady's permission to choose her 'friend' (II.i. 72), Buc has pencilled a marginal cross and the substitute word 'servant' in the margin. Despite the King's despotic nature, Buc no doubt objected to the familiarity of the reference. In

Helvetius's next speech, as we have seen, Buc has altered 'courtier' to 'woman', thereby removing the general charge of corruption at court. Subsequent lines of the speech have been marked for removal, although the colour of the ink provides no certain evidence of Buc's hand. Here Helvetius almost incidentally exposes the Tyrant's lust with his allusion to the 'twenty feathered mistresses/That glister in the sun of princes' favours' and conveys his willingness to act as a pander: 'But I come/To bear thee gently to his bed of honours,/All force forgotten.' Most of Govianus's furious denunciation of Helvetius which follows has been similarly bracketed for omission. Moreover, one line of the long passage has been struck through. Here Govianus anticpates Helvetius's defence of panderism merely on account of its prevalence in high places: 'as you perhaps will say your betters do'. This deletion appears to have been made by Buc. Later in the act, the reformed Helvetius confronts the Tyrant and contemptuously unmasks his libidinousness and his corrupting influence upon his courtiers:

> You'll prefer all your old courtiers to good services!
> If your lust keep but hot some twenty winters,
> We are like to have a virtuous world of wives,
> Daughters, and sisters, besides kinswomen
> And cousin-germans removed up and down
> Where'er you please to have 'em!   (II.iii. 40–5)

In the same speech he proceeds to deplore the ignoble treatment he has suffered at the hands of the Tyrant: 'And must I take my pay all in base money?/I was a lord born! – set by all court grace/And am I thrust now to a squire's place?' (II. 50–2) These passages have been delineated in ink, possibly by Buc. Anne Lancashire has suggested that one specific reason for the cuts in this part of the plot would be that the offending comments could be applied to a scandal at James's Court involving the Earl of Northampton's niece, Frances Howard, Lady Essex, and James's favourite Robert Carr.[25] Northampton was rumoured to have acted as pander in the affair. The ready applicability of lines to particular events at Court may well have induced their censorship, but since the affair did not become public knowledge until 1612,[26] this view assumes that the play was further reformed some time after it received Buc's licence in 1611. It may not be necessary to assume any specific reference in the excised passages. The explicit focus on a sovereign's wantonness and on dissolute habits at court in a play to be performed by James's own company, possibly before the King, would surely have caused Buc some anxiety and produced prudent excisions.

That the play was intended for Court performance is suggested by further cuts evident in the manuscript. Anselmus's wife reprimands her servant, Leonella, for her impudence and her sexual indiscretions. The Wife's cynical comparison – 'There's many a good knight's daughter is in service/And cannot get such favour of her mistress/ But what she has by stealth; she and the chambermaid/ Are glad of one between 'em' (IV.i. 74–7) – is a slur on the gentry which has drawn another stroke of Buc's pen. He has deleted 'knight's' and inserted 'men's'. In a somewhat different context, the Tyrant makes a similar point about what he sees as the rampant promiscuity of women. He contrasts the Lady's sense of honour with the conduct of others of her sex: 'Nothing hurt thee but want of woman's counsel/Hadst thou but asked th' opinion of most ladies,/ Thou'dst never come to this' (IV.iii. 99–101). Buc has moderated the judgement by altering 'most ladies' to 'many ladies'. Distraught, Govianus addresses the dead Lady, who following her suicide should have been released from the world but through the Tyrant's preservation of her corpse is kept at court, 'in the worst cornor' (V.ii.56). Buc has again deleted the derogatory allusion to the court. When the Tyrant employs Govianus, disguised as a painter, to vitalise the features of the dead Lady, he asks him if he expects payment in money. Govianus replies that he would not accept credit at court by choice: 'I would not trust at court and I could choose' (V.ii.80). Buc has deleted heavily the words 'at court' and has substituted 'but few'. The impact of the censorship is obviously to dissipate the social satire. Buc's concern is to remove explicit slurs on the nobility and court mores, regardless of the dramatic context or the speaker. This is particularly so in the deletion of Anselmus's line 'all honest courtiers' (I.ii.15), a reference to the spirits of heaven. The allusion seems innocuous enough, but presumably Buc inferred a marked contrast with earthly counterparts and may have anticipated the sardonic nuances in the line's delivery. Again, at first sight, Buc's censorship of slighting remarks about women seems curious. Ribaldry at women's expense is common enough in Jacobean drama; but because the critiques of women's easy sexuality in *The Second Maiden's Tragedy* are directed specifically at court ladies, they have been censored.

One further issue engaged Buc's attention, that of the justifiable murder of a tyrant. Regicide as the ultimate response to oppression was clearly a subject fraught with danger and *The Second Maiden's Tragedy* is subversive in so far as it endorses the death of a tyrannous monarch as the inevitable outcome of despotic government. Excisions in the manuscript suggest that someone, although apparently not Buc, has deleted lines in which Govianus vows to kill the King for his idolatrous treatment of the dead Lady: 'Tyrant, I'll run thee on a dangerous shelf,/Though I be forced to fly this land myself.' (V.i. 201–2). Buc's hand itself is in evidence in censoring the climactic statement of regicide. Racked with pain, the Tyrant calls out 'Your King's poisoned' (V.ii. 167). Buc has registered his disapproval by drawing a marginal cross, deleting the exclamation and replacing it by 'I am poisoned' (Plate 2). Moments before his death, when the Tyrant recognises Govianus as his assassin, he desperately threatens to devise a death for him 'beyond the Frenchmen's tortures'(I. 140). Here the prospect of hideous retribution would have called to mind an actual event, namely the appalling death meted out to Ravaillac, murderer of Henri IV of France. Henri's assassination had left James fearful for his own life and, as has been noted, resulted in the prohibition of any publication relating to the event. Buc has thought it expedient to remove the contemporary connotation, scoring through 'Frenchmen's' and interlining 'extremest'. Significantly, there are cuts elsewhere in the final scene leading to the Tyrant's death and its immediate aftermath. The tyrannicide is accompanied by all the techniques of sensational theatre. Govianus, legitimate ruler and avenger, has contrived the death of the King in an elaborate, stage-Italianate tradition: disguised as a painter, he anoints the dead Lady's face with poison so that the Tyrant meets his death through his own necrophiliac lust. But there are obvious attempts to abridge the scene. Marginal rules and traces of an erased pencil cross can be seen alongside Govianus's final searing denunciation of the Tyrant as a 'sacrilegious villain' whose sins are so heinous that no partner will ever share his torments (V.ii. 126–37). Political considerations are likely to have determined the removal of the passage in which Helvetius joins with the courtiers in defecting from the Tyrant to Govianus (V.ii. 173–7) and the following one in which Govianus thanks his supporters for bringing about his elevation. Although Govianus is the legitimate ruler, the censor was presumably wary of permitting the portrayal of courtiers transferring their loyalties from the tyrant King to his murderer, who then basks in their favour. There are signs of an erased cross and lines are drawn against a passage in which the courtiers judge the Tyrant's death as the inevitable outcome of his despotic behaviour and rapacious life:

Mem. Long-injured lord,
    The tyranny of his actions grew so weighty,
    His life so vicious –
Hel. To which this is witness –
    Monster in sin! – this, the disquieted body
    Of my too resolute child in honour's war –

2 *The Second Maiden's Tragedy*: the scene of regicide.

Mem. That he became as hateful to our minds –
Hel. As death's unwelcome to a house of riches,
        Or what can more express it.
Gov. Well, he's gone,
        And all the kingdom's evils perish with him.   (V.ii. 187–94)

The faint traces of erased pencil marks suggest that Buc objected to this rationalisation of tyrannicide, although the ink colour of the lines around the passage seems to indicate that they were drawn by a different hand. Brackets enclosing Helvetius's speech imply that his judgment on the Tyrant and the part played by his daughter in his downfall were unwelcome to a censor anxious to root out any justification for regicide.

As Buc's rejection of such allusions to the Court and courtiers illustrates, the censor's perceptions are principally attuned to verbal excesses. There are, however, signs that Buc also attempted to diminish the impact of subversive and arguably sacrilegious visual imagery. One of the reasons for the cutting of so many lines at the end of the play may have been to limit the time span when the audience's attention is focused on the retribution meted out to the Tyrant. Rather than have members of the court cluster around his body and deliver their verdicts on him, the revised ending has a simple proclamation of Govianus's kingship and several lines in which Govianus praises the Lady. Moroeever, the play's visual images and language, from the point where the Lady's corpse is brought on to the stage, suggest a distorted form of Catholic ritual. Passages have been excised, apparently in order to tone down the blasphemous aspects of the stage business. One of the soldiers employed to remove the Lady's body from the tomb and – as the stage direction demands – forced by the Tyrant to 'make obeisance' to it, looks on in horror and realises his own damnation as the Tyrant kisses the Lady's hand: 'By this hand, mere idolatry. I make curtsy/To my damnation. I have learned so much,/ Though I could never know the meaning yet/Of all my Latin prayers, nor ne'er sought for't.' (V.ii. 20–3). The excision of these lines removes the specifically anti-Catholic reference to incomprehensible 'Latin prayers'; but the cut could well have been a result of orders to modify the action described in the stage direction. The omission of the soldier's aside from the text suggests that he may not, in performance, have bowed or genuflected to the Lady's corpse. Such a travesty of Catholic ritual would have been an offensive spectacle in a court where there were a number of crypto-Catholics and Catholic guests, and the marking for exclusion of the soldier's lines in ink which seems to be the censor's own suggests that Buc was not prepared to tolerate the full realisation of the scene. A similar reason may explain the omission of lines in Govianus's final pronouncement, in which he commands the Lady to be placed on a throne and crowned queen before she is returned to her tomb. The honours so bestowed raise a vestigial association with the Catholic teaching of the Assumption and Coronation of the Virgin.

The revisions in *The Second Maiden's Tragedy*, whether by Buc or under his influence, suggest a policy of countering the satirical thrust of plays which had dominated the stage during the early years of James's reign. The censor here seems to be taking a stand against the free scope assumed by some dramatists in their vivid and explicit lampoons of court life; only if they troubled to disguise their targets within a specific foreign setting as did Webster in his court plays, might they avert interference. The play is among the most subversive of the period in its challenge to the dominant Jacobean ideology of non-resistance to the anointed ruler. The removal from the text of lines which confront the issue and which prolong interest in its debate shows that Buc was uneasy about the liberties thus taken. The fact that the play was never published, and that apart from the names of two actors of the King's Men in a stage direction on folio 50r there is no external evidence for its performance, may well have been because its production and circulation were officially discouraged.

The Maid's Tragedy

Buc's name for *The Second Maiden's Tragedy* has remained with it and it seems evident that he discerned similarities in its dramatic content with Beaumont and Fletcher's *The Maid's Tragedy*, which he must have perused a short time before. The point of contact is the pivotal act of the killing of a king. In both plays regicide is the dramatic climax, both providing a powerful theatrical image and posing in sublimated form the moral and political implications of the act. Since Buc has substantially interfered with *The Second Maiden's Tragedy*, we might expect *The Maid's Tragedy* also to have suffered some censorship. There is of course no manuscript of the latter play. As the text has come down, it is a much more cautious and evasive play. Unlike the author of *The Second Maiden's Tragedy*, who invokes the legitimacy of resistance to a tyrant, Beaumont and Fletcher avoid any such endorsement. Despite such prudence, two discrepancies between the early printed editions do point to a degree of censorial interference. The play was first printed in 1619, nearly a decade after its composition; a second edition, advertised as 'newly perused, augmented, and inlarged', appeared in 1622. The second quarto, which appears to have been based on a different manuscript from that of the first edition, contains about eighty additional lines.[27] From the content and political connotations of a few lines present only in the 1622 edition, it may reasonably be inferred that they were not in fact additions, but lines which had originally been censored by Buc c. 1610, and finally restored. Absent in the first quarto is Amintor's murderous threat to the King that he will not be satisfied unless he sends the latter's 'limbs through all the land/ To show how nobly I have freed myself' (III.i. 230–1).[28] The first quarto conflates two lines, 'Unlesse I show how nobly I have freed my selfe', and omits the brutal expression of regicide. That Buc targeted and deleted references to regicide is irrefutable from another omission in the 1619 edition. When Evadne relays the news that she has murdered the King, expecting Amintor's approbation, Amintor's response is one of distraught horror: '. . . and to augment my woe/ You now are present, stained with a king's blood/ Violently shed' (V.iii. 145–7). This graphic image of Evadne as the King's assassin is lost in the first quarto, where Amintor's grief stems only from the death of Aspatia. As T. W. Craik notes, the contents of the following half-line and line – 'This keeps night here,/And throws an unknown wilderness about me' – make it clear that Amintor's allusion to the King's murder must always have been part of the text.[29]

Regicide appears as the focus of dramatic interest in *The Maid's Tragedy* as soon as Evadne informs Amintor that the King is her lover. Thomas Fuller's celebrated anecdote about the meeting of Beaumont and Fletcher in a tavern 'to contrive the rude draft of a tragedy' in which Fletcher 'undertook to kill the King therein' embellishes the playwrights' imaginative point of departure.[30] Yet censorship demanded that the theme be treated with considerable circumspection. Structurally, there is a degree of tension between the dynamic of the play, which demands the King's murder, and the foregrounding of the counter-argument. Any suggestion that the act might have a moral and political rectitude is corrected by commonplace expressions of the King's divinity. Buc was presumably satisfied that, at least superficially, the play did not appear to endorse regicide, however great the provocation. Only for an instant, when he accuses the King of tyranny, does Amintor contemplate retribution, but then he recoils in horror at the thought:

> As you are my King,
> I fall before you and present my sword

To cut my own flesh if it be your will.
                    ... But fall I first
Amongst my sorrows, ere my treacherous hand
Touch holy things!   (III.i. 240–50)

In some respects Beaumont and Fletcher side-step the issue: Melantius
has no such fear or scruple about the consequence of touching 'holy
things', yet his obsession with restoring the family honour takes the
form of tangential plotting against Calianax for control of the fort,
while at the same time he urges Evadne to do the deed which Amintor
refuses to countenance. In spite of her brief remonstrance that 'all the
gods forbid it', Evadne assumes the role of avenger, transforming the
act into one of expiation. The plot is so constructed that in effect the
King's murder becomes a crime of passion rather than, as in *The
Second Maiden's Tragedy*, a political act against a tyrannical and
dissolute ruler. The ambiguities which surround an act of requital
against an unjust king are present in Lysippus's final pronouncement:
'May this a fair example be to me/To rule with temper, for on lustful
kings/Unlooked-for sudden deaths from God are sent;/But curs'd is he
that is their instrument' (V.iii. 292–5).

The playwrights are evidently trying to have it both ways: their
warnings are directed both at kings who abuse their prerogative and
at those who would presume to purge the state of such rulers. The
sententious admonitions, the introduction at crucial moments of
counter-arguments against regicide and the use of a woman as agent
can be seen as strategies employed to bring within the parameters of
the permissible potentially subversive material which was otherwise
liable to be censored.

There is an added piquancy in both *The Second Maiden's Tragedy*
and *The Maid's Tragedy*, in that they exploit the most terrible of the
King's known phobias while simultaneously undermining Jacobean
ideology. As we have seen, the assassination of Henri IV of France in
1610 had intensified James's fear of sudden death[31] and it was no
doubt this event which particularly induced Buc's censorship of overt
references to regicide in *The Maid's Tragedy*, in spite of the playwrights' efforts to shroud their work in the veil of orthodoxy.

Despite the return to a more centralised system of censorship
under the Master of the Revels, it was still possible that individuals
might use influence to suppress productions of allegedly libellous
plays. In 1609 and again in 1613, the performances of two plays at
Whitefriars were suspended after personal complaints had been made
about their contents. Only a year after the theatre opened in 1608,
Jonson's *Epicoene* was temporarily disallowed and Robert Tailor's

The Hog Hath Lost His Pearl was also suppressed four years later. Neither of these minor instances appears to have generated much controversy or tells us a great deal about the concerns of Jacobean censorship; but they do illustrate the frustrations of working within a system which also accommodated the private interests of individual complainants.

Epicoene

Evidence that the early performances of *Epicoene* by the newly formed Children of the Queen's Revels aroused protests is fragmentary and has to be pieced together from a variety of sources, textual and documentary. There are several anomalies arising from the early publication of the play which imply that it encountered some official opposition. An entry in the Stationers' Register on 20 September 1610 attests to the fact that the play had been licensed both by Buc and by one of the wardens: the reference to Buc's licence in addition to that of the warden implies that Buc had already licensed the play for the stage. However, the play first appeared in print only in the 1616 folio. Some reason for the failure to publish earlier can be deduced from a study of the Prologue and dedicatory letter which accompany the folio text and in which Jonson implies that accusations of libel had been levelled against him. There are two Prologues to the play. The first, in which Jonson expresses his wish to please a wide audience, is conventional, although, as one editor of the play has noted, it contrasts with the earlier satirical comedies, where the playwright's insinuation is that his art can be appreciated only by a select few.[32] The levity of tone is not maintained in the second Prologue, which was apparently written after the early performances at Whitefriars. The motive for the later Prologue is indicated by the marginal note: 'Occasion'd by some persons impertinent exception'. The Prologue closes with a commonplace defence of satire: 'If any, yet, will, (with particular slight/ Of application) wrest what he doth write;/ And that he meant or him, or her, will say:/ They make a libell, which he made a play'. All that can so far be inferred is that Jonson considered it necessary to defend his dramatic intention and to deny that personal satire was part of it. The dedicatory letter to Francis Stuart corroborates what has been said in the Prologue: complaints have been lodged against the play. With typical indignation, he castigates his enemies for having spread malicious allegations about him:

Sir,

... And, when you shall consider, through the certaine hatred of some, how much a mans innocency may bee indanger'd by an un-certaine accusation; you will, I doubt not, so beginne to hate the iniquitie of such natures, as I shall love the contumely done me, whose end was so honorable, as to be wip'd off by your sentence.   Your unprofitable, but true lover,
                                                                        BEN. JONSON.

It is evident that Jonson had cause to be grateful to his influential patron; but the address is vague about the exact nature of the complaint. More information can be deduced from documentation elsewhere. On 10 February 1610, the Venetian ambassador in London wrote to the Doge and Senate about the King's cousin, Lady Arabella Stuart:

> She complains that in a certain comedy the play-wright introduced an allusion to her person and the part played by the Prince of Moldavia. The play was suppressed. Her Excellency is very ill pleased and shows a determination in this coming Parliament to secure the punishment of certain persons, we don't know who.[33]

The sensitive nature of the news is implied by its communication through the medium of cipher. The view that the play which had annoyed Lady Arabella Stuart was *Epicoene* has been generally accepted.[34] The offending lines have been taken to be those spoken by Amorous La Foole to Clerimont in a typically discursive passage on the talents of Epicoene's servant, John Daw. La Foole states that Daw can draw maps of contemporary persons and proceeds to name the subjects: 'Yes, sir, of NOMENTACK, when he was here, and of the Prince of *Moldavia*, and of his mistris, mistris EPICOENE' (V.i. 23–5). A reference to the Prince of Moldavia in the first decade of the seventeenth century was highly topical. Jonson's audience would doubtless have been familiar with the picaresque career of Stephano Janiculo, who claimed the principality of Moldavia.[35] His entitlement was tenuous; but he had succeeded in enlisting support from both Elizabeth and later James, much to the exasperation of the English ambassador in Turkey, who wrote that he wished his sovereign would not 'harken to these compterfitt and conicatching fellowes that give themselves names of princes'.[36] Janiculo's notoriety in England increased when he stated his intention of marrying Arabella Stuart, in order to assist him in making a claim to the English throne. Arabella Stuart was subsequently interrogated by the Privy Council.[37]

As the syntax and punctuation stand in the folio, Jonson's allusion to the Prince of Moldavia appears quite innocuous: La Foole is referring to Epicoene as Daw's mistress. As Herford and Simpson have observed, however, the remark could be and apparently was interpreted as a reference to a mistress of the Prince. In view of the publicised claims of Stephano Janiculo, Arabella Stuart presumably believed, or was led to believe, that some satirical allusion was intended at her expense in the role of Epicoene. The ambiguity of La Foole's statement is not dispelled by Clerimont's rejoinder and *double entendre*: 'Away! he has not found out her latitude, I hope'.

From the testimony of the Venetian ambassador it appears that, as a result of Lady Arabella Stuart's objection, performances of *Epicoene* were suppressed. It seems probably that her complaint also in some way hindered publication. As has been noted, the play was licensed for the press in 1610. Two years later, copyright was transferred from Browne and Busby to Burre, which would seem to suggest Burre's intention to print the play. But there is no extant text earlier than the folio. It has been conjectured that a quarto was printed in 1612.[38] In the dedicatory epistle, Jonson attests that 'there is not a line, or syllable in it changed from the simplicity of the first Copy', which could mean that this is the first text to represent his original composition and, by inference, that any earlier edition, if there was one, has been censored, but the line is ambiguous: Jonson could merely be stating that the 1616 text is the only one to be published and consists entirely of what he originally wrote. Perhaps more confidence can be placed in Herford and Simpson's conjecture that if the play had been printed in 1612, it is unlikely that a reference to the Prince of Moldavia would have been included. If the play was not printed in 1612, this may have been because Arabella Stuart was once more the focus of interest. Her assumption of an epicene identity in order to escape from her guardians and marry William Seymour had brought about her disgrace in the eyes of the King. It may well have been considered inexpedient to allow the circulation of a play which in the minds of the public still held associations with her cause. By 1616, however, Arabella Stuart was dead and Jonson could publish with impunity.

The composition and performance of *Epicoene* coincided with one of the most creative and active periods of Jonson's career: he had been writing plays for the adult and children's companies and composing masques for the Court of King James. Nevertheless, his royal patronage and the prestige gained from his Court service clearly did not carry any form of immunity from official interference with his plays. Allegations of dramatic satire by its influential victims continued to be a hazard to the professional dramatist, even when a work was performed before a more popular audience in a theatrical venue distant from the Court.

The Hog Hath Lost His Pearl

By the time of James's accession, the local authorities no longer exercised much control over dramatic production. The suppression of Robert Tailor's *The Hog Hath Lost His Pearl* in January 1613, however, following an irregular performance by London apprentices, illustrates a readiness to use such powers as they retained. The affair is documented and is of interest for the alertness to topical satire which it demonstrates on the part of the City governors. The details are recorded in a letter from Henry Wotton to Edmund Bacon. Wotton reports that the apprentices had secretly learnt their parts 'without book' and had staged the play at the private Whitefriars theatre before a specially invited audience. The performance was abruptly ended:

> towards the end of the Play the Sheriffs (who by chance had heard of it) came in (as they say) and carried some six or seven of them to perform the last act at *Bridewel*; the rest are fled. Now it is strange to hear how sharp-witted the City is, for they will needs have *Sir John Swinerton*, the Lord Maior, be meant by the Hog, and the late Lord Treasurer, by the Pearl.[39]

From Wotton's circumspect comments, it is difficult to say exactly what had brought about the sheriffs' intervention: the illicit nature of the performance or a suspicion of satire against the mayor, John Swinnerton. Swinnerton, a client of Northampton, had recently attempted to acquire the lucrative patents for the farming of wines, an enterprise which is undoubtedly reflected in the gulling of the usurious Hog. In spite of his attempts to prove that the current farmers of the customs were defrauding the King, Swinnerton, opposed by Salisbury, was unable to secure the desired imposts.[40] In the play, Hog is duped by counterfeit spirits into believing that his gold will be metamorphosed into pearl. The 'spirits', personated by Haddit the young gallant and his accomplices, can be seen as a punning allusion to Swinnerton's rapacious designs on the wine patents. Hog's obsession with the jewel would also have evoked thoughts of Swinnerton: he had presented a chain of oriental pearl to James's daughter, Elizabeth, Queen of Bohemia, a week before the apprentices had performed the play. Since the satire was so elusive, it would have been a self-defeating ordinance to have suppressed the play on that score; but the irregular nature of the performance would have served as a pretext for the ban.

Like a number of other Jacobean plays which encountered some kind of censorship for dealing with contemporary issues, *The Hog Hath Lost His Pearl* was demanded in print soon after it was first performed. Indeed, the Prologue boasts that despite all obstacles the drama has received Buc's approbation: 'Our long time rumor'd

Hogge, so often crost/By unexpected accidents, ... Hath a Knights licence, and may raunge at pleasure.' With a certain audacity, the Prologue draws attention to the play's satirical purpose by affecting to deride any such intention:

> And thus much let me tell you, that our Swyne
> Is not as divers Crittickes did define,
> Grunting at State affaires, or invecting
> Much, at our Citty vices; no, nor detecting
> The pride, or fraude, in it,

Presumably Swinnerton, despite his connection with Northampton, was not an important enough figure to be able to sabotage the play's publication. It is, however, unlikely that the text of the play, as performed in 1613, is faithfully transmitted in the printed text of the following year. The circumstances of the original performance, acted without recourse to a prompt book, suggest that the actors would have made their own interpolations and that the satire, drawing on the resources of the stage, was more personalised.

The Hog Hath Lost His Pearl is not a play of great dramatic value, but in its composition and structure it does show how playwrights endeavoured to make their plays topical and yet evade censorship. Tailor mischievously draws attention to the irrelevance of a play's title when Haddit tells a player that he is writing a play called *Who buyes my fowre ropes of hard Onions*, 'by which fowre ropes is meant fowre several kind of livers, by the onions hangers on' and promises to enlighten the actor further about his 'hidden and obscure a mistery'. In the absurdity of his plot, Tailor is similarly oblique. The play's satiric aims are diffused by the inclusion of a conventional romantic plot built upon Albert, who deceives Maria by pretending to be his friend Carracus and gains access to her bedroom. Albert then imposes penitential exile in the forest upon himself. He eventually meets with Carracus and Maria, now married, and the three are reconciled. It is, of course, possible that the romantic plot was introduced, or expanded, just prior to publication and was not part of the production at Whitefriars. It certainly has no bearing on the remainder of the plot, which revolves around the trickery of Hog, and with its exaggerated romanticism it may well have been developed to camouflage more personalised matters.

Foreign affairs on the Jacobean stage

James's policy of European rapprochement meant, as we have seen, that the nationalistic, sometimes xenophobic, perspective through which Elizabethan dramatists viewed foreign affairs did not find the same expression in Jacobean drama. Safeguarding diplomatic relations with foreign powers was self-evidently one of the principal concerns of censorship during the final decade of James's reign. Several plays incurred censorship – to different degrees – because in dramatising foreign matters, whether explicitly or analogically, they were perceived as jeopardising James's amicable relations with his European allies. The change in attitude of the censor can be discerned in a minor textual variant between the two early editions of *Much Ado About Nothing*. In the quarto of 1600, Don Pedro jokes about German and Spanish dress; Benedict, if he is in love, might affect to dress 'in the shape of two countries at once, as a German from the waist downward, all slops, and a Spaniard from the hip upward, no doublet' (III.ii. 30–3). The derogatory comment about German and Spanish dress has been omitted from the folio text. R. A. Foakes regards the cause of the omission as political and suggests that the words may have been removed when the play was revived in 1612 for the marriage of Princess Elizabeth and Frederick of the Palatinate.[41] The lines may originally have been excised for a specific performance; but, since they are absent in the folio, they were in all probability not restored in ensuing Jacobean performances of the play. Either the Master of the Revels or the stage reviser, for the mere loss of a laugh, thought it expedient to avoid a remark which might displease the King or foreign guests. This is a comparatively trivial instance of Jacobean censorship of material containing a foreign element. In other cases, however, the interference of the Master of the Revels threatened the dramatic integrity of the text or frustrated performance altogether.

Marquis d'Ancre

Nothing is known about the auspices of the authorship of the now lost play *Marquis d'Ancre*; but documentary evidence that it was banned in 1617 further illustrates how foreign affairs were circumscribed on the Jacobean stage. Presumably the play described the career and recent murder of the French noble, who had been a favourite of the Queen Dowager but disliked by her son. Although the play itself is lost, a contemporary record mentions the initial reaction which it had provoked. In the Privy Council minutes of 22 June 1617 is an injunction to Buc ordering him to suppress a play currently in production:

> Wee are informed that there are certayne players or comedians wee knowe not of what company that goe about to play some enterlude concerning the late Marquesse d'Ancre, which for many respectes wee thincke not fitt to be

suffered. Wee doe therefore require you upon your perill to take order that the same be not represented or played in any place about this citty or ellswhere, where you have authoritie. And hereof have you a speciall care.[42]

The threat to Buc is an indication that the Master of the Revels was himself at risk of sanctions if he failed to censor plays in accordance with attitudes expressed in Council. The 'many respectes' which persuaded the members of the Privy Council that the play was 'not fitt to be suffered' can only be surmised. D'Ancre had been slain in April 1617 and the play must have been composed and performed almost immediately thereafter. Louis XIII was implicated in the death; he was reported as being present and remarking that now he was King of France.[43] Such an event might be good theatre; but the Privy Council perhaps anticipated – or even received – French complaints and thus considered it judicious to prohibit a play which exposed machinations at the French court. Moreover, the theme itself would surely have caused alarm. The Marquis d'Ancre was representative of a certain type of tragic hero who set himself up in opposition to the Crown. Here was a subject which aroused considerable disquiet, as has been illustrated in official reactions to *Sejanus, Philotas,* and *The Conspiracy* and *Tragedy of Charles Duke of Byron.*

The Tragedy of Sir John van Olden Barnavelt

The reaction of the Privy Council against the *Marquis D'Ancre* may well have persuaded Buc to be particularly vigilant in his perusal of any further plays which dealt with near contemporary foreign affairs. Indeed, following the short run of *Marquis D'Ancre*, no new play on a foreign political theme was staged until the King's Men produced Massinger and Fletcher's dramatisation of the recent civil conflicts in the Netherlands, *The Tragedy of Sir John van Olden Barnavelt*, in 1619. Evidence of the censor's response is here extensive, since the manuscript which contains Buc's deletions, annotations and comments has survived.[44] There are, moreover, contemporary allusions to further difficulties which the players encountered from the church authorities once the play had been licensed by Buc.

Massinger and Fletcher present the much publicised struggle between Johan van Oldenbarnevelt, Advocate of Holland, and the Stadtholder Maurice of Nassau, Prince of Orange, for supremacy in the United Province. In the play, Barnavelt is portrayed acting to consolidate the support of the States, the Army and the Arminian sect within the church in opposition to Orange. Against this background, however, the dramatic focus is concentrated on the defeat of Barnavelt's party

and his subsequent imprisonment, trial and execution. John Chamberlain, writing to Dudley Carleton, Ambassador in the Netherlands,
reported that the fate of Oldenbarnevelt was the subject of considerable debate in England and that he was considered to be a victim of
factiousness and intrigue. Moreover, it was felt that his downfall and
sentence betrayed an injustice which ill became a new republic:

> divers of goode judgement thincke he had hard measure, considering that
> no cleere matter of conspiracie with the ennemies of the state appeares, or
> can be proved, so that yt seemes to be meere matter of faction and
> opposition rather than infidelitie or treacherie, which though perhaps in
> England might be found treasonable or within that compasse, yet in a new
> upstart commonwelth that hath so long contended and stands so much
> upon libertie, they were not to proceed with such rigour against a man of
> his yeares and service, specially when the sparing of the rest makes manifest
> shew that they shot only at him. And though he were nothing gracious here,
> yet now he is gon, his protestations both by word and writing, together
> with his matter of dieng so constantly and religiouslie move much com-
> miseration and breed these discourses. But there is hope that neither they
> nor wee shall have any misse of him, but rather that we shall grow neerer
> and lincke together the surer.[45]

That Chamberlain should write about Oldenbarnevelt's fate in such
an ambivalent fashion, suggesting sympathy for him while apparently
endorsing the official line that neither the British nor the Dutch should
'have any misse of him', points to the sensitiveness of the matter.
Massinger and Fletcher respond with similar circumspection: Barnavelt
in his opposition to Orange is seen as a schemer and political
opportunist, yet he evokes sympathy during his unjust trial and
through his demeanour on the scaffold before his execution. Buc's
heavy censorship of the manuscript, particularly during the trial scene,
indicates his disapproval of a play which appeared so soon after the
events it described and which, by sustaining interest in Oldenbarnevelt's
defeat and projecting a tragic end to his career, conflicted with the
official counsels.

The hands which may be seen in the manuscript have been identified
as those of the scribe, Ralph Crane, Buc, and an unknown bookkeeper
or stage manager of the King's Men.[46] Crane's deletion of lines and his
reworking of passages censored by Buc provide further evidence of a
collaboration between the Revels Office and the playhouse also
manifested in the manuscript of *The Second Maiden's Tragedy*.
Whether or not Crane was responsible for the actual composition of
the revised lines which he has written in the manuscript is uncertain,
although their poor quality suggests that he, rather than the playwrights, devised them.

Buc's presence is felt more heavily in the manuscript of *Barnavelt* than in that of *The Second Maiden's Tragedy*. The same square crosses, in pencil and in ink, are to be found in both. Faint pencil lines in the margins of several pages may also point to Buc's initial disapproval of certain passages during a preliminary reading. He has deleted words, phrases and lines, sometimes substituting blander alternatives or leaving Crane to render the line politically inoffensive. Most tellingly, Buc has made two marginal comments which convey the rationale behind much of the censorship of the play, and indeed other cases of Jacobean censorship. Around a passage in which guards refuse the Prince of Orange entry into the council chamber, Buc has drawn rules and crosses. His marginal, initialled remarks indicate the range of his displeasure: 'I like not this: neither do I think that the prince was thus disgracefully used. besides he is to much presented. [her]. G.B.' (Plate 3). The Master was evidently disturbed at such a display of physical opposition to the Prince, an offence against the principle of sovereignty, and in any event felt uneasy that a living ruler should figure so prominently on the stage. His deletion of his own word 'here' is significant, suggesting that on reconsidering his comment, he maintained his objection to Orange's representation not only in this particular scene but throughout the play. Buc's other explicit prohibition relates to a passage in which Barnavelt draws an elequent historical parallel between the Netherlands under Orange and the Rome of Octavius Caesar:

> *Octavius*, when he did affect the Empire,
> and strove to tread upon the neck of *Rome*,
> and all hir auncient freedomes, tooke that course
> that now is practisd on you: for the *Cato's*
> and all free speritts slaine, or els proscribd
> that durst have stird against him, he then sceasd
> the absolute rule of all: you can apply this:
> and here I prophecie, I that have lyvd
> and dye a free man, shall, when I am ashes
> be sensible of your groanes, and wishes for me;
> and when too late you see this Government
> changd to a Monarchie, you'll howle in vaine
> and wish you have a *Barnavelt* againe.   (ll. 2434–46)

Buc was intent on removing the analogy between the United Provinces and the Roman Republic transmuted into the Roman Empire: from the speech he has deleted 'tooke that course that now is practisd on you' and 'you can apply this', writing by the former excision 'cutt off his opposites' (Plate 4). He has also disapproved the disparaging reference to monarchical government which Barnavelt claims will in time elicit despair from his accusers: 'to a Monarchie' has been deleted by Buc and replaced by the anodyne 'another forme'. Buc's interference here betrays the censor's habitual distrust of historical parallels drawn by playwrights to comment by comparison or default on the present. Buc has altered the meaning of the passage so that the ideological critique of monarchy – more apposite to the condition of England than to the United Provinces – is lost.

Buc's censorship of the play exhibits throughout a concern that the dignity of the Prince of Orange should not be violated and that he should not be represented, either personally or as a ruler, in an unfavourable light. In the opening scene in which the enraged Barnavelt and his supporters discuss Orange's ascendancy, Buc has censored Barnavelt's more denigratory opinions. A cross has been drawn against a line in which Orange's courage is in question, with the insinuation that his personal authority, having 'increased with all the Armyes', is dependent solely on force of arms. There is a further cross by another line in which Barnavelt claims that Orange is 'usurper of what's mine'. In the next scene, Buc has altered Barnavelt's reference to 'this prowd Prince of Orange' to read simply 'this Prince'. Later, Barnavelt and his faction try to persuade the English mercenaries to abandon the garrisons and to enlist instead in their service. Buc has placed two marginal crosses against lines spoken by Barnavelt in which he suggests to the soldiers that Orange is disloyal to the States (fol. 7v). Angered by his failure to persuade them to desert the Prince's cause, Barnavelt wildly denounces the Stadtholder's ambitions, arguing that it is preferable to be subjects of Spain than slaves to him:

> slaves to the pride of one we have raisd up
> unto this g[ian]t height, the *Spanish* y[oa]k
> is soft, and easie, if compared with what
> we suffer from this popular S[na]ke, that hath
> stolne like a cunning theif the Armyes harts
> to serve his owne ambitious ends   (ll. 724–9)

Buc has drawn his familiar crosses in the margin and ruled through the lines, so making some letters illegible. Above the deleted lines, Crane has substituted new ones which omit Barnavelt's references to the Prince as a 'popular snake' and 'cunning theif' and his allusion to the former subjugation of the States to Spain, so that he charges only the people as 'Slaves so contemptible: as no worthie *Prince*/that would have men, not sluggish Beaste his Servants/would ere vouchsafe the owning, Now my Frends'. Crane's addition makes little dramatic sense since, with the removal of references to Orange and the people's allegiance to him, there is no reason for Barnavelt's invective. Along

stayed the matter was not so forward yet
the least may patience to winn owen betray me
the shee find time and eyes rayse: now Clowde
1.Gu.   like my Lords the States set yet

Or.   an howre agoe Sir

1.Gu.   we know ye Gentlemen, yt have made not tardy
open the dre

1.Gu.   yt befores yr Guard to pardon md

Or.   dost thou know wt I am?

1.Gu.   yes Sir, and how vp

Or.   wey dost thou keep the dre fast then?

Henry
wise   thou ffellow
thou sawry feddo: and yt that stand by gaping
is the Prince of no more valew, no more respect

2.Gu.   then like a Player?
we before yr Excellencies
to pardon vs: our duties are not wanting,
yor dare we entertaine a request to passe ye

Or.   we are plac'd here on command
to here me out
haue I lost my place in Councell? are my seruices
growne to so poore regard, my worke, so baancerupt,
or am I stayned wth disgrace actions
that I am thus shutt from ranchies businesse?

1.Gu.   we plac'd by ye
the body of the Councell,
and we before yr Guard make it not a synn

Or.   then glue the shirt continued to the ye passage
Will.   I was friendly dn, and let my noble Masters
Henry   deny yr Coland

Or.   make good the dre against yt?

Coll.   tis is much fferible, much troubleraable
now it begin to fell the dubts, I feard shee
so far to dare wowe ys tis too monstrous,
and yt begett ye ye Conir worke yr Crowd,
the name of Coollr it ye suffer the
suffer hom then, then frinds, then you wont
those neodds of men made worlds by yr founders
ye daylie threatts

1.Cap.   it must not be endured ye

2.Cap.   the wrong extends to vs, we feele it seuerally
the sweet familtie hes made vs strud the
and vs, (and all the world that stood togir ws
and sink them downe in hearte maistes? frinds,
allmost now gods twi, hundred yt now faileos

Coll.   wele bred yor way
let's see then only dare stop ys

Guard   not we, we am sure

Coll.   let's see my shirt dried vp

Or.   ye poland, and esyert of Counnell
ye yt continued hs
the right putts ferward hast to his wild action
hes lost my love, and is bcom enuie Enduw)
my mortall enemie put vs yr wadexons
yr draw'n em against orders, duty, skall

Guard at dore

I like not this: neye
do I think this was
thus disgracefully ysd
... is to
presented ... C.H.

with Barnavelt's inapposite commendation of Orange as a 'worthie *Prince*', these lines were clearly composed with the aim of appeasing the censor.

The trial scene (IV.v), in which Barnavelt attracts considerable sympathy, has been subjected to quite intensive censorship which distorts the playwrights' original design.[47] Altogether, Buc's annotations throughout this scene indicate that he was concerned about the way Barnavelt was shown as upstaging the Prince of Orange. Traces of a faint pencil rule from the point where Barnavelt's alleged crimes are pronounced and alongside his spirited defence suggest that Buc disliked Barnavelt's affirmative stance before his accusers. A marginal

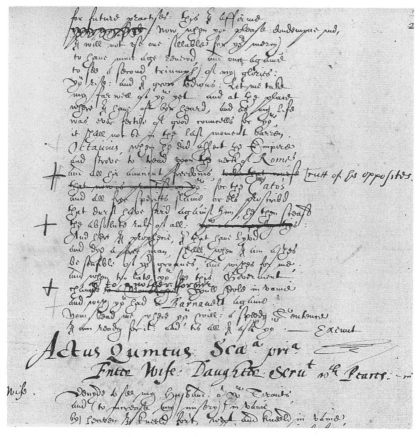

Sir John van Olden Barnavelt: (*facing* 3) the treatment of the Prince of Orange; (*above* 4) censorship of the parallel between the United Provinces and the Roman Republic.

cross by the line in which Barnavelt is given his formal title, 'late Advocate of *Holland*, and *West Frizeland* and *Councellor of State*' (l. 2194) conveys Buc's discontent at attention being thus drawn to Barnavelt's eminent status.[48] It is significant that Crane has scribbled over a speech in which Barnavelt boasts of his 'glorious Actions' and proudly defends his acts of disobedience to the Prince's authority because 'it lookd not towards the generall good' (ll. 2287–311). It seems probable that Crane was here acting under instructions from Buc to remove such a celebration of Barnavelt's successful military career. Crane's deletion of part of Barnavelt's defence, whilst Orange's counter-attack remains, discloses an attempt to load the scales against the former. Buc has further cancelled an exchange between the two during which Barnavelt, in accusing Orange of an ignoble remoteness from the conflict in the Battle of Flanders, undermines the Prince's military reputation (Plate 5):

> *Or.* I was in person there –
> *Bar.* and yet you clayme
>   as little in the victory as I,
>   that then was absent: I was in *Ostend*,
>   you with three troopes of horsse were on the hill
>   and saw the battaile fought, but strook no stroak in't.
>   I must confes 'tis fitt a Generall
>   should looke out for his safetie: and you therefore
>   are to be held ex[cu]sd: But that great day,
>   that memorable day in which our honors,
>   our lives, and liberties were at the stake,
>   [we owe to] the dir[e]ct[i]on and the vallor
>   of those unparalelld paire of warlike Brothers
>   the ever-noble *Veres*: and who takes from them
>   usurpe on what is theirs.   (ll. 2347–61)

In the shorter passage composed to replace Buc's excision and written in the right-hand margin, Barnavelt states limply:

> *Bar.* I was not there,
>   but what in Councell freely I deliverd
>   before 'twas sought, your Grace must graunt was honest:
>   You were in person there and pro[vi]dent
>   nor tax I that: 'tis fit a Generall.   (fol. 23r)

Crane's substitution, like that on folio 7v, distorts the dramatic purpose; the lines themselves are effectively meaningless. It seems that Crane thought better of his attempt at revision, since he has scribbled the passage out, with the same looped strokes and apparently at the same time as his excision of the remainder of the exchange on folio 23.
  A determination to remove references to the international arena and

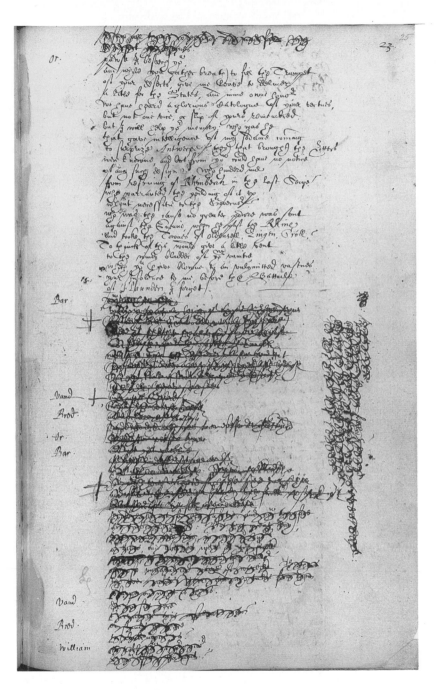

5 *Sir John van Olden Barnavelt:* the trial of Barnavelt.

possibly also to the French partisanship of Barnavelt's cause, can be inferred from further instances of Buc's censorship in the final scenes of the play. During the trial scene, Barnavelt recalls his role as ambassador to England and France. Buc has drawn a marginal flourish by Barnavelt's assertion that he has spoken 'with mightie Kings; twyce with that virgin Queene/our Patronesse of happie memory' (ll. 2262–3). Later, French ambassadors arrive to mitigate on Barnavelt's behalf. There is a faint pencil line in the margin alongside a passage in which Beisises praises Barnavelt and pleads for leniency, while Orange refuses to be swayed by Louis XIII's intervention (fol. 25v). Buc has expressed his disapproval by marking with crosses specific lines which refer to the French King and in which the ambassador remonstrates that the King 'must thinck himself/slighted in his requests' (ll. 2629–30) if the States refuse to be influenced by his counsel. Presumably the Master's objection to such references to Barnavelt's formidable political allies lay in the prospect of their enhancing his international reputation and inviting a more sympathetic audience response to his cause.

The struggle for political domination in the Netherlands was viewed with interest in England because it also represented a clash of doctrinal interests which impinged on the beliefs and practices of the Anglican Church. Oldenbarnevelt's defeat and execution in 1619 signified the triumph of high Calvinism and the decline in influence of the more liberal doctrines of the Arminians. In the English Church and Court, sympathies were sharply divided between the rival factions. In matters of doctrine, James was increasingly attracted by the Arminians' lack of fanaticism, whilst remaining suspicious of the ideology of a sect which condoned opposition to the Prince of Orange. At the time of the composition and censorship of *Barnavelt*, the Puritans were in the ascendancy, among them Abbot, the Archbishop of Canterbury, who was encouraging James to endorse anti-Arminian policies at the 1619 Synod of Dort.[49] In *Barnavelt*, Massinger and Fletcher only touch on the confrontation of the religious leagues, presenting the Advocate's espousal of Arminianism purely as a form of political opportunism to extend his influence in the States. There are signs, however, of alterations in the manuscript which strengthen anti-Arminian sentiments. The first instance occurs when Leidenberch assures Barnavelt that he has religious backing for his campaign: 'the *Preachers* play their parts too,/and thunder in their Pulpitts, hell and dampnation/ to such as hold against us' (ll. 587–9). Crane has here deleted 'Preachers', with its connotation of Puritanism, and overwritten 'Arminians' and has replaced 'Pulpitts' by 'meetings'.[50] In a later scene (II.ii), aspersions cast on preachers by one of a group of Dutchwomen have been modified by the alteration to 'teachers'. The verbal shifts are slight, but not insignificant. Crane, acting either on his own initiative or under direction from Buc, wanted to differentiate between Arminian and Calvinist clergy and to ensure that it was the Arminians who suffered the opprobrium.

The religious controversy dramatised, albeit peripherally, in *Barnavelt* may have incurred the interference of the Bishop of London. When rehearsals for the play were well under way, Thomas Locke conveyed the news to Carleton that the Bishop of London had intervened to prevent its performance. A fortnight later, however, Locke was able to report that the players had found 'the meanes to goe through with the play of Barnavelt' and that it had attracted large audiences. There are, as we have seen, precedents for such interference with the production of a play once it had been licensed by the Master of the Revels; but, unlike other cases of post-censorship intervention, the reasons here can only be conjectured. The Bishop of London, John King, was a moderate who was opposed to high Calvinism, a preacher at Court and friend of Launcelot Andrewes,[51] and would have reacted against an account of events which showed the Arminian sect in a treacherous light. He may, moreover, have disliked the whole notion of dramatising the defeat of Oldenbarnevelt, which had helped to bring about the Calvinist triumph in the United Provinces and which had further polarised religious allegiances in England.

Locke's account of the difficulties encountered by the King's Men prior to the production of *Barnavelt* includes a notable comment about the way in which contemporaries perceived the dramatic version of events:

> yet some say that (according to the proverbes) the devill is not so bad as he is painted, and that Barnavelt should perswade Ledenberg to make away himself (when he came to see him after he was prisoner) to prevent the discov'i of the plott, and to tell him that when they were both dead (as though he meant to do the like) they might sift it out of their ashes, was thought to be a point strayned. When Barnevelt understood of Ledenbergs death he comforted himself which before he refused to do, but when he perceaveth himself to be arested then he hath no remedie, but with all speedes biddeth his wife send to the French Ambassador.[52]

From Locke's remarks, it is clear that the play was received by some with the feeling that it had distorted recent history, particularly to the detriment of its tragic protagonist. In delineating the character and fate of Oldenbarnevelt, Massinger and Fletcher were in fact governed by their sources.[53] But the bias against the Advocate is weighted by

Buc's censorship of lines which are critical of Orange and of others which disclose Barnavelt's qualities as a soldier and statesman. Whether those well versed in foreign affairs who witnessed the performance of *Barnavelt*, and who in Locke's words judged that 'the devill is not so bad as he is painted', thought that the playwrights had wilfully chosen to present a partial, one-sided view of their noble subject, or whether they were conscious that the stage portrayal of recent international affairs was to some extent dictated by the censor, is a tantalising question.

Massinger and Fletcher should have anticipated that James's distaste for Dutch republicanism and his support for the Prince of Orange against Oldenbarnevelt would have elicited Buc's interference with their tragedy. They may have taken the risk knowing that, whilst relations with the Netherlands were strategically significant, they were not predominant on the foreign agenda. Here Anglo-Spanish relations prevailed.[54] When it comes to the dramatisation of matters relating to Spain, playwrights were faced with the dilemma of catering for popular anti-Spanish sentiment while thereby provoking interference from a censor wishing to protect James's policy of rapprochement with Spain. Only Beaumont, Fletcher and Middleton appear to have been prepared to take the gamble of playing to their audiences' inveterate hispanophobia.

Philaster

In Beaumont and Fletcher's *Philaster*, the King of Sicily and Calabria is shown initially in his quest for an alliance with Spain through the marriage of his daughter, Arethusa, to the Spanish Prince, Pharamond. Dion, a gentleman of the Sicilian court, draws attention in the first scene to the King's foreign policy: 'the King labours to bring in the power of a foreign nation, to awe his own with'. The dramatic situation does, of course, immediately suggest James's long cherished ideal of the marriage of the Infanta with Prince Henry and, after Henry's death in 1612, with Prince Charles. The analogy is enhanced by the fact that the occupant of the throne of Sicily, is, like James, ruler of two kingdoms, although the former owes his crown to his father's act of usurpation.

The play is a good example of a text which acquired greater political significance after its composition. Some of the dramatic material could be said to mirror, if unobtrusively, the political situation immediate to the play's composition c.1609. A Spanish match for Prince Henry had been broached early in the reign and, although not immediately followed up, continued to be favoured by James as an entrée into Catholic Europe. But by the next decade, when the play came to be published, negotiations for the marriage of Charles with the Infanta were well under way and *Philaster* had undoubtedly become more overtly topical.

It was this topicality which at some time between composition and the publication of the first quarto in 1620 seems to have drawn the interference of the censor. Two years after the publication of the first quarto, a second quarto was published by the same publisher, Thomas Walkley. Walkley took the unusual step for a publisher of including his own address to the reader, in which he claims that the first impression of the play had 'dangerous and gaping wounds' which he affirms were caused neither by himself nor by the printer. The metaphor of bodily injury has resonances of Chapman's reference to 'dismemberd poems' in the dedication to the *Byron* plays. In the case of *Philaster*, there is no external evidence of censorship and Walkley's extended metaphor side-steps any explanation for the corrupt nature of the 1620 text. There is, however, a hint that Walkley had been encouraged to make good the text by individuals who had taken a special interest in the play: 'I, knowing and finding by experience how many well-wishers they have abroad, have adventured to bind up their wounds, and to enable them to visit upon better terms such friends of theirs as were pleased to take knowledge of them, so maimed and deformed as they at the first were.' Such a cryptically elaborate justification for the second quarto seems designed to arouse interest in the play rather than merely to offer an apology for the publication of an earlier, corrupt text.

Variations between the two editions are suggestive of censorship: The two texts depart most markedly from each other at the beginning and the end of the play, specifically in Act I. scene i, lines 1–115 and Act V. scene iv.[55] In the first scene as it appears in the first quarto, references to the Spanish alliance are more guarded and less readily applicable to the projected Stuart union with the Spanish branch of the Hapsburgs. The second quarto opens with three Sicilian gentlemen gathering expectantly in response to a royal summons: Dion comments, 'Sir it is plain about the Spanish Prince that's come to marry our Kingdom's heir and be our sovereign.' The opening discourse of the first quarto is more casual in tone and Lyon's equivalent remark to Clerimon – 'but come and speake your thoughts of the intended marriage with the Spanish Prince'– carries less sense of a power-broking alliance. Dion's reference to the King seeking to bring in the power of a foreign nation to subdue his own subjects becomes in the first quarto less explicit: '[the King] makes this contract to make his faction strong'. The meaning remains essentially the same, but the words fail to convey the objective of forging international cohesion.

The two texts again diverge during the final scenes of the play, which depict Pharamond at the mercy of the citizens, the quelling of the riot by Philaster, the revelation that Bellario is the lost daughter of Lord Dion and the reconciliation of the King with Philaster and Arethusa. A comparison of the mob scene in the first quarto with that of the second quarto reveals, as Peter Davison has noted, that part of the brutal baiting of Pharamond by the mob is omitted from the former.[56] In the second quarto, in lines absent in the first quarto, the citizens try to outdo each other in devising horrible torments for the Prince:

> *1 Cit.* I'll have a leg, that's certain.
> *2 Cit.* I'll have an arm.
> *3 Cit.* I'll have his nose and at mine own charge build a college and clap't upon the gate.
> *4 Cit.* I'll have his little gut to string a kit with, for certainly a royal gut will sound like silver.
> *Pha.* Would they were in thy belly and I past my pain once.
> *5 Cit.* Good Captain, let me have his liver to feed ferrets.
>
> (V. iv. 58–65)

In the citizens' manhandling of Pharamond, Beaumont and Fletcher are clearly pandering to popular xenophobia. The first quarto is significantly different in that it is the soldiers, and not the citizens, who hurl abuse at Pharamond. Pharamond's Spanishness is again more pronounced in the second quarto's version of the final scene, where Philaster addresses him as 'Prince of Spain' and grants him leave 'to make an honourable voyage home'.

There are other notable discrepancies between the two texts. In the first quarto, the King is described in the cast list as King only of Cycele and on two occasions references to 'Kingdoms' have become 'Kingdom'. Such textual differences prompted J. E. Savage to argue that the 1620 edition of *Philaster* represents a censored text and the only version of the play to appear on the Jacobean stage.[57] Although Savage's argument for censorship as the reason for some of the discrepancies in the 1620 quarto is not in every respect convincing, his general thesis that the text has suffered at the hands of the censor prior to performance seems a reasonable supposition. The Master of the Revels, in considering a play which so explicitly depicted an unpopular Spanish marriage alliance and the citizens' vociferous objections to that union, would no doubt have felt compelled to demand that the anti-Spanish element be toned down. The argument that the first quarto is scarred by theatrical censorship is borne out by features of the text. The detailed stage directions and the marking of entrances before the characters appear on stage indicate that the manuscript behind the 1620 quarto must have been prepared for theatrical use. This is no less true of the alternative version of the first and last scenes, which appear to have been written to replace lines censored by the Master of the Revels. The opening stage direction of the first quarto – 'Enter at severall doores Lord LYON, TRASILINE followes him, Clerimon meetes them' – clearly suggests the playhouse and the play in performance.

The scenes may have been hack work, as has been suggested, [58] but they are nonetheless versions which Jacobean audiences would have seen on the stage. In contrast, the second quarto bears no obvious signs of contamination by playhouse use. Savage conjectures that the text derived – like that of the first quarto of Beaumont and Fletcher's *A King and No King* – from a private transcript. Presumably such transcripts were produced directly from authorial papers and their limited circulation obviated the need to defer to any later corrections by the theatrical or press censor.

It is difficult to ascertain when in its theatrical life *Philaster* was censored. James was set on maintaining cordial relationships with Spain throughout his reign. The play could have been censored as early as its first performance in 1609. But anti-Spanish sentiment was more vociferous during the latter part of the next decade when the marriage negotiations were well advanced and censorship may have taken place in response to this climate of opinion, upon a revival of the play for Court performance.[59] The respective attitudes of nation and monarch had by then diverged to such an extent that in 1621 James insisted in Parliament that public discussion of foreign matters be prohibited as an infringement of the prerogative. By 1622, the King was faced with growing demands for a repudiation of the Spanish treaties and for active engagement with the Protestant cause in Europe. Walkley, sensing that the risky enterprise of publication would satisfy the popular mood, may well have considered it an opportune moment to boost sales in *Philaster* by bringing out the uncensored version which so closely mirrored the contemporary international scene.

The Revels in transition 1622–23

In March 1622, coinciding with a critical juncture in international relations, there was a transfer of power in the Revels Office. Chamberlain, writing to Carleton, reported bluntly that 'Poore Sir George Bucke master of the Revells is in his old age falne starke madde and his place executed by Sir John Ashley [sic] that had the reversion'.[60] Buc's successor was in fact Sir John Astley, who had acquired the reversion to the Office in 1612.[61] A second reversion to the Office had also been granted by patent dated 5 October 1621 to Ben Jonson,[62] who may seem an extraordinary choice in the light of his earlier misdemeanours, but Jonson had evidently rehabilitated himself over the years through the popularity of his masques and other Court productions. He was therefore poised to succeed to the Revels, should Astley die or vacate the Office.

Astley was accordingly sworn in as Master of the Revels as a result of Buc's apparent indisposition. Buc, in fact, died on 31 October 1622. The new Master received his special commission investing him with the powers associated with the Office on 22 May 1622. Yet, little more than a year later, on 20 July 1623, Astley sold a life tenancy of the Mastership to Henry Herbert for the sum of £150 per annum.[63] This transaction must have been a source of considerable chagrin to Jonson, whose prospects of displacing Herbert and claiming the benefit of his reversion would be fulfilled only if Astley pre-deceased him. In fact, those prospects remained unfulfilled, for Jonson died in 1637 and Astley in 1640.

Astley's active tenure of the Office under his commission therefore lasted a mere fifteen months.[64] Immediately upon purchasing his investment, Herbert proceeded to exercise the powers of Master and was addressed as such, even though the title still officially belonged to Astley. Despite the fact that Astley evidently did not consider it necessary to seek James's prior consent to his taking early retirement or to his disposal of the Office, Herbert's assumption of the Master's powers must have met with the King's approval. Two weeks after the transaction, on 7 August 1623, Herbert attended the King at Wilton House and recorded that 'it pleased the King, at my Lord Chamberlain's motion, to send for me unto his chamber ... and to knight me, with my Lord Marquis Hamilton's sword ... and to receive me as Master of the Revels'.[65] James appears to have recognised that, notwithstanding the unorthodox way in which his new purveyor of Court entertainment and censor had obtained his privileges, his government had acquired in the person of Herbert a vigorous custodian of its interests.

As we shall see from his unfortunate experience with *A Game at Chess*, Herbert's judgment was perhaps not entirely sure during his early years. But the strictness of his regime and his careful husbandry of the powers of his Office ensured the longevity of his tenure, which was to extend into three reigns and beyond the Restoration.

The Life of the Duchess of Suffolk

One of the first plays to be censored by the new Master of the Revels was Thomas Drue's *The Life of the Duchess of Suffolk*, licensed on 2 January 1624.[66] It depicts the eponymous Protestant Duchess, widowed but now remarried to her steward Richard Bertie, fleeing the persecution of the Catholic bishops Bonner and Gardiner during the reign of Mary Tudor. In the presentation of the vindictive bishops and their zeal to purge the land of Protestant influence, the drama is in the popular anti-Catholic vein, in keeping with its principal source, Foxe's *Acts and Monuments*. But, during a period when a Catholic alliance had appeared for the first time in seventy years to be a distinct prospect, the play had an obvious topical resonance.

Herbert evidently found plenty to arrest his eye. He records in his office book that he had 'much reformed' the play since it had been 'full of dangerous matter'. Herbert's licence is again referred to in the Stationers' Register entry on 13 November 1629 and it is probable that the play which was printed in 1631 contains his amendments and is thus not representative of Drue's original composition. The nature of Herbert's alterations can only be conjectured. It is notable that there is no reference to the Spanish match between Mary Tudor and Philip II, detested by contemporaries. Although as Robert Raines has pointed out, the play's strong Protestant bias is quite apparent, specific doctrinal issues are not raised.[67] Moreover, the foreign and domestic policies of the three reigns which fall within the play's compass are altogether subordinate to the domestic aspects of the Duchess's wanderings.

But the play contains more than a generalised image of a Catholic counter-offensive. The 'good applause' which, according to the title page, the play received, was no doubt earned because of the audience's identification of the protagonists with contemporary figures. As Margot Heinemann has said, the appearance of the play in 1624 would have promoted the analogy between the Duchess's sufferings as a refugee in Europe and those of Queen Elizabeth of Bohemia, a Protestant heroine.[68] In the character of the Count Palatine there is also a tribute to Elizabeth's husband, Frederick of the Palatinate,[69] whose company performed the play at the Fortune. Significantly, Drue departs from his source in drawing upon three figures – the Prince Palatine of the Rhine, the Count Palatine of Vilna and King Sigismund of Poland – as models for the composite character of the Palsgrave,[70] who in the first act becomes King of Poland. The Count's unhistorical accession to the Polish throne would have brought to mind Frederick's acceptance of the crown of Bohemia in 1619. Significantly, the passage in which news of the Palsgrave's election is announced and marriage between him and the Duchess is proposed and rejected (Br), is so short as to suggest truncation.

As he perused the play, Herbert must have judged it 'dangerous' precisely because it fuelled attitudes antagonistic to the Crown's interests. Whilst ready to defend Frederick's claim to the Palatinate, James was opposed to his acceptance of the crown of Bohemia, refusing to address him by the title. Unsympathetic towards apocalyptical protestantism, he had no wish to adopt the mantle of champion of the Protestant cause throughout Europe.[71] Without suppressing the play altogether, there was little Herbert could do to prevent perception of the likeness between the Duchess of Suffolk and the Queen of Bohemia. But parallels were no doubt considerably more explicit before Herbert's intervention and the original play may well have contained an anti-Spanish element which did not survive the Master's scrutiny.

A Game at Chess

Middleton's *A Game at Chess* also served to satisfy fervent anti-Catholic as well as anti-Spanish hostility. In the guise of a game of chess between the Black House and the White House, the play exploits the conviction that Spain nourished a grand design for 'universal monarchy'. The strategy is masterminded by the Black Knight who, according to contemporary witnesses, was presented on the stage as a lively caricature of the former Spanish ambassador, Diego Sarmiento de Acuna, Conde de Gondomar. The members of the White House are successively duped by the cunning and casuistic arguments of the Black House, before the White Knight – identifiable as Prince Charles – exposes the latter's duplicity. The play, composed in the early summer of 1624, cunningly refers to events of the previous year when Charles and the royal favourite George Villiers, Duke of Buckingham, had journeyed to Madrid to formalise the long purposed marriage alliance. In the autumn of the same year, after a protracted sojourn during which the Spanish continued to temporise, the Prince and Duke returned to England without the Infanta. The failure of the mission became a cause of celebration, as it was projected as a politic manoeuvre undertaken to reveal the grandiose designs of the Spanish and was followed by clamours for war.[72] In the Parliament which convened in February 1624, James, who was becoming increasingly isolated, was pressed to terminate diplomatic relations with Spain and to rescind the Spanish treaties.[73] As ever, he was reluctant to change the direction of his foreign policy and refused to commit himself to any declaration of war, emphasising his limited engagement in the Palatinate and the priority of diplomacy and strategy. But the hand of the war party was strengthened by its new alliance with Buckingham and Charles.

In the midst of such a heightened atmosphere, *A Game at Chess* was performed in August 1624. It was an immediate success, relished, no doubt, as much because of a consciousness that such an audacious piece of theatre was bound to excite state interference and would therefore be performed for only a limited period. Even those who had not seen the play were sufficiently intrigued to comment. After only two performances, George Lowe reported to Sir Arthur Ingram at York that it was thought that the play, 'which describes Gondomar and all the Spanish proceedings very boldly and broadly' would 'be called in and the parties punished'.[74] A week later, Sir Francis Nethersole wrote to Carleton about a new play, containing a plot based on a game of chess 'under which the whole Spanish businesse is ripped to the the quicke' and commented on the extraordinary financial success of the drama. The players had apparently increased admission charges 'knowing ther time cannot be long'. The most detailed account of the play and of the remarkable diversity of its audience is recorded in Chamberlain's letter to Carleton of 21 August 1624, written several days after royal intervention brought about its suppression:

I doubt not but you have heard of our famous play of Gondomar, which hath ben followed with extraordinarie concourse, and frequented by all sorts of people old and younge, rich and poore, masters and servants, papists and puritans, wise men et ct., churchmen and statesmen as Sir Henry Wotton, Sir Albert Morton, Sir Benjamin Ruddier, Sir Thomas Lake, and a world besides; the Lady Smith wold have gon yf she could have persuaded me to go with her. I am not so sowre nor severe but that I wold willingly have attended her, but I could not sit so long, for we must have been there before one a clock at farthest to find any roome. They counterfeited his person to the life, with all his graces and faces, and had gotten (they say) a cast sute of his apparell for the purpose, and his Lytter, wherein the world sayes lackt nothing but a couple of asses to carrie yt, and

Sir G. Peter or Sir T. Mathew to beare him companie. But the worst is in playeng him, they played sombody els, for which they are forbidden to play that or any other play till the Kings pleasure be further knowne; and they may be glad yf they can so scape scot-free: the wonder lasted but nine dayes, for so long they played yt.[75]

The description of *A Game at Chess* as 'our famous play of Gondomar' suggests that the play's popular success lay in the stage caricature of the ex-ambassador, although it would seem that the play had been forbidden principally on the grounds that 'somebody els', a wry allusion to King James, had been personated on the stage.

A Game at Chess had been licensed for performance by Herbert on 12 June 1624. That Herbert should have licensed such an audacious piece of political satire at first seems curious. It has been suggested by way of explanation that Buckingham, who was identifiable with the joint hero of the play, the White Duke, and who was by this time at the forefront of the war party, encouraged Herbert to license the play.[76] Margot Heinemann has suggested that the Lord Chamberlain, William Herbert, third Earl of Pembroke, might well have protected the play.[77] Pembroke was the most prominent member of the Puritan wing of the Privy Council.[78] He was, moreover, a cousin of the new Master of the Revels and recommended Herbert for the Office. As a client of his, Herbert may well have been pre-disposed to allow a play which was broadly in sympathy with the Lord Chamberlain's ideology. But there are other factors which help to explain why so topical a satire passed the censor. Amid the sense of impending conflict with Spain at the prorogation of Parliament in May, it is not necessary to pre-suppose the existence of an eminent protector. When Herbert licensed the play, the foreign policy of the Crown had virtually collapsed. Although the King continued to equivocate, the coercive stance of Parliament and the efforts of Charles and Buckingham in persuading him to abandon the notion of alliance with Spain were undoubtedly causing a weakening of his purpose.[79] Herbert must have felt that neither James nor the Privy Council would take exception to a play which reflected the officially propagated version of the fruitless expedition and heightened hispanophobia in the Commons, at Court and in the country. The prime target of the satire, Gondomar, had left England two years previously. Although it was rumoured he would return, his prolonged absence from the capital would surely have encouraged the actors to take impressionists' liberties. It is also probable that Herbert did not read the actual text of the notorious production. There was an interval of six weeks between the date of Herbert's licence, 24 June 1624, and the date of the play's first performance on 7 August 1624. The King's

Men may have been biding their time waiting for James to leave the capital and possibly also for the departure of Gondomar's successor, Don Carlos de Coloma.[80] Whatever the cause of the delay in production, Middleton appears to have made use of the time to sharpen his original composition so that the satire became still more expressly topical.

The earlier text of the play seems to have survived in the so-called Archdale manuscript, one of several private transcripts which circulated in 1624, attesting to the play's considerable appeal.[81] The text has been transcribed by Ralph Crane who, as scribe for the King's Men, would have had easy access to any early prompt book. The main differences between the text of the Archdale manuscript and that of the other extant transcripts and quartos lie in the parts of the 'turncoat' Fat Bishop and the White King's pawn. The Fat Bishop does not appear at all in the former text and the part of the White King's pawn is here less significant. Those figures are recognisably the notorious Marco de Dominis, Archbishop of Spalato and the deeply unpopular pro-Spanish Lord Treasurer, the Earl of Middlesex. Originally a Catholic, de Dominis had on his arrival in England converted to Anglicanism and had subsequently been honoured by James. His motives were regarded with suspicion by the English clergy, an attitude which seemed to be justified when, on the accession of a new Pope, he reverted to Catholicism.[82] Just as the White Knight's pawn is revealed as a traitor to his own house, Middlesex was similarly accused of, and impeached for, alleged intrigue with Spain in May.[83]

If the hypothesis that the Archdale manuscript contains an earlier version of the text and that it was later revised to accommodate more current material is correct, then it is almost certain that the play book which Henry Herbert licensed was somewhat less provocative than the play seen on the stage of the Globe. The Archdale manuscript lacks the ebullient satire of the rapacity and hypocrisy of de Dominis. Also missing are lines of such political significance as the White King's pawn's revelation to the Black Knight of his manoeuvrings on behalf of the Black House:

> there shall nothing happen,
> Believe it, to extenuate your cause
> Or to oppress her friends, but I will strive
> To cross it with my counsel, purse and power,
> Keep all supplies back, both in means and men,
> That may raise strength against you.   (I.i. 318–23)

Nor does it include the White King's denunciation of his pawn, containing pertinent references to Middlesex's lowly origins and to

King James's advancement of his career: 'From a condition next to popular labour,/Took thee from all dubitable hazards/Of fortune, her most insecure advantures/And grafted thee into a branch of honour' (III.i. 266–9). The satire against the White King, alias King James, is likewise sharper in the revised text, where it is implied that he is an easy victim of Spanish machinations. With the absence of such material, the satire is focused less on factional politics than on the general strategies of Catholic expansionism.[84] While the additional passages are not among the most inflammatory parts of the play, they tend to locate the satire in a more precisely contemporary context. If they had been included in the manuscript which was submitted to the Master, Herbert might have discerned how comprehensively the satire was directed at actual principals in the Spanish débâcle and might better have anticipated how explosively those likenesses could be realised in performance.

The appearance of the King on the stage, according to Chamberlain, was the main cause of the suppression of *A Game at Chess*. Secretary Conway, in his letter to the Privy Council on 12 August 1624, written after complaints had been received from the Spanish ambassador, also refers to the players' offence in flouting the prohibition against presenting a contemporary monarch on the stage:

> His Majesty hath receaved informacion from the Spanish Ambassador, of a very scandalous Comedie acted publickly by the King's Players, wherein they take the boldnes, and presumption in a rude, and dishonorable fashion, to represent on the Stage the persons of his Majesty, the King of Spaine, the Conde de Gondomar, the Bishop of Spalato &c. His Majesty remembers well there was a commaundment and restraint given against the representinge of anie modern Christian kings in those Stage-plays, and wonders much both at the boldnes nowe taken by that companie, and alsoe that it hath been permitted to bee so acted.[85]

The 'commaundment and restraint given against the representinge of anie modern Christian kings' may refer to the promise extracted from the theatre companies, following the *Byron* plays, that they would not perform any contemporary history upon the stage.[86] Alternatively, this may be an allusion to a convention taken for granted since the beginnings of theatre censorship, that the part of the monarch should not be interpreted by an actor. It is, in any event, symptomatic of James's isolation towards the close of his reign that the players were prepared to transgress the boundaries of censorship and trespass so impudently both on the ruins of his Spanish strategy and on his personal dignity.

James's anger at the players' audacity provoked an investigation into the licensing of *A Game at Chess*. Conway directed the Council to discover who had in fact licensed the play, implying perhaps that an unofficial performance was at first suspected. The Council reported to Conway that the actors had 'produced a Booke being an Orriginall and perfect Coppie thereof (as they affirmed) seene and allowed by Sir Henry Herbert Knight Master of the Revels under his owne hande and subscribed in the last page of the said Booke',[87] and that they had denied that any passages other than those in the licensed book had been spoken on the stage. But performance is ephemeral and it would of course have been impossible to tell how far the actors had strayed from their written parts. The tone of the Council's letter to Conway suggests that they were not unduly concerned by the international commotion which *A Game at Chess* had aroused. They evaded the responsibility of locating 'offensive and Scandalous' passages by sending the book to the King and advising him to summon Herbert, then in attendance with the Court at Woodstock, to explain why he had licensed the play. We do not know whether the King did in fact call Herbert to account for his apparent lapse in concentration, but when Conway next wrote to the Council on 27 August, he was clearly in possession of more detail about the play and about those parts which had caused particular offence:

> his [James's] pleasure is that your Lordships examine by whose direction, and application the personating of Gondomar, and others was done. And that beinge found out, that partie or parties to bee severely punished. His Majestie beinge unwillinge for ones sake, and only fault to punish the innocent or utterly to ruine the companie.

The King's orders make it quite clear that it was the accuracy of the actors' impersonations, which removed any element of ambiguity from the dramatic situation and from the identities of its characters, which had caused the affront. In Pembroke's letter to the President of the Council sent on the same day as Conway's letter, the Lord Chamberlain instructs the Council to 'to take such course' with the actors 'as might give best satisfaction to the Spanish Ambassador' and preserve the honour of the King of Spain and his ministers. From these letters, it seems reasonable to suppose that Herbert had exculpated himself and that the King was satisfied that the true offence lay in the impersonations and other aspects of performance which were beyond the censor's apprehension or control.

The play's suppression and the temporary restrictions placed on the King's Men were related both to James's determination not to exacerbate relations with Spain further and to his indignation at his own stage representation. In his letter to the Duke of Olivares of

20 September 1624, Coloma wrote angrily of the contents of *A Game at Chess* and the attendance thereat of 'all the nobility still in London'. He describes the plot of the play which, he affirms, did little but show 'the cruelty of Spain and the treachery of Spaniards'. The presentation of Spain was such, he continues, that audiences were inflamed against his country and his own person and he was consequently no longer safe. Coloma's reaction to a play which he deemed 'so scandalous, so impious, so barbarous and so offensive' to his sovereign, as it is communicated in the same letter to Olivares, was to present James with the choice of punishing the actors or accepting a severance of relations between the two nations:

> I have given the King of England this choice between punishing this roguery and sending me my papers, because every good reason and conjecture require that he should choose the first alternative, and it seemed to me that if he chose the second, he would find his actions condemned, not only by God, but also by the world.[88]

James chose the former course: the company were called before the Council and forbidden to play until they were licensed again by the King. A warrant was sent out for the arrest of Middleton after it was discovered that he was 'shifting out of the way, and not attending the Board with the rest'. Although his son was examined before the Privy Council, it has not been proved whether Middleton was imprisoned and (as it has been suggested) released after he had written and presented the verse petition to King James which appears in one of the extant quarto texts.[89] In the long term, the repercussions for the King's Men of the staging of *A Game at Chess* were limited: the Privy Council was informed independently by Secretary Conway and the Earl of Pembroke on 27 August 1624 that the company were to be allowed 'to act as before', providing that plays had been 'lycensed by authority'. Order was given, however, that *A Game at Chess* was to be 'antiquated and sylenced'. The injunction to continue investigations to discover what is rather unspecifically referred to as the 'originall roote of this offence' might be interpreted as a diplomatic gesture to appease the Spaniards, since there was very little else the Council could do once the play book had been examined.

The short duration of the prohibition on the company, together with the publication of the play the following year, invites the conclusion that the King had intervened largely to placate the Spanish ambassador. According to the Venetian ambassador's second dispatch referring to the controversy, James had been concerned not to involve himself unduly in investigations:

The comedians who presented what I reported, have been condemned not to perform until further order. The Council pronounced this sentence, the King having referred the case to them. He willingly refers such cases to them, in order to give them some employment and rid himself of the odium of such decisions.[90]

Nevertheless, King James emerges with some credit for his tactful handling of the affair. He knew that the vast majority of his subjects were fervently sympathetic to Middleton's political stance in *A Game at Chess*, even had they not demonstrated it in their response to the play. He was aware also, as he made clear in a speech to Parliament in March 1624, that he had 'to deal with allies as well as subjects'.[91] To have forbidden the play on the ground that it promulgated anti-Spanish propaganda would have been to court further the antagonism among members of the war party. Not to have ordered its suppression may well have precipitated the destruction of the concord to which he had devoted so much of his foreign strategy and for which even in his isolation he so tenaciously strove. Confronted by such a potential crisis, James was circumspect: he banned the play, though stressing disapproval at the stage impersonation of himself as much as at the Spanish satire, and prohibited – but only briefly – the professional activity of his company.

The Dedication attached to one of the private transcripts of the play donated to William Hammond in late 1624 draws attention to the play's notoriety and to the prohibition of circulation:

This, Which no Stage, no Stationers Stall can Showe,
(The Common Eye maye wish for, but ne're know)
Comes in it's best love with the New-yeare forth,
As a fit Present to the Hand of worth.

Yet *A Game at Chess* was published the following year. Publication was no doubt facilitated by the death of King James and the fact that open hostilities between Spain and England had broken out. The existence of three printed quartos, however, probably all printed in 1625,[92] indicates, unsurprisingly, continuing interest in the play's political allegory, made explicit on the engraving of the title page.[93] Here, ten *dramatis personae* are presented. The Fat Bishop and the Black Knight can easily be recognised as caricatures of the Archbishop of Spalato and Gondomar. The two Kings, James I and Philip IV, and two Queens, Anne of Denmark and the French-born Isabella of Bourbon, are conspicuously contrasted. There are other close resemblances: the White Bishop to Abbot, Archbishop of Canterbury; the Black Duke to Olivares, the White Duke to Buckingham; and the

White Knight to Prince Charles. Considering the original furore aroused by the play's performance only the previous year, such an unambiguous identification of the stage characters with their actual counterparts seems highly provocative, yet illustrates the vicissitudes of censorship. Once Spanish protests had subsided, the climate was fluid enough to permit publication; the stage ban presumably remained in place, but was not tested.

The number of extant documents relating to the investigation into and suppression of *A Game at Chess* have made it a *cause célèbre* of Jacobean censorship. Its importance in international politics cannot be over-estimated: its dramatised political currents, embodying half a century's fear and hatred of Spanish power, produced threats of war. But it is as a case of non-censorship that *A Game at Chess* is of greatest interest in any study of Jacobean censorship. An apparent puzzzle surrounding the performance of *A Game at Chess*, as we have seen, concerned the fact that Herbert at first licensed the play. The breakdown in Anglo-Spanish diplomacy and his contact with the anti-Spanish faction no doubt initially persuaded Herbert to give the play a licence although if he had envisaged the boldness of the theatre production he would surely have withheld it. To a great extent censorship, falling short of complete suppression, is rendered inoperable by the nature of the extended metaphor. Whilst Herbert could not have failed to detect allusions to Catholic and Spanish manoeuvrings in the metaphor of the chess game, he may well have judged that the dramatic artifice would deflect any offence registered by the emissaries of Spain. He could not have predicted that the players would have impersonated the Spanish ambassador so brazenly or that they would use as stage properties Gondomar's actual litter and chair of ease. There are no references to such accoutrements in the stage directions. Students of drama will recognise that the text contains the actors' directions, but the sensibilities of the late Jacobean Master of the Revels were not so attuned. Textual references to the properties which contributed to such vivid identification of the Black Knight with Gondomar (IV.ii. 3) are easily missed. To a lesser extent, the mild satire of James as the ineffectual and sententious White King would have been fully realised only in performance. To be effective in its purpose, theatrical censorship must be alert to all aspects of the relationship between text and performance. Few censors possess the imagination necessary to the task and Henry Herbert, at least at the beginning of his career, seems to have been no exception.

Notwithstanding the changes in the personnel of the Revels and the shifts of power within the Privy Council, the censorship of foreign affairs remained remarkably consistent throughout James's reign. The box-office success of *Barnavelt* and *A Game at Chess* gives some indication of the popularity of international relations and personalities as subjects for dramatic treatment: yet the infrequency of such productions shows that playwrights regarded this field of theatrical activity as a risky enterprise. James may have been comparatively lenient towards personal and Court satire, but when plays impinged upon his foreign policy he was quick to respond. Pre-performance censorship and post-performance suppression of plays on foreign matters disclose the restraints operating on plays which might undermine James's image of Rex Pacificius or the sovereign interests of foreign rulers. The circumstances which brought about the suppression of the *Byron* plays in 1608 are comparable to those in which *A Game at Chess* was prohibited in 1624. Both plays were licensed by the Master of Revels, performed in a more audacious or embellished version than that approved by the censor, and at a time when the Court was out of town. In each case, protests by representatives of the injured nation were instrumental in the play's suppression. In contrast to Elizabeth I, who paid lip service to complaints from foreign powers,[94] James acted promptly to appease the anger of France and Spain.

In these instances, royal policy was clearly at odds with the currents of public opinion which dramatists strove to gratify. Since coded accounts of foreign issues would have been less easily deciphered by the audience of the popular playhouse, it was not open to dramatists to employ the techniques of veiled reference. The explicitness of the satire in *A Game at Chess* is the consequence and demonstrates playwright and players pushing at the boundaries. The state reaction guaranteed that the boundaries remained in place.

Richard III

It has been one of the contentions of this study that the censorship of texts is governed by the vagaries of the political climate. This is further illustrated in the probable censorship of *Richard III*, two decades after its first production c.1592. In the folio of 1623, a passage which appeared in all six earlier quartos is lost from the text. The lines comprise part of an exchange between Richard, who is now ruminating over Richmond's ascendancy, and the Duke of Buckingham, who persistently importunes the King for the earldom of Hereford:

Buck. My lord –
K. *Rich.* How chance the prophet could not at that time
    Have told me, I being by, that I should kill him?
Buck. My lord, your promise for the earldom –
K. *Rich.* Richmond! When last I was at Exeter,
    The Mayor in courtesy show'd me the castle,
    And call'd it Rugemount, at which name I started,
    Because a bard of Ireland told me once
    I should not live long after I saw Richmond.
Buck. My lord –
K. *Rich.* Ay, what's o clock?
Buck. I am thus told to put your Grace in mind
    Of what you promis'd me.
K. *Rich.* Well, but what's o clock?
Buck. Upon the stroke of ten.
K. *Rich.* Well, let it strike.
Buck. Why let it strike?
K. *Rich.* Because that like a Jack thou keep'st the stroke
Betwixt thy begging and my meditation.
I am not in the giving vein to-day.   (IV.ii. 102–20)

It has been suggested that this 'stageworthy' scene was not in the text of the authorial papers which served as the folio copy text and that it represents Shakespeare's afterthought.[95] But the evidence of expurgated oaths and doctrinal reference in the text underlying the folio indicates that this version must have been prepared for performance. It seems probable that the exchange between Richard and Buckingham was removed from the play book in contemplation of a revival because it had acquired a new topical resonance. R. B. McKerrow suggests that the passage was deleted because the prophecy of the Irish bard, that the King would not live long after he had seen Richmond, would have played upon the susceptibilities of the superstitious and ageing James I. More plausible is William Griffin's conjecture that the lines were removed because they would evoke associations with the patronal relationship of James and his protege, the unpopular George Villiers,[96] who became Marquis of Buckingham in 1619 prior to his elevation to the dukedom in May 1623, a month before the folio appeared. The precise reason for the disappearance of the passage is not, however, as important as the evidence it provides that there existed a system of continuous surveillance of dramatic texts, with a view to removing lines which, however coincidentally, suggested contemporary events.

The Honest Man's Fortune

The censor's reconsideration of an earlier play in a different political context is again evident in the prompt book of Beaumont and Fletcher's *The Honest Man's Fortune*, which was brought to Herbert to be relicensed by Joseph Taylor of the King's Men.[97] Herbert's autograph licence appears on the final folio of the manuscript: 'This Play, being an olde One and the Originall Lost was reallowed by mee. This 8 Febru 1624 Att the Intreaty of Mr. Taylor'. It is impossible to tell, on the sole basis of the colours of ink used by the scribe Edward Knight and by Herbert respectively, which of them was responsible for the several cuts made to the texts. But in the style in which the cuts are made, there are indications of two different hands at work: some passages are marked for omission simply by marginal rules, others, much more heavily obliterated, suggest the censor. It is not, however, wholly essential to differentiate between the hand of the scribe and that of the official censor, for we know from Herbert's letter to Edward Knight in 1633, in which he commends Knight for saving him labour,[98] that the prompt book was prepared in the theatre in deference to the anticipated objections of the censor.

The apparent objectives underlying the censorship of *The Honest Man's Fortune* bring together the concerns of the Master of the Revels throughout James's reign and yet, also, herald changes in the scope of Jacobean and Caroline censorship. A passage which could be interpreted as a satirical gloss on James's foreign policy has been excised. Criticism of the Court and the nobility has been toned down by the deletion of several derogatory remarks and the disappearance of various obscene and bawdy comments indicates a new intolerance of vulgar language.

At the beginning of Act II, Longaville and Dubois consider their careers now that 'swords are out of use,/and words are out of credit'. These lines are left to stand, but a passage which follows in which they jestingly propose to set up 'male stewes' (II.i. 15–27) has been marked for exclusion and the dialogue heavily excised by loops and scribbles. The excision has been made either because of the implicit indictment of a foreign policy which was seen as inviting dissolute behaviour among the younger uncommissioned gentry, who were frustrated in their desire for active military service; or because of the sheer obscenity of the lines. Other deletions in the manuscript evidently stem from disapproval of the kind of bawdy repartee and sexual innuendo which had been commonplace in Jacobean drama. Laverdure, a coarse and unsavoury courtier, attempts unsuccessfully to woo the Lady

Lamira and makes light of his rejection, comparing her to 'manye mistresses, that will so mistake, as to take their horse keepers, and ffootemen insteed of theire husbands' (III.iii. 158–60). Also marked for omission by brackets drawn in heavy ink is Viramour's comment to his master, the honest Montaigne, on Charlotte's gross sexual appetite:

> *Vir.* why truely she devoures more mans flesh
> *Mont.* I but she roares not boy.
> *Vir.* no sir, why she is never silent, but when hir mouthes full. (IV.i. 103–5)

Later in the same scene Viramour, trying to repel the unwelcome advances of Laverdure who believes him to be a woman, tells the latter that he smells 'like a womans chamber,/she newly up, before she have pincht hir vapours in with/hir cloathes' (IV.i. 266–8). The lines, despite their dramatic purpose, were apparently considered too indecorous, for they too have been rejected. In view of the steps taken to remove lewd remarks from the text, it is interesting to note a short scene printed in the 1647 Beaumont and Fletcher folio (V.iii), but missing from the manuscript, in which four servants pruriently speculate about Lamira's wedding night. It may have been deliberately omitted when the play was transcribed because Knight was aware that Herbert took a stricter attitude towards scurrility.

Censorship of *The Honest Man's Fortune* also extends to the familiar territory of pejorative references to the Court where, in two instances, Herbert's hand may be detected in the heavy scoring out of offending lines. The first case affects a passage in which Laverdure boasts that he has assisted a poor widow in a suit without remuneration. In response to Lapoop's comment that this is nothing unusual, Laverdure counters: 'by *Mars* Captaine, but it is, and a verie strange thinge/to in a Courtier' (II.ii. 52–3). The line is inked out. In identical fashion, Longaville's sneer at the turpitude of members of the aristocracy – 'pretious, tis allmost as common/as to have a lord arrested, and lye by it'[99] (III.ii. 56–7) – is taken out. Marginal rules signify the exclusion of part of a dialogue between Montaigne and Viramour, in which Viramour compares Montaigne's standards of honour with the prevailing decadence of his contemporaries:

> Indede
> you never taught me how to handle cardes
> to cheate and cozen men with oaths and lyes:
> those are the worldlye quallities to live
> some of our scarlet gallants teach their boyes.
> since stumbling fortune then leaves vertue thus,
> let me leave ffortune ere be vicious.   (IV.i. 74–80)

Further lines have been cut from Montaigne's soliloquy in which he condemns an aristocracy that has abandoned its claims to a status built upon virtue:

The greatest harted man supplyed with meanes,
nobilitye of birth, and gentlest parts,
I, though the right hand of his soveraigne,
yf vertue quit hir seate in his high soule,
glitters but like a pallace set on fire,
whose glorye whilst it shines but ruins him
and his bright showe each houre to ashes tending
shall at the last be raekt up like a sparkle,
unlesse mens lives and fortunes feede the flame.   (IV.i. 8–16)

The lines may have been removed in the playhouse simply because they were considered dramatically superfluous, but the strength of the rebuke, coupled with the implication that the foundations of the social order are jeopardised by corruption among the aristocracy, may have been perceived as too obviously vulnerable to Herbert's censure. Another rejected passage with socio-political overtones contains Viramour's assertion that a person's social origins determine status and cannot be transcended:

Doves beget *Doves*: and *Eagles Eagles* madame, a
cittizens heire tho' left never so rich, seldome at
the best proves but a griffin gent;
... she that of a chambermaide is
metamorphosed into a madame, will yet remember
how oft her daughter by hir mother venterd to lye
upon the rushes, before she coo'd get in that which
makes manye ladyes   (III.i. 81–90)

It is probable that such sentiments endorsing the supremacy of rank and blood were interpreted as too overt a comment upon Jacobean courtiers, Buckingham in particular, who had risen to positions of power in spite of their relatively lowly origins.

The timing of the revival of *The Honest Man's Fortune*, which took place a month before the death of King James in March 1625, no doubt impinged on its censorship. Herbert would have been aware of an impending succession and that the ambience of a Caroline court would be very different from that of the permissive Jacobean Court. Assuming that an awareness of change did indeed prey upon his mind, the Master must have sensed that under Charles, drama which aspired to be admitted to Court circles would have to conform to new standards of seriousness and decorum. Later notes in his office book suggest that Herbert was certainly anxious to contain indecorous language as well as attacks on both the aristocracy and courtiers.[100] Such concerns are anticipated in the removal of passages in *The Honest Man's Fortune*. From the deletions made in the manuscript there is an intimation of shifting values and a changing perspective. A reign whose mode of Court life betrayed a certain lack of social refinement and which was to some extent prepared to countenance occasional assaults upon its dignity was giving way to a new regime which would seek from its drama a more constrained ethos of morals and manners.

Notes

1 It is difficult to say when Buc took over from Tilney the task of licensing plays for the stage. He had no allowance from government until 1611, retrospective to 1608. See Mark Eccles, 'Sir George Buc, Master of the Revels', *Thomas Lodge and other Elizabethans*, ed. C. J. Sisson, p. 435.

2 See W. W. Greg, *A Companion to Arber* (Oxford, 1967), p. 157.

3 Arber, *SR*, III, 433.

4 *A Companion to Arber*, p. 156.

5 *CSPD 1619–23*, CX, p. 79. Frederick and his wife, Elizabeth, were immensely popular in England.

6 *The Letters of John Chamberlain*, II, p. 331.

7 See Margot Heinemann, *Puritanism and Theatre: Thomas Middleton and Opposition Drama Under the Early Stuarts* (Cambridge, 1980), pp. 155–7.

8 See *The Letters of John Chamberlain*, II, pp. 336, 339.

9 In December 1621, for example, when ill health prevented James's presence in the Commons, he wrote to the Speaker admonishing the House for its behaviour and its reported dabbling in 'state mysteries'; saying that he had heard 'that his detention by ill health at a distance from Parliament has led some fiery spirits to meddle with matters far beyond their capacity, and intrenching upon the prerogative; forbids any further meddling with state mysteries, as the Prince's match, attacks on the King of Spain', (*CSPD 1619–23*, CXXIV, p. 316). Yet by the following Parliament of 1624, the climate had changed and relations with Spain were freely debated.

10 *CSPD 1623–5*, CLIX, p. 172.

11 *The Letters of John Chamberlain*, I, p. 568.

12 See *The History of the World*, ed. C. A. Patrides (London, 1971), p. 179.

13 See Fulke Greville, *Life of Sir Philip Sidney*, p. 218.

14 *Life of Sir Philip Sidney*, p. 220.

15 See Joan Rees, *Fulke Greville, Lord Brooke, 1554–1628: A Critical Biography* (London, 1971), pp. 4–5.

16 The precise date of composition cannot be ascertained. Since Greville refers to his play on Antony and Cleopatra which he feared might be applied to Essex's fate as a 'younger brother to the rest', *Mustapha* must have been composed before 1600–1.

17 *Life of Sir Philip Sidney*, pp. 224–5.

18 *Poems and Dramas of Fulke Greville, First Lord Brooke*, ed. Geoffrey Bullough (2 vols., London, 1938), p. 26. Quotations are from this edition.
19 The play's ending in the manuscript is printed as Appendix B in vol. II of Bullough's edition.
20 Although it must be added that apart from the plays, Greville did not attempt to publish his writings. Whilst a coterie comprising his friends and admirers probably read and discussed ideological issues presented in manuscript, it was not judged prudent to make them available for wider reading.
21 Henry Herbert licensed Greville's *Workes* on 10 November 1632 (Arber, *SR*, IV, 288). Although Herbert claimed the re-perusal of old plays revived in performance as part of his duties as Master of the Revels, it is unlikely that he would have assiduously re-examined a play thirty years old, not intended for the stage, and already licensed by his predecessor. Interestingly, the *Workes* did encounter some censorship *after* Herbert had licensed them (see Bullough, I, p. 26).
22 Folio 56r. The manuscript, Lansdown 807, is in the British Library.
23 The play was entered in the Stationers' Register as '*The Maids Tragedie*, 2^d part', on 9 September 1653. It was never printed.
24 'Marginal Markings: the censor and the editing of four English prompt books', *Studies in Bibliography*, 36 (1983), 168–77, at 175.
25 *The Second Maiden's Tragedy*, ed. Anne Lancashire (Manchester, 1978), p. 278. In Appendix A, Professor Lancashire gives a detailed description of the censorship of the manuscript and classifies the cuts according to their contents.
26 See G. P. V. Akrigg, *Jacobean Pageant or the Court of King James I* (London, 1962), pp. 181–3.
27 See *The Maids Tragedy*, ed. T. W. Craik (Manchester, 1988), pp. 33–4. It is difficult to determine the provenance of the texts. There are no obvious signs that either is based on performance. Since quarto 1 bears traces of censorship it may have been printed from authorial papers submitted to Buc before the copy for the playhouse was made.
28 Professor Craik accepts Theobald's emendation of 'limbs' where quarto 2 has 'lives'. See p. 118 note. Whichever, a savage image of regicide is evoked.
29 *The Maid's Tragedy*, p. 190 note.
30 Thomas Fuller, *The Worthies of England*, ed. J. Freeman (London, 1952), p. 439.
31 James's fear of assassination was such that he was known to have slept behind a barricade of empty beds. After the death of Henri IV, further precautions were taken to guard the King. See D. Harris Willson, *King James VI and I* (London, 1956), pp. 279, 367.
32 See *Epicoene*, ed. R. V. Holdsworth (London, 1979), p. 8 note.
33 *CSP Venetian 1607–10*, p. 42.
34 See Logan Pearsall Smith, *The Life and Letters of Sir Henry Wotton* (2 vols., London, 1907), I, p. 414; Chambers, *ES*, III, p. 317; *Ben Jonson*, V, p. 146; *Epicoene*, ed. Holdsworth, pp. xvii–xviii. Marion A. Taylor, 'Lady Arabella Stuart and Beaumont and Fletcher', *Papers on Language and Literature*, 8 (1972), 252–60, has argued, however, that Arabella Stuart was angry about the use of Moldavia as a setting for Beaumont and

Fletcher's *The Knight of the Burning Pestle*. This theory is open to some doubt. Although the latter play was not well received (according to its authors its 'irony' went unappreciated), there is no record of its being officially suppressed. The cumulative evidence of the Prologue, Dedication and Register entry all point to the censorship of *Epicoene*.

35 See *Ben Jonson*, V, p. 145.

36 *The Travels of John Sanderson in the Levant 1584–1602*, ed. Sir William Foster (London, 1931), p. xxxvi.

37 Chamberlain wrote to Carleton on 30 December 1609, that the Lady Arabella was 'again before the Lords' (*The Letters of John Chamberlain*, I, p. 292). McClure notes that she was released with the assurance that the King did not object to her marriage with any subject of his.

38 W. W. Greg, 'Was there a 1612 quarto of *Epicoene?*', *The Library*, Fourth Series, 15 (1935), 306–15.

39 See *The Hogge Hath Lost His Pearl*, prepared by D. F. McKenzie for the Malone Society (Oxford, 1972), p. vi.

40 See *CSPD 1611–18*, LXX, p. 147. On 8 October 1612 the Earl of Northampton informed the King that Sir John Swinnerton had offered a large advance for the patent, 'but the Lord Treasurer rated him soundly for it, and declared he should not have it, let his best friends in court strain as they would', *CSPD 1611–18*, LXXI, p. 150. The topical references of the play are discussed in detail by E. M. Albright, 'A stage cartoon of the Mayor of London in 1613', *The Manly Anniversary Studies in Language and Literature* (Chicago, 1923), 113–26.

41 *Much Ado About Nothing*, ed. R. A. Foakes (Harmondsworth, 1968), p. 167.

42 *APC 1616–17*, p. 267.

43 See Sir Horace Vere's letter to Carleton, 21 April 1617, *CSPD 1611–1618*, XCL, p. 461.

44 The manuscript, Add. 18653, is in the British Library.

45 *The Letters of John Chamberlain*, II, p. 239.

46 See *Sir John van Olden Barnavelt*, prepared by T. H. Howard-Hill for the Malone Society (1980), pp. vi–x. In 'Buc and the censorship of *Sir John van Olden Barnavelt in 1619*', *RES*, 39 (1988), 39–63, Howard-Hill discusses lucidly the censorship of the manuscript in the context of Buc's experience of and James's interest in the Netherlands.

47 On the basis that folios nineteen to twenty-six are written in a different ink and bear a different watermark, T. H. Howard-Hill believes that this part of the text (including the trial scene) was re-written to comply with Buc's earlier censorship (*Sir John van Olden Barnavelt*, p. xx and 'Buc and the censorship of *Sir John van Olden Barnavelt* in 1619', p. 50). This may well have been the case although, as Buc's censorship of the arraignment indicates, he was clearly not satisfied with the re-writing. It is not uncommon for leaves of different watermarks to be bound together. The manuscript of *The Honest Man's Fortune* consists of seven different papers.

48 In the manuscript, the cross is placed a little higher than it appears in the *Malone Society Reprint*. Buc could, therefore, have been registering his disapproval of the previous line in which Barnavelt's alliance with the Arminian faction is stated.

49 See Lockyer, *The Early Stuarts*, pp. 116–7 and Hugh Trevor-Roper, *Catholics, Anglicans and Puritans: Seventeenth Century Essays*, pp. 57–62.

50 The censorship here may have had nothing to do with Buc: from Crane's verses it appears that he had Puritan sympathies. See F. P. Wilson, 'Ralph Crane, scrivener to the King's Players', *The Library*, Fourth series, 7 (1927), 194–215, at 194.

51 According to the entry in *Dictionary of National Biography*, after King's death it was rumoured that he had died a Catholic; there is no evidence of this.

52 *State Papers Domestic, James I*, CX, no. 37.

53 Wilhelmina Frijlinck in her edition of the play (Amsterdam, 1922) offers a thorough discussion of the several sources known to the playwrights. She concludes that much of the contemporary broadside against Olden-barnevelt was written 'in a time of confusion, intense hatred and blind-eyed prejudice' (p. 58). Massinger and Fletcher ignored the more libellous pamphlets.

54 See S. L. Adams, 'Foreign policy and the Parliaments of 1621 and 1624' in *Faction and Parliament: Essays in Early Stuart History* (Oxford, 1978), 139–71 for a discussion of the debates on foreign policy during the last years of James's reign.

55 Andrew Gurr in the Revels edition (London, 1969) reprints the variant sections of the first quarto in Appendix A.

56 'The serious concerns of *Philaster*', *English Literary History*, 30 (1963), 1–16, at 13.

57 'The "gaping wounds" in the text of *Philaster*', *Philological Quarterly*, 28 (1949), 443–58.

58 *Philaster*, ed. Gurr, p. lxxviii. See, also, R. K. Turner, Jr., 'The printing of *Philaster* Q1 and Q2', *The Library*, Fifth Series, 15 (1960), 21–32.

59 *Philaster* was played at Court in the 1612–3 and 1619–20 seasons. See *Philaster*, ed. Gurr, pp. lxxi–lxxii.

60 *The Letters of John Chamberlain*, II. p. 430.

61 See Richard Dutton's forthcoming article 'Patronage, politics and the Master of the Revels: the case of Sir John Astley, Master of the Revels 1622–40' in *English Literary Renaissance*.

62 *CSPD 1619–23*, CXXIII, p. 296.

63 *Dramatic Records* ed. J. Q. Adams, p. 8.

64 The only play which seems to have caused any controversy during Astley's mastership was *Osmond, The Great Turk*. The case was unusual in that Astley initially prohibited the play, but it would seem that he was overruled by the Lord Chamberlain, Pembroke, who intervened and gave his own permission for performance. See G. E. Bentley, *The Jacobean and Caroline Stage*, (7 vols., Oxford, 1956), III, pp. 119–22 and, especially, Dutton, 'Patronage, politics and the Master of the Revels'.

65 Quoted by Michael G. Brennan, *Literary Patronage in the English Renaissance: The Pembroke Family* (London, 1988), p. 139.

66 *Dramatic Records of Henry Herbert*, ed. J. Q. Adams, p. 18.

67 See Robert Raines, 'Thomas Drue's *The Duchess of Suffolk*: a critical old spelling edition' (unpublished doctoral dissertation, University of Dela-ware, 1968), p. 37. Raines points out that the play differs from Foxe, who has the bishops accusing the Duchess of staying away from the Mass.

68 Margot Heinemann, *Puritanism and Theatre*, p. 205. See also Jerzy Limon, *Dangerous Matter: English Drama and Politics 1623–24* (Cambridge, 1986), pp. 53–61.
69 See Leslie M. Oliver, 'Thomas Drue's *Duchess of Suffolk*: a Protestant drama', *Studies in Bibliography*, 3 (1950), 241–6, at 242.
70 See Raines, pp. 26–7 and Limon, *Dangerous Matter*, pp. 48–9.
71 See Adams, 'Foreign policy and the Parliaments of 1621 and 1624', p. 148.
72 See Thomas Cogswell, 'Thomas Middleton and the Court, 1624: *A Game at Chess* in context', *Huntington Library Quarterly*, 47 (1984), 273–88. Cogswell discusses the broad-based 'patriot' coalition in 1624 which, he argues, would have supported the wider dissemination of events in Madrid as reported by Buckingham represented in *A Game at Chess*.
73 For a detailed account of the parliamentary sessions of 1624 see Cogswell, *The Blessed Revolution: English Politics and the Coming of War, 1621–1624* (Cambridge, 1989), pp. 135–261.
74 Quoted in R. C. Bald's edition of the play (Cambridge, 1929), p. 159. Unless otherwise stated, contemporary references to the play are cited from Bald's edition (pp. 159–66).
75 The Letters of John Chamberlain, II, pp. 577–8.
76 See John Robert Moore, 'The contemporary significance of Middleton's *Game at Chesse*', *PMLA* 50 (1935), 761–68 at 767–8.
77 Margot Heinemann, 'Middleton's *A Game at Chess*: Parliamentary-Puritans and Opposition Drama', *English Literary Renaissance*, 5 (1975), 232–50, at 241.
78 See Adams, 'Foreign policy and the Parliament of 1621 and 1624', pp. 143, 156. Pembroke was, however, sensitive to James's reluctance to be drawn into war and he refused to go along with Buckingham's proposal to repudiate the Spanish treaties without parliamentary debate.
79 In April 1624, for example, the King replied to both Houses stating that he 'grants their desire for a proclamation to banish priests and Jesuits; will command the Judges to execute all the laws against recusants, which were suspended, not dispensed with, by the treaties, including those for disarming them ... will yield to no interference of foreign princes' (*CSPD 1623–5*, CLXIII, p. 221). Encouraged by Buckingham, James was now contemplating a French alliance. Dudley Carleton Jr. wrote to his uncle in June: 'The King is almost as much in love with France as he was with Spain ... The King of Spain told Sir Walter Aston that he had done his part to settle his Majesty, but if he was weary of peace, he might take his course' (*CSPD 1623–5*, CLXVIII, p. 284).
80 Dudley Carleton Jr. informed his uncle in June 1624 that one of the ambassadors, the Marques de la Inijosa, had already departed, 'leaving his residence, Exeter House, in a filthy state, and Don Carlos de Colonna follows him' (*CSPD 1623–5*, CLXVIII, p. 284). Coloma in fact left in October without, as Chamberlain reported, 'kissing the Kings hand as he desired' (*The Letters of John Chamberlain*, II, p. 581).
81 See R. C. Bald's edition of the play for its invaluable discussion of the various texts. In a later article, 'An early version of Middleton's *Game at Chesse*', *Modern Language Review*, 28 (1943), 177–81, Bald argues that, in spite of the haste with which it was written, the play underwent revision

and enlargement, probably during the period between licensing and performance, (p. 180). The most recent edition is that prepared by J. W. Harper (London, 1966). All quotations are from this edition.

82 James honoured Marco Antonio de Dominis, Archbishop of Spalato, when he arrived in England announcing his conversion from Rome (see *CSPD 1611–18*, XCII, p. 474). He was made Dean of Windsor, which increased his unpopularity amongst the English clergy. On 16 September 1620, Chamberlain wrote to Carleton that he had heard him 'generally ill spoken of, so that if he continues this course, his conversion will deserve and do litle honor to religion'. Later, Chamberlain reported, somewhat sceptically, 'Your great bishop of Spalato is undertaking such another adventure, having required and obtained leave to go for Rome. ... he pretends auncient acquaintance and familiaritie with this Pope' (*The Letters of John Chamberlain*, II, p. 423). See also Trevor-Roper, *Catholics, Anglicans and Puritans*, p. 59.

83 Dudley Carleton Jr. wrote to his uncle on 14 April 1624: 'He [Middlesex] will be made a sacrifice, for the King has forsaken him, and he has no friend ... The world cries "Down with him"; there has been no man in England these 200 years whose ruin has been so thirsted after by all sorts of people' (*CSPD 1623–5*, CLXII, p. 214).

84 Jerzy Limon takes up the idea advanced by T. H. Howard-Hill that the play was originally intended as a religious allegory. See *Dangerous Matter*, p. 119.

85 Bald, *A Game at Chess*, pp. 159–60.

86 See above, p. 140.

87 Bald, *A Game at Chess*, p. 162.

88 See Edward M. Wilson and Olga Turner, 'The Spanish protest against *A Game at Chess*', *Modern Language Review*, 44 (1949), 476–83 at 481.

89 An epigram in a commonplace book, compiled between 1620–30, which belonged to Sir Thomas Dawes, may be evidence that Middleton was arrested and imprisoned. The 'Verses' were copied into the Dyce quarto without the last two lines present in the Dawes version:

Verses sent to King James

A harmeless Gaime rais's meerely for delight
Was lately plaide bye *black* howse and *White*
The White side wann but nowe the black side bragg
They changd the Gaime and putt me in the bagg
And that which makes malicios joy more sweete
I lye nowe under hatches in the ffleete.
Yet use your Royall hand! my hopes are free;
Tis but removing of one man, that's mee.   T.M.

(See Geoffrey Bullough, '*The Game at Chesse*: how it struck a contemporary', *Modern Language Review*, 49 (1954), 156–63.)

90 *CSP Venetian 1623–5*, no. 568, p. 432.

91 Reply of the King to a Declaration from both Houses, 15 March 1624 (*CSPD, 1623–5*, CLX, 188).

92 Bald notes that the second edition, bearing the date 1625, seems to have been in demand before the type used for the first had all been broken up, (*A Game at Chess*, p. 30).

93 See John Robert Moore, 'The contemporary significance of Middleton's *Game at Chess*'. p. 762.

94 The Spanish ambassador had reported to Philip II on 29 April 1559 that the Queen had said 'that she wished to punish severely certain persons who had represented some comedies in which your majesty was taken of' (quoted in *Tudor Royal Proclamations*, II, p. 115). Hughes and Larkin link this to the proclamation of 1559 'Prohibiting Unlicensed Interludes and Plays, Especially on Religion or Policy'; but there is no evidence that the representation of Spanish affairs greatly impinged on subsequent censorship. In *Midas* (1589) the satire of the grandiose ambitions, greed and cruelty of Philip of Spain as Midas are little disguised by the play's allegorical mode. In Paris 1602, objections were raised to the presentation of Henri IV and the death of the Duke of Guise in Marlowe's *The Massacre at Paris*. See Sir Ralph Winwood, *Memorials of Affairs of State in the Reigns of Queen Elizabeth and King James I* (3 vols., London 1725), I, p. 425.

95 See *King Richard III*, ed. Antony Hammond (London, 1981), p. 44. The editors of the Oxford Shakespeare describe the dialogue as 'a dramatic gem, which could easily result from an inspired afterthought' and, ignoring the role of the censor, assert that 'it is difficult to believe that anyone would have deliberately singled it out as the only passage in the play which should be cut': Stanley Wells and Gary Taylor, *William Shakespeare: A Textual Companion* (Oxford, 1987), p. 228.

96 William J. Griffin, 'An omission in the folio text of *Richard III*', RES, (1937), 329–32. In a note attached to Griffin's article, McKerrow puts forward his view.

97 The prompt book (Dyce 25 F9) is in the library of the Victoria and Albert Museum. Quotations are from J. Gerritsen's edition (Groningen, Djakarta, 1952).

98 *Dramatic Records*, ed. J. Q. Adams, p. 21. Herbert appears here to be referring to the expurgation of the text. But it seems reasonable to suppose that other likely objections by the censor were anticipated in the playhouse.

99 The expression 'lye by it' is an idiom for 'lie in prison'. See *OED*, entry 'LIE v^1 B. 3'.

100 On 25 January 1625, Herbert licensed the now lost play *The Widow's Prize* and recorded that it contained 'much abusive matter' and was allowed only on condition that his reformations were observed (*Dramatic Records*, ed. J. Q. Adams, pp. 18–19). In November 1632, he reacted strongly against Shirley's *The Ball* because 'ther were divers personated so naturally, both of lords and others of the court' (*Dramatic Records*, p. 19).

Some conclusions

Thus we have the split engendered by Society and Self, Art and Authority, governmental demands as to what the poet should say and how he should use his talent, and the great navigating excursions of the free spirit against the limits of consciousness and the imagination. (Alan Sillitoe, Introduction to *Poems for Shakespeare*, 1979).

We have seen that Tudor proclamations regulating the stage and the commission which invested the Revels Office with its extended responsibilities were vague but all-encompassing. Early theatrical censorship was, thus, able effectively to drive a wedge between the drama and religious discourse. It developed not according to pre-determined formulae, but from the individualistic responses of a Crown servant anxious to justify his novel privileges. The generality of his commission allowed the Master of the Revels to wield his authority selectively according to his perception of the Crown's interests. Thus, under Elizabeth, anti-Catholic and anti-Puritan propaganda were admitted whilst assaults on the Anglican episcopacy were not. Plays might project the evils of rebellion or the ineptitude of its proponents, but the portrayal of an insurrection which had any ideological or economic *raison d'être* was not be be tolerated. What particularly characterises theatrical censorship during the early modern period, however, is its dynamic quality. There are no consistent political, moral or cultural criteria to be discerned; instead, the historical moment determined the censor's response in each case. Nationalism and militant Protestantism flourished in the drama of the 1580s and 1590s, but scarcely figure in the Jacobean canon since James's ideal of grand European alliances forbade hostile treatment of foreign policies and personages. Thus, in 1588, the year of the Armada, Robert Wilson could exploit national hatred of Spain in *The Three Lords and the Three Ladies of London*; in 1624, when Middleton sought to gratify a like xenophobia in *A Game at Chess*, the play was suppressed. The scale of the disorders in London during 1592 and 1596–7, among the most serious in the decades preceding the Civil War, similarly dictated the censor's prohibition of scenes ranging from popular discontent and riot in *The Book of Sir Thomas More* to deposition in *Richard II*. To some extent, the shackles restraining such material were eased under James.

Theatre of the late sixteenth and early seventeenth centuries, more than at any subsequent time, belonged to popular culture. But unlike the constraints which operated in that other great age of popular theatre, the Victorian period, censorship was not at one with the mass of public opinion. John Russell Stephens has demonstrated that Victorian stage censorship reflected a widespread middle-class belief that politics was an inappropriate subject for the theatre; and that the censors saw themselves in the role of interpreters of the public conscience, trying to objectify the often deeply subjective responses of prospective audiences.[1] This identification of ideology and interest between stage licenser and public audience did not exist during our period. The Elizabethan populace, in spite of its diet of official sermons, could not have subscribed to an ideology which maintained absolute condemnation of any form of insurrection as an heinous act; playwrights, however, were coerced into such a presentation whenever rebellion made its appearance in historical drama. Likewise, anti-Scots satire would have greatly appealed to English courtiers and to the Blackfriars audience; the sensibilities of King James and of his Scottish entourage prevented any such comedy. The Master of the Revels, in attempting to bring about a more compliant stage, was quite prepared to frustrate audience predilections.

If censorship was not identified with popular opinion, it is necessary to ask whether the censors were aligned with factional interests at Court or whether they practised unswerving loyalty to the Crown. From the immediate evidence of the Master's hand in extant manu-scripts, there are few signs of any factional partisanship. The censors' concerns, reflected in their various excisions and imperatives, relate to those spheres in which the Crown's interests were judged to be at risk, principally and successively, the topics of rebellion, foreign relations and the reputation of the Court. A notable exception was the short period when Daniel, acting as licenser for the Queen's Revels 1604–6, seems to have allowed satires which ridiculed the King because they were countenanced by the Queen.

The Master of the Revels censored plays, not productions; his function ceased once he had examined the book and returned it to the theatrical company, although he obviously had a vested interest in seeing that his conditions were observed. If the play was to be performed at Court, almost certainly the company would have observed the Master's strictures. Whether or not the actors generally adhered to the licensed text in the public playhouses or during provincial tours is less certain. The furore over the performance of the *Byron* plays and *A Game at Chess* and, to a lesser extent, the textual features of *The Merry Wives of Windsor*, indicate that the players did on occasion perform plays in a form materially different from that licensed by the Master of the Revels. Chapman's defence, in his letter to Buc, of his intentions in respect of the *Byron* plays, on the ground that 'the action of the mynde is performance sufficient of any dewtie', could equally be applied to the censor's activity. Covert textual allusions might elude his attention on a cursory reading of the play; with the aid of mimicry, gesture and costume the text would acquire a sharper edge in performance. This was certainly the case with the personation of Gondomar in *A Game at Chess* and probably also with the Scots satire in *Eastward Ho*. There may have been more than a hint of King James in the stage presentation of the King in *The Fawn*, *Philaster* and *A Game at Chess*, all of which bypassed the censor.

Certain instances of censorship seem trivial, ill-judged or heedless of dramatic requirements. The suppression of the line about German and Spanish costume in *Much Ado about Nothing* and of the line, in *The Second Maiden's Tragedy*, 'all honest courtiers', which refers to the spirits of heaven, are cases in point. The intervention brought about by alleged satire in *Epicoene* seems to represent an insubstantial case of censorship. Lines in *Mustapha* and *King Lear* appear to have been censored irrespective of dramatic context. The censors of the Elizabethan and Jacobean stage were not faceless bureaucrats. Tilney, Buc and Herbert were cultivated men; but ultimately they placed a premium on their duties to government and the associated privileges of their Office. In such moods they were not averse to the exercise of an obtuse literal-mindedness in expunging lines regardless of dramatic situation.

For playwrights of our period it was, then, never quite clear what was prohibited and what would be permitted. The ill-defined terms of censorship encouraged some playwrights to take risks (which sometimes succeeded) and drove others into timidity or self-censorship. While it is a commonplace that there are two types of censorship, external and internal, the extent of the latter is difficult to assess. Undoubtedly, playwrights must consciously or otherwise have imposed restraints on themselves, fearful of sanctions as arbitrary as the censorship they sought to avoid. That out of the hundreds of plays which came before the Master of the Revels in the early decades of censorship, only a comparatively small number tell – or have survived to tell – a tale of censorship, could be seen as indicative of the irregularity or ineffectiveness of censorship. Yet there are extant few plays which challenge and are uncontaminated by the censor. The absence of plays dealing with recent history, doctrinal conflict, the debate over the justification of tyrannicide and the royal prerogative, all of which subjects featured prominently in the national conscious-ness but rarely surfaced in the drama, must surely be attributed to circumspect self-censorship.

It is frequently acknowledged that censorship gives birth to metaphors which thrive on ambiguity. Elizabethan and Jacobean dramatists were adept at giving themselves alibis by re-siting their political and satirical plays in the ancient world, or in imaginary courts of Arcadia, Genoa or Ferrara, or by dislocating the action altogether, thus creating a familiar dilemma for the censor. If he penetrated such camouflage and recognised parallels with his royal patron or courtly milieu, the Master of the Revels stood to be accused of excessive ingenuity in uncovering references which, it could be maintained, were not intended. Other manoeuvres were adopted to circumvent censorship. As we have seen, political drama contains its quota of orthodox declamation and articulates the dominant ideology of non-resistance and the evils of rebellion. Yet the validity of such sentiments is often ironically undermined by the self-interest and motivation of the speaker or by their very incongruity amid the general thrust of events or ideas elsewhere in the play.

Arguably, such ambiguity can enrich a play and censorship can actually mould style and composition to positive effect. Yet, in its incursions against freedom of expression and in its distortion of the text, censorship has more pernicious consequences. The prohibitions on performance and circulation of *The Isle of Dogs, Marquis D'Ancre* and *The Old Joiner of Aldgate* account for the fact that these plays are no longer extant. We do well to remember that behind some of the standard historical, political and biographical dramatic texts of the period, there may lie a censored manuscript. The tampering by the Master of the Revels with certain plays has ensured that they have come down to us only in the altered, approved form: *Sejanus, Eastward Ho, The Isle of Gulls, The Hog Hath Lost His Pearl, The Conspiracy* and *Tragedy of Charles Duke of Byron* and *The Duchess of Suffolk*, are amongst those works which, as they now stand, do not fully represent their authors' original intentions. The texts of *Jack Straw* and *Macbeth* also suggest that they too may in parts have suffered interference from the censor. These constraints should induce caution in evaluating the projection of politics in sixteenth and seventeenth century drama.

However universal the appeal of a dramatic work, it cannot in form transcend its own historicity. The text cannot be disengaged from what Stephen Greenblatt has described as 'the circulation of social energy'.[2] Censorship, which is of necessity determined by the specific historical moment, is perhaps the most potent external force which interacts with the creative consciousness. The dramatist's first priority is to ensure that his work will command an audience and then, in most cases, a degree of permanence through publication; to that end compromises will inevitably be made. Some texts may, by a combination of good luck and judgment, ultimately be recovered from the depredations of censorship. It is salutary to recall, however, that all the plays of our period were written in the shadow of the censor and that no dramatist could unchain his thoughts from the agent of that most arbitrary and punitive instrument of state control.

Notes

1 John Russell Stephens, *The Censorship of English Drama 1824–1901* (Cambridge, 1980).
2 See *Shakespearean Negotiations*, pp. 1–20.

INDEX

Day, John, *The Isle of Gulls*, 124–7, 214
Dominis, Marco de, Archbishop of Spalato, 193, 197
Dekker, Thomas, 88
  Old Fortunatus, 66, 107
  Sir Thomas Wyatt, 107
  The Whore of Babylon, 107
Dollimore, Jonathan, 71, 73
Doran, Madeleine, 136
Drayton, Michael, 101
Drue, Thomas, *The Duchess of Suffolk*, 189–90, 214
Drummond, William, 52, 112, 119, 121
Dutton, Richard, 146 n. 11

Edmondes, Thomas, 14, 126
Edmund Ironside, 46–7, 55
Edward VI, 2, 4, 5
Edwards, Philip, 71
Elizabeth I, Queen, 4, 5, 11, 43, 45, 60, 70, 98, 107, 199
  contrast with James I, 98, 199
  and *Cynthia's Revels*, 84–5, 107
  and Essex, 62–3, 70
  and *Every Man out of His Humour*, 82–3
  excommunication, 28, 55
  execution of Mary Stuart, 45
  and *2 Henry IV*, 70
  identification with Richard II, 43, 70
  proclamation against interludes, 5
  and *Thomas of Woodstock*, 45
Elizabeth, Queen of Bohemia, 153, 171, 173, 189
Essex, Robert Devereux, Earl of, 33, 61, 62–7
  and *Henry V*, 71, 77
  and *Old Fortunatus*, 67
  and *Philotas*, 113, 127–31
  and *Sejanus*, 112–13
  trial of, 64–5

Falstaff, and Oldcastle/Falstaff

controversy, 68, 76–9
Fehrenbach, Robert J., 77
Finkelpearl, Philip J., 141, 144
Fleay, F. G., 112
Fletcher, John, 166
  and Beaumont, *see* Beaumont, Francis
  and Massinger, *see* Massinger, Philip
  The Honest Man's Fortune, 103
Foakes, R. A., 173
Fortune playhouse, 9, 190
Foxe, John, *Acts and Monuments (Book of Martyres)*, 93, 189
Frederick of the Palatinate, 153, 173, 189
Fuller, Thomas, 166

Glascock, Edward, 14
Globe playhouse, 9, 65, 80, 83, 193
Goldberg, Jonathan, 101
Gondemar, Conde de, 190, 191, 192, 195, 197, 198
Goodale, Thomas, 37
Greenblatt, Stephen, 68, 215
Greene, Robert, 24
  James IV, 54
Greg, W. W., 28, 34, 35, 102, 103, 106
Greville, Fulke, Lord Brooke, 129
  Life of Sir Philip Sidney, 67, 155
  Mustapha, 155–7, 213
Griffin, William, 200
Grindal, Edmund, Archbishop of York, 5, 7
Gurr, Andrew, 49

Hall, Edward, 50
Hall, Joseph, 153
  Byting Satyres, 62
Hanky, John, Mayor of Chester, 6
Hardware, Henry, Mayor of Chester, 6
Harsnett, Samuel, 62
Hart, Alfred, 70
Hatton, Sir Christopher, Lord Chancellor, 84